U.S. Fish & Wildlife Service

Pea Island National Wildlife Refuge

Comprehensive Conservation Plan

Whimbrel
Photo courtesy of Michael Halminski

Comprehensive Conservation Plans provide long-term guidance for management decisions; set forth goals, objectives, and strategies needed to accomplish refuge purposes; and identify the Fish and Wildlife Service's best estimate of future needs. These plans detail program planning levels that are sometimes substantially above current budget allocations and, as such, are primarily for Service strategic planning and program prioritization purposes. The plans do not constitute a commitment for staffing increases, operational and maintenance increases, or funding for future land acquisition.

Pea Island National Wildlife Refuge

Comprehensive Conservation Plan

U.S. Department of the Interior
Fish and Wildlife Service
Southeast Region

September 2006

SUBMITTED BY: _____ DATE: 3-28-06
MIKE BRYANT , REFUGE MANAGER

CONCUR: _____ DATE: 7/14/06
PETE JEROME, REFUGE SUPERVISOR

CONCUR: _____ DATE: 7/14/06
BUD OLIVEIRA, REGIONAL CHIEF

APPROVED BY: _____ DATE: 7/17/06
SAM HAMILTON, REGIONAL DIRECTOR

COMPREHENSIVE CONSERVATION PLAN

PEA ISLAND NATIONAL WILDLIFE REFUGE
Dare County, North Carolina

U.S. Department of the Interior
Fish and Wildlife Service
Southeast Region
Atlanta, Georgia 30345

September 2006

TABLE OF CONTENTS

SECTION A. COMPREHENSIVE CONSERVATION PLAN

SECTION B. APPENDICES

LIST OF FIGURES

LIST OF TABLES

Executive Summary

The Fish and Wildlife Service prepared this Comprehensive Conservation Plan to guide the management of Pea Island National Wildlife Refuge in Dare County, North Carolina. The plan outlines programs and corresponding resource needs for the next 15 years, as mandated by the National Wildlife Refuge System Improvement Act of 1997.

Before the Service began planning, it conducted a biological review of the refuge's wildlife and habitat management program and conducted public scoping meetings to solicit public opinion of the issues the plan should address. The biological review team was composed of biologists from federal and state agencies and non-governmental organizations that have an interest in the refuge. The staff held the public scoping meetings at four locations on four evenings. The staff also held another round of public meetings to solicit public reaction to the proposed alternatives.

The Service developed and analyzed five alternatives. Alternative 1 was a proposal to maintain the status quo. The refuge currently manages its impoundments very intensively by managing water levels and vegetation to create optimum habitat for migrating waterfowl, shorebirds, wading birds, and aquatic organisms. It also manages marshes with prescribed fire. The staff surveys sea turtles, waterfowl, shorebirds, and wading birds on a routine basis. The refuge allows five of the six priority public use activities: fishing, wildlife observation, wildlife photography, and environmental education and interpretation. The staff conducts extensive environmental education and interpretation programs with the assistance of 25,000 hours of volunteer service every year. There is one staff public use specialist (0.9 FTE) stationed on the refuge. Staff from the Alligator River National Wildlife Refuge (an additional 6.3 of the 23 FTEs) manages the refuge, administers budgets and contracts, maintains the facilities, manages impoundment and marsh habitat, and conducts wildlife surveys.

Alternative 2 proposed moderate program increases. The refuge would continue to manage its impoundments very intensively by managing water levels and vegetation to create optimum habitat for migrating waterfowl, shorebirds, wading birds, and aquatic organisms. It would manage for fall shorebird habitat. It would also manage marshes with prescribed fire. The staff would survey a wider range of wildlife on the refuge, adding regular surveys of land birds. The refuge would continue to allow five of the six priority public use activities, but would have the capacity to increase the number of opportunities. The staff would continue to conduct extensive environmental education and interpretation programs with the assistance of 30,000 hours of volunteer service every year. There would be five staff members (4.4 FTEs) stationed on the refuge, including an assistant refuge manager, biologist, two public use specialists, and a maintenance worker. Staff from the Alligator River National Wildlife Refuge (an additional 8.85 of 39 FTE) would still administer budgets and contracts and manage impoundment and marsh habitat.

Alternative 3 proposed optimum program increases. The refuge would continue to manage its impoundments very intensively by managing water levels and vegetation to create optimum habitat for migrating waterfowl, shorebirds, wading birds, and aquatic organisms. It would manage for fall shorebird habitat. It would also manage marshes with prescribed fire. The staff would survey a wider range of wildlife on the refuge, adding regular surveys of land birds, wading birds, mammals, invertebrates, reptiles, and amphibians. The refuge would continue to allow five of the six priority public use activities, but would have the capacity to increase the number of opportunities. The staff would continue to conduct extensive environmental education and interpretation programs with the assistance of 35,000 hours of volunteer service every year. There would be twelve staff members (11.4 FTEs) stationed on the refuge, including an assistant refuge manager, biologist, three biological technicians, two public use specialists, and five maintenance workers. Staff from the Alligator River National Wildlife Refuge (an additional 13.9 of the 69.5 FTEs) would still administer budgets and contracts and manage marsh habitat.

Alternative 4 assumed that vehicular access to the refuge on a paved road would be eliminated from the north but would be maintained from the south as far north as the Visitor Center. The alternative assumed that natural processes would dominate the area north of the Visitor Center and habitat for colonial nesting shorebirds would increase. The refuge would continue to manage impoundments and marshes. The staff would survey wildlife on the refuge. The refuge would provide public use opportunities, but the number of visitors would decrease due to the limited access. Staffing would be the same as Alternative 3.

Alternative 5 assumed that access to the refuge on a paved road would be totally eliminated. The Service would provide other means of accessing the refuge. The alternative assumed that natural processes would dominate the entire refuge and habitat for colonial nesting shorebirds would increase substantially. The refuge would continue to manage impoundments and marshes. The staff would survey wildlife on the refuge. The refuge would provide public use opportunities, but the number of visitors would decrease due to the limited access. Staffing would be the same as Alternative 3.

The planning team selected Alternative 2 as its preferred alternative. It advances the refuge program considerably, and is more realistic than Alternative 3 in terms of expected staffing levels to conduct the proposed program. The staff evaluated Alternatives 4 and 5 in the event that the North Carolina Department of Transportation would close the Bonner Bridge over Oregon Inlet and eliminate access from the northern end of the island. The North Carolina Department of Transportation is considering the bridge's closure, but has not yet made a decision.

SECTION A. COMPREHENSIVE CONSERVATION PLAN

I. Background

INTRODUCTION

The U.S. Fish and Wildlife Service (Service) developed this Comprehensive Conservation Plan for Pea Island National Wildlife Refuge in Dare County, North Carolina, to provide a foundation for the management and use of the refuge. The Service designed the plan as a working guide for the refuge's management programs and actions over the next 15 years.

However, with the pending Herbert C. Bonner Bridge replacement project, the North Carolina Department of Transportation proposes several alternatives, each affecting future refuge management in significant ways. The "status quo" alternative in this plan should not be interpreted in any way as a statement that the Service prefers the Bonner Bridge or North Carolina Highway 12 remain where it is currently located. The alternatives merely reflect planning strategies with the road and bridge located in their current positions. The potential exists for the refuge portion of the North Carolina Highway 12 to be relocated west of the refuge in the Pamlico Sound as early as 2010. If this occurs, this comprehensive conservation plan may require revision to reflect new methods of access that would result if the North Carolina Department of Transportation chooses to abandon its existing right-of-way through the refuge. The North Carolina Department of Transportation has indicated that if it chooses to replace the bridge by paralleling the existing alignment and using the existing right-of-way, it will request permits for work outside the existing right-of-way, such as large-scale, repetitive beach building and dune building over at least the next 50 years; and permits for many miles of a major new right-of-way west of the existing right-of-way in an attempt to maintain North Carolina Highway 12 for the life of the new bridge. Requests for large-scale, long-term, repetitive beach building and dune building permits or for major new right-of-way permits are not likely to be compatible. The Service would work with federal, state, county and local officials, and other groups to identify feasible public use access and management actions that are compatible with the purposes for which the refuge was established.

The U.S. Army Corps of Engineers dredges the Oregon Inlet navigation channel adjacent to the refuge. This dredging affects the amount and kind of sand that natural processes bring to the refuge beach face and the beach-face organisms. Annually, the Corps requests a refuge permit to dispose dredged sand on the refuge. Dredge disposal timing and placement, sand suitability characteristics, and monitoring and remediation of impacts are addressed in permit conditions. Long-term trends are analyzed to monitor changes in beach sediment and beach-face organisms associated with sand disposal on and near the refuge. Present trend analysis indicates that the Corps' Oregon Inlet dredge disposal has changed the refuge beach over time to a beach with finer grain-sized sand, a greater percentage of heavy (dark) minerals, and decreased abundance of beach-face organisms. Compatibility of this permitted use can only be determined if long-term monitoring and adjustments to other permit conditions continue.

The permitted activities of both the North Carolina Department of Transportation and the Corps of Engineers are long-term and large-scale. They have significant effects on the physical environment of the refuge and on all management planning and actions. To achieve the refuge's desired condition, the actions of these two agencies must be considered when refuge management decisions are made.

The Service developed this plan in compliance with the National Wildlife Refuge System Improvement Act of 1997 and Part 602 (National Wildlife Refuge System Planning) of the Fish and Wildlife Service Manual. When fully implemented, this plan will strive to achieve the vision and purposes of Pea Island National Wildlife Refuge. The actions described within this plan also meet the requirements of the National Environmental Policy Act of 1969. The refuge staff achieved compliance with this Act through the involvement of the public and the preparation of an Environmental Assessment, which was Section B of the Draft Comprehensive Conservation Plan for Pea Island National Wildlife Refuge. The environmental assessment contained a description of the alternatives considered and an analysis of the environmental consequences of the alternatives.

The plan's overriding consideration is to carry out the purposes for which the refuge was established. Fish and wildlife are the first priority in refuge management, and the Service allows and encourages public use (e.g., wildlife-dependent recreation) as long as it is compatible with the refuge's mission and purposes.

A planning team prepared the plan. The planning team was made up of representatives from various Service programs, including the divisions of Refuges, Fisheries, Ecological Services, Realty, and Migratory Birds. In developing this plan, the planning team and refuge staff incorporated the input of the North Carolina Wildlife Resources Commission, other governmental organizations, local citizens, and the general public through a series of stakeholder and public scoping meetings.

The plan represents the Service's preferred alternative and is being put forward after considering four other alternatives, as described in the environmental assessment referred to above. After reviewing a wide range of public comments and management needs, the planning team developed the alternatives in an attempt to determine how to best meet the goals and objectives of Pea Island National Wildlife Refuge. The preferred alternative is the Service's recommended course of action for management of the refuge, and forms the basis for this comprehensive conservation plan.

PURPOSE AND NEED FOR THE PLAN

The purpose of this comprehensive conservation plan is to identify the role that Pea Island National Wildlife Refuge will play in support of the mission of the National Wildlife Refuge System, and to provide long-term guidance to the refuge's management programs and activities for the next 15 years. The plan is needed to:

- provide a clear statement of direction for the future management of the refuge;

- provide refuge neighbors, visitors, and local, state, and federal government officials with n understanding of the Fish and Wildlife Service's management actions on and around the refuge;

- ensure that the Service's management actions, including land protection and recreational and educational programs, are consistent with the mandates of the National Wildlife Refuge System Improvement Act of 1997;

- ensure that the management of the refuge is consistent with federal and state laws; and

- provide a basis for the development of budget requests for the refuge's operational, maintenance, and capital improvement needs.

Perhaps the greatest need of the Service is to communicate with the public and include public participation in its efforts to carry out the mission of the National Wildlife Refuge System. Many agencies, organizations, institutions, businesses, and private citizens have developed relationships with the Service to advance the goals of the Refuge System. This plan supports the Partners in Flight Initiative; South Atlantic Coastal Plain Migratory Bird Conservation Plan; North American Waterfowl Management Plan; Western Hemisphere Shorebird Reserve Network; and National Wetlands Priority Conservation Plan.

U.S. FISH AND WILDLIFE SERVICE

The U.S. Fish and Wildlife Service is the primary federal agency responsible for the conservation, protection, and enhancement of the Nation's fish and wildlife populations and their habitats. Although the Service shares some conservation responsibilities with other federal, state, tribal, local, and private entities, it has specific trustee obligations for migratory birds, threatened and endangered species, anadromous fish, and certain marine mammals. In addition, the Service administers a national network of lands and waters for the management and protection of these resources.

As part of its mission, the Service manages more than 540 national wildlife refuges covering a total of more than 93 million acres. These areas comprise the National Wildlife Refuge System, the world's largest collection of lands and waters specifically managed for fish and wildlife. The majority of these lands, 77 million acres, lie in Alaska. The remaining 16 million acres are spread across the other 49 states and several island territories.

NATIONAL WILDLIFE REFUGE SYSTEM

The mission of the Refuge System, as defined by the National Wildlife Refuge System Improvement Act of 1997, is:

> ... to administer a national network of lands and waters for the conservation, management, and where appropriate, restoration of the fish, wildlife and plant resources and their habitats within the United States for the benefit of present and future generations of Americans.

The National Wildlife Refuge System Improvement Act of 1997 established, for the first time, a clear mission of wildlife conservation for the National Wildlife Refuge System. The Act states that the Service will manage each refuge to:

- fulfill the mission of the Refuge System;

- fulfill the individual purposes of each refuge;

- consider the needs of fish and wildlife first;

- fulfill the requirement of developing a comprehensive conservation plan for each unit of the Refuge System, and fully involve the public in the preparation of these plans;

- maintain the biological integrity, diversity, and environmental health of the Refuge System; and

- recognize that wildlife-dependent recreational activities including hunting, fishing, wildlife observation, wildlife photography, and environmental education and interpretation are legitimate and priority public uses.

Following passage of the Act in 1997, the Service immediately began efforts to carry out the direction of the new legislation, including the preparation of comprehensive conservation plans for all refuges. The development of these plans is now ongoing nationally. Consistent with the Act, the Service is preparing all refuge comprehensive conservation plans in conjunction with public involvement, and is requiring each refuge to complete its own plan within a 15-year schedule.

Approximately 37.5 million people visited the country's national wildlife refuges in 1998, mostly to observe wildlife in their natural habitats. As this visitation continues to grow, the visitors generate substantial economic benefits to the local communities that surround the refuges. Economists have reported that national wildlife refuge visitors contribute more than $400 million annually to the local economies. In addition, the National Survey of Fishing, Hunting, and Wildlife Associated Recreation reports that nearly 40 percent of the country's adults spent a combined $108 billion on wildlife-related recreational pursuits in 1996 (U.S. Fish and Wildlife Service 2001).

Volunteerism continues to be a major contributor to the successes of the Refuge System. In 1998, volunteers contributed more than 1.5 million person-hours on refuges nationwide, a service valued at more than $20.6 million.

The wildlife and habitat vision for national wildlife refuges stresses the following principles:

- Wildlife comes first.

- Ecosystems, biodiversity, and wilderness are vital concepts in refuge management.

- Refuges must be healthy.

- Growth of refuges must be strategic.

- The National Wildlife Refuge System serves as a model for habitat management with broad participation from others.

Pea Island is one of ten national wildlife refuges in eastern North Carolina. Those refuges—Alligator River, Cedar Island, Currituck, Great Dismal Swamp, Mackay Island, Mattamuskeet, Roanoke River, Pocosin Lakes, Swanquarter, and Pea Island—and the Back Bay National Wildlife Refuge in Virginia are all located in the watersheds of the Roanoke, Tar, Neuse, and Cape Fear rivers, which the Service has classified as Ecosystem Unit #34. This watershed unit covers a 40,000-square-mile-area in southeast Virginia and eastern North Carolina, extending from the piedmont to the Atlantic Coast. Specifically, Pea Island National Wildlife Refuge is located within the Pasquotank River basin that encompasses 3,635 square miles of low-lying lands and vast open waters, including the Albemarle and Pamlico sounds, in the state's northeast outer coastal plain.

LEGAL POLICY CONTEXT

A variety of international treaties, federal laws, federal regulations, departmental and Service policies, and presidential executive orders guide the administration of Pea Island National Wildlife Refuge. The documents and acts listed in Appendix III contain management options under the refuge's establishing authority, the National Wildlife Refuge Administration Act of 1966, and the National Wildlife Refuge System Improvement Act of 1997 (the legal and policy guidance for the operation of national wildlife refuges).

NATIONAL CONSERVATION PLANS AND INITIATIVES

Along with the Service's legal mandates and initiatives, other planning activities directly influence the development of the comprehensive conservation plan. Various groups and agencies develop and coordinate planning initiatives involving federal, state, and local agencies; local communities, non-governmental organizations, and private individuals to help restore habitats for fish and wildlife on and off public lands.

The Service is initiating cooperative partnerships in an effort to reduce the declining trend in biological diversity. Biological planning for species groups targeted in this plan reflects the North American Waterfowl Management Plan. The North American Waterfowl Management Plan of 1986 brings together international teams of biologists from private and government organizations from Canada and the United States. The partnerships, called joint ventures, are working to restore waterfowl and other migratory bird populations to the levels of the early 1970s by protecting about 6 million acres of priority wetland habitats from the Gulf of Mexico to the Canadian Arctic.

The United States Shorebird Conservation Plan and the Waterbirds for the Americas outline approaches to conserving those species groups. Restoration of migratory songbird populations is a high priority of the Partners in Flight Plan. It also provides strategies for conserving and managing wintering, breeding, and migration habitat for midcontinental wood duck and colonial bird populations.

The Partners in Flight Plan emphasizes land bird species as a priority for conservation. Habitat loss, population trends, and the vulnerability of species and habitats to threats are all factors used in the priority ranking of species. Further, biologists have identified focal species for each habitat type from which they will determine population and habitat objectives and conservation actions. This list of focal species, objectives, and conservation actions will aid migratory bird management on the refuge.

The Farm Bill programs administered by the U.S. Department of Agriculture provide cost-share funding and technical assistance to private landowners to install and manage conservation practices on working farms and forests, and to restore cropland to natural habitats. The programs provide opportunities for landowners in the vicinity of national wildlife refuges to manage their land better as wildlife habitat, or to protect it with easements.

RELATIONSHIP TO STATE PARTNERS

A provision of the National Wildlife Refuge System Improvement Act of 1997, and subsequent agency policy, is that the Service shall ensure timely and effective cooperation and collaboration with other federal agencies and state fish and wildlife agencies during the course of acquiring and managing refuges. This cooperation is essential in providing the foundation for the protection and sustainability of fish and wildlife throughout the United States.

The North Carolina Wildlife Resources Commission is a state-partnering agency with the Service charged with enforcement responsibilities for migratory birds and endangered species, as well as managing the state's natural resources. It also manages approximately 1.8 million acres of game lands in North Carolina.

The Commission coordinates the state's wildlife conservation program and provides public recreation opportunities, including an extensive hunting and fishing program, on several game lands and from several boat ramps located in Dare County. The Commission's participation and contribution throughout this comprehensive conservation planning process have been valuable. It is continuing its work with the Service to provide ongoing opportunities for an open dialogue with the public to improve the condition of fish and wildlife populations on the Outer Banks. Not only has the Commission participated in biological reviews, stakeholder meetings, and field reviews as part of the comprehensive planning process, it is also an active partner in the coordination, planning, and execution of various wildlife and habitat surveys. The Commission also assists refuge staff in providing special wildlife observation opportunities. A key part of the comprehensive planning process is the integration of common mission objectives between the Service and the Commission, where appropriate.

II. Refuge Overview

INTRODUCTION

LOCATION

Pea Island National Wildlife Refuge is located within the Dare County, North Carolina, coastal barrier island chain known as the Outer Banks. The refuge is between Oregon Inlet to the north, the village of Rodanthe (2000 population: 206) to the south, the Atlantic Ocean to the east, and the Pamlico Sound to the west. The refuge also lies within Cape Hatteras National Seashore, which is managed by the National Park Service. The town of Nags Head (2000 population: 2,700) is 13 miles north of the refuge, just north of Cape Hatteras National Seashore (Figure 1).

Pea Island National Wildlife Refuge is located within the Pasquotank River basin that encompasses 3,635 square miles of low-lying lands and vast open waters, including the Albemarle and Pamlico sounds, in the state's northeast Lower Coastal Plain.

ESTABLISHMENT

Executive Order 7864 established Pea Island National Wildlife Refuge on April 8, 1938, as a refuge and breeding ground for migratory birds and other wildlife. Presidential Proclamation 2284 closed a 25,700-acre area encompassing the refuge and a portion of the Pamlico Sound west of and adjacent to the refuge to migratory bird hunting. The refuge covers approximately 5,000 acres (reduced by erosion from the original 5,915 acres).

IMPORTANCE

The Bureau of Biological Survey named the refuge for the beach peas (*Stropostyles helvula*) that once dominated the backsides of the coastal dunes. The peas mature in October as geese arrive. The beach face and exposed areas of the dunes are also nesting habitat for colonial nesting birds, such as oystercatchers. The beaches provide foraging habitat for shorebirds and nesting habitat for sea turtles. Piping plovers nest on unvegetated sand areas with shallow pools of water. Ducks rest and feed in the bodies of water west of the refuge. Marsh birds and wading birds inhabit the marshes.

REFUGE HISTORY AND PURPOSES

HISTORY

In the early days, Pea Island had only a sand pathway traversing the refuge. Ferry transportation began to the area that is now Pea Island in the mid-1920s, when Captain J.B. Tillet established a tug and barge service across Oregon Inlet. In 1934, the North Carolina Highway Commission recognized the importance of this service to residents and began subsidizing Tillet's business. In 1942, full reimbursement by the state began and Tillet eliminated the tolls. This continued until 1950 when Tillet sold his business to the state. The Service authorized a specific road easement for the State of North Carolina in October 1951, and the state constructed a clay-surface road. The state initially paved the road that is now North Carolina Highway 12 in the mid-1950s. Ferry service ceased with the opening of the Herbert C. Bonner Bridge on November 20, 1963.

Figure 1. Location of Pea Island River National Wildlife Refuge in Dare County, North Carolina

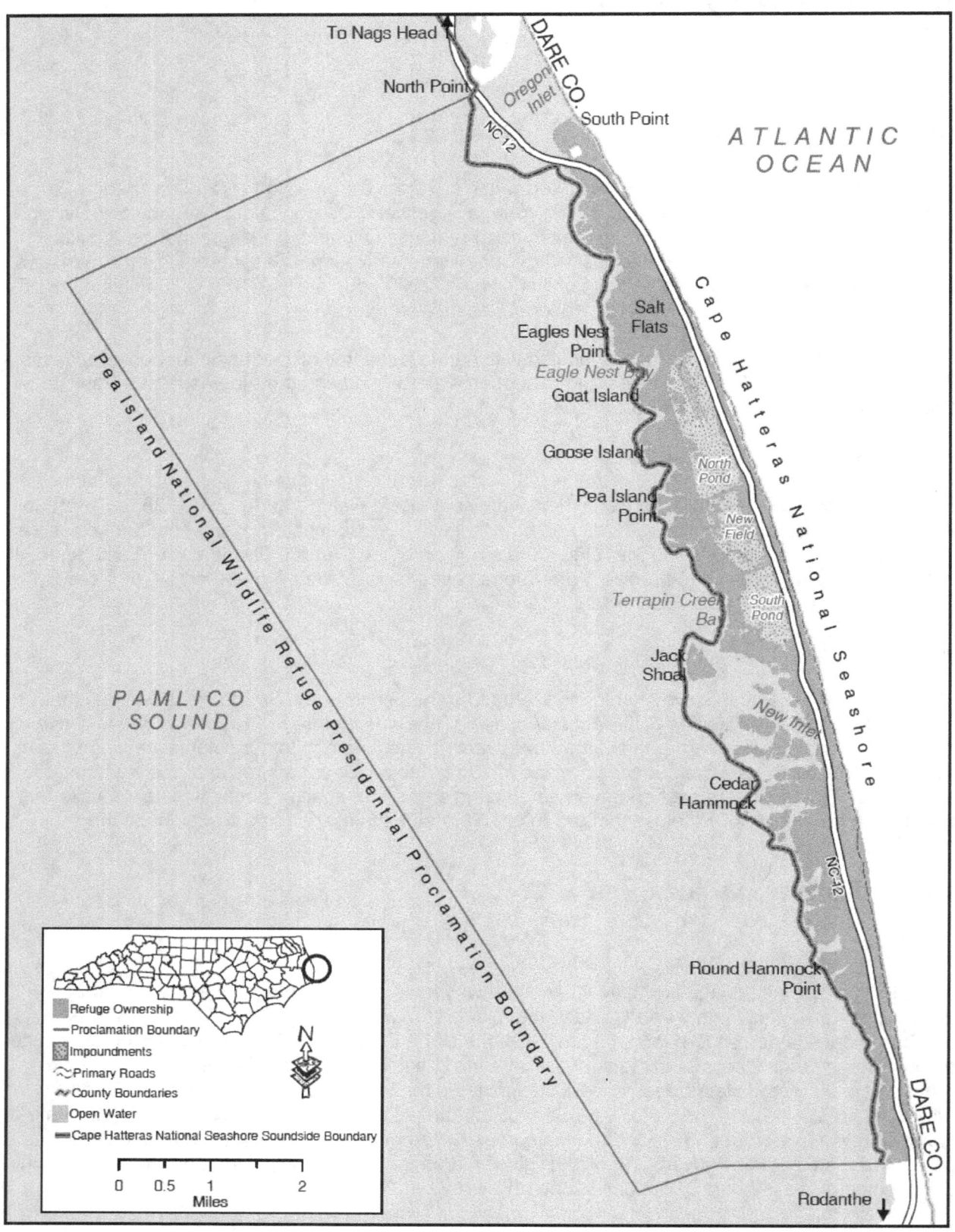

Upon its establishment, the U.S. Department of Agriculture, Bureau of Biological Survey, managed "Pea Island Migratory Waterfowl Refuge." A U.S. Army Civilian Conservation Corps (CCC) camp (Camp BF-2, Company 436, 1933-1942) in the area was responsible for numerous jobs, including dike construction; dune enhancement; water control structure installation; planting to prevent erosion; land surveys; building fences; maintaining truck trails; marking boundaries; and planting trees and shrubs. One of the most significant jobs the CCC accomplished was the construction of dikes. The initial purpose of the dike system (according to historic narratives) was to prevent salt water from contaminating the inland freshwater areas.

In 1939, the administration placed the Bureau of Biological Survey and Bureau of Fisheries under the U.S. Department of the Interior. The following year, these two bureaus were combined to create the U.S. Fish and Wildlife Service, and the refuge was officially renamed Pea Island National Wildlife Refuge. The first manager at Pea Island Refuge was Sam A. Walker, who served in this capacity from 1938 through 1944. The staff grew to a high of eight permanent full-time employees in the mid-1980s.

Pea Island Refuge is an overlay of a portion of Cape Hatteras National Seashore. Through a Memorandum of Understanding signed in July 1975 and amended in 1987, the National Park Service and Fish and Wildlife Service work together to manage the refuge and the national seashore. The National Park Service is responsible for interpreting historical and cultural assets, maintaining all parking lots and the restroom facility adjacent to the Visitor Center, and assisting with law enforcement patrols along the beach. The Fish and Wildlife Service is responsible for all wildlife and habitat management activities, operation of the Visitor Center, recreational access, and uses on the refuge. The current Memorandum of Understanding is under review and the agencies will update it in the near future.

Pea Island Refuge remained a stand-alone refuge until 1984 when the Service started administering it as part of a two-refuge complex with the newly created Alligator River National Wildlife Refuge. Today, the refuge complex staff administers both the Pea Island and Alligator River refuges from an office located in Manteo, North Carolina.

PURPOSE

The purpose of Pea Island National Wildlife Refuge is to protect and conserve migratory birds and other wildlife resources through the protection of wetlands, in accordance with the following:

> *"...as a refuge and breeding ground for migratory waterfowl and other wildlife..."* (Executive Order 7864, August 8, 1938)

SPECIAL DESIGNATIONS

The North Carolina Natural Heritage Program has designated most of the refuge, with the exception of its moist-soil areas, as a Significant Natural Heritage Area. The Nature Conservancy ranks certain vegetative communities as imperiled or rare (Table 1).

The North Carolina Division of Water Quality has designated several water bodies in the vicinity of Pea Island Refuge as outstanding resource waters or high-quality waters (Table 3).

The North Carolina Division of Marine Fisheries has designated water bodies within and off the borders of the refuge as anadromous fish spawning habitats.

Table 1. The Nature Conservancy ranking of vegetative communities of Pea Island National Wildlife Refuge

Vegetative Community	State Rank	Global Rank
Maritime Dry Grassland	S2	G3
Dune Grass	S3	G3
Maritime Shrub	S3	G4

S1 = Critically imperiled in North Carolina because of extreme rarity or otherwise very vulnerable to extirpation in the state.
S2 = Imperiled in North Carolina because of rarity or otherwise very vulnerable to extirpation in the state.
S3 = Rare or uncommon in North Carolina.
G1 = Critically imperiled globally because of extreme rarity or otherwise very vulnerable to extinction throughout its range.
G2 = Imperiled globally because of rarity or otherwise very vulnerable to extinction throughout its range.
G3 = Either very rare or local throughout its range, or found locally in a restricted area.
G4 = Apparently secure

ECOSYSTEM CONTEXT

Pea Island National Wildlife Refuge lies within a physiographic area known as the South Atlantic Coastal Plain (Figure 2). The South Atlantic Coastal Plain was once a 25 million-hectare (62 million-acre) complex of forested wetlands and uplands, dunes, and marshes that extended from Florida to North Carolina. Historically, the extent and duration of seasonal flooding along the ecosystem's rivers have fluctuated annually, recharging the South Atlantic Coastal Plain's aquatic systems and creating a rich diversity of dynamic habitats that supported a vast array of fish and wildlife resources.

On the Lower Coastal Plain, the daily tidal cycles flooded beaches and marshes maintaining the hydrology that kept the area's flora and fauna vigorous. Coastal breezes blew salt spray over the barrier islands trimming the woody vegetation behind the low broad dunes and depositing fresh sand on the herbaceous dune vegetation. Periodic storm events cut inlets through the barrier islands bringing tidal fluctuations to the sounds. Periodic storm events also overwash the barrier islands. Ocean overwash can deposit fresh layers of sand across the islands that sometimes extend new layers of sand to the sounds. Within a period of sea level rise where ocean overwash occurs, the elevation of the island can be raised and the whole island effectively moves toward the mainland to the west.

REGIONAL CONSERVATION PLANS AND INITIATIVES

Along with the Service's legal mandates and initiatives, other planning activities directly influence the development of the comprehensive conservation plan. Various groups and agencies develop and coordinate planning initiatives involving regional, state, and local agencies; local communities; non-governmental organizations; and private individuals to help restore habitats for fish and wildlife on and off public lands.

The Service is initiating cooperative partnerships in an effort to reduce the declining trend in biological diversity. Biological planning for species groups targeted in this plan reflect the North American Waterfowl Management Plan, which includes the Atlantic Coast Joint Venture; the joint venture between the North Carolina Wildlife Resources Commission and the Fish and Wildlife Service; the Partners in Flight Plan; and the South Atlantic Migratory Bird Initiative.

Figure 2. Pea Island National Wildlife Refuge in the South Atlantic Coastal Plain Physiographic Area

The Atlantic Coast Joint Venture focuses on the middle and upper Atlantic coast. Within the Atlantic Coast Joint Venture is the joint venture formed between the North Carolina Wildlife Resources Commission, Fish and Wildlife Service, and private conservation organizations.

The South Atlantic Coastal Plain serves as a primary migration habitat for migratory songbirds returning from Central and South America. It also provides wintering, breeding, and migration habitat for midcontinental wood duck and colonial bird populations. Restoration of migratory songbird populations is a high priority of the Partners in Flight Plan for the South Atlantic Physiographic Region.

The Partners in Flight Plan emphasizes land bird species as a priority for conservation. Habitat loss, population trends, and the vulnerability of species and habitats to threats are all factors used in the priority ranking of species. Further, biologists from local offices of the Service, the North Carolina Wildlife Resources Commission, and conservation organizations, such as Audubon Society and The Nature Conservancy, have identified focal species for each habitat type from which they will determine population and habitat objectives and conservation actions. This list of focal species, objectives, and conservation actions will aid migratory bird management on the refuge.

The Farm Bill programs administered by the U.S. Department of Agriculture have state-level plans and priority ranking systems in which the Service has input. For private landowners who own lands in the vicinity of national wildlife refuges, the Service uses these programs to help them manage habitat for wildlife, or protect their lands with easements.

The North Carolina Wildlife Resources Commission has its own Comprehensive Wildlife Conservation Strategy to help direct the state's allocation of funds from the federally funded State Working Grants Program. The Service has provided input to the development and execution of the strategy.

ECOLOGICAL THREATS AND PROBLEMS

HABITAT LOSS AND FRAGMENTATION

The South Atlantic Coastal Plain has changed markedly over the last 100 years as civilization spread throughout the area. Scientists have estimated that land conversion has cleared 40 percent of the natural vegetation. The greatest changes to the landscape have been in the form of land clearing for urban development and agriculture (Hunter et al. 2001).

Although these changes have allowed people to settle and earn a living in the area, they have had a tremendous negative effect on biological diversity, biological integrity, and environmental health of the South Atlantic Coastal Plain. The changes have reduced vast areas of forests, pocosins, marshes, and coastal beaches to fragments ranging in size from very small tracts of limited functional value to a few large areas that have maintained many of the original functions and values. Severe fragmentation has resulted in a substantial decline in biological diversity and integrity. Species endemic to the South Atlantic Coastal Plain that have become extinct, threatened, or endangered include the extinct passenger pigeon, Carolina parakeet, and Bachman's warbler; the threatened piping plover and sea turtles; and the endangered red wolf. Federal species of concern for this area include the black rail and the "Buxton Woods" white-footed mouse. Table 2 provides a complete list of the threatened and endangered animals in North Carolina.

Breeding bird surveys show continuing declines in species and species populations. The avian species most adversely affected by fragmentation include those that are area-sensitive (dependent on large continuous blocks of hardwood forest); those that depend on forest interiors; those that depend on special habitat requirements such as mature forests or a particular food source; and/or

Table 2. Threatened and endangered animals of the North Carolina Coastal Plain

Status	Common Name	Scientific Name
Endangered	Manatee, West Indian**	*Trichechus manatus*
Endangered	Sea Turtle, Hawksbill**	*Eretmochelys imbricata*
Endangered	Sea Turtle, Kemp's Ridley**	*Lepidochelys kempii*
Endangered	Sea Turtle, Leatherback**	*Dermochelys coriacea*
Endangered	Sturgeon, Shortnose	*Acipenser brevirostrum*
Endangered	Tern, Roseate**	*Sterna dougallii*
Endangered	Whale, Finback	*Balaenoptera physalus*
Endangered	Whale, Humpback	*Megaptera novaeangliae*
Endangered	Whale, Right	*Balaena glacialis*
Endangered	Whale, Sea	*Balaenoptera borealis*
Endangered	Whale, Sperm	*Physeter catodon*
Endangered	Wolf, Red**	*Canis rufus*
Endangered	Woodpecker, Red-cockaded**	*Picoides borealis*
Threatened	Eagle, Bald*	*Haliaeetus leucocephalus*
Threatened	Plover, Piping*	*Charadrius melodus*
Threatened	Sea Turtle, Green*	*Chelonia mydas*
Threatened	Sea Turtle, Loggerhead*	*Caretta caretta*
Threatened	Silverside, Waccamaw	*Menidia extensa*

Presence Documented on Pea Island National Wildlife Refuge
**Presence Not Documented on Pea Island National Wildlife Refuge*

those that depend on good water quality. Habitat loss has also affected species dependent on coastal marshes, exposed sandy areas on beaches and sandbars, and within dune ecosystems.

More than 300 species of breeding migratory songbirds occupy the region. Some inland species, including the Swainson's warbler, prothonotary warbler, swallow-tailed kite, wood thrush, and cerulean warbler, have declined substantially and need the benefits of large forested blocks to recover and sustain their existence. On the Outer Coastal Plain, songbirds, such as the seaside sparrow, saltmarsh sharp-tailed sparrow, and Nelson's sharp-tailed sparrow, depend on declining marsh habitat. The black rail and yellow rail, secretive marshbirds, require brackish marsh. The red knots, least terns, black skimmers, American oystercatchers, and threatened piping plovers are shorebirds that nest on the decreasing acreage of unvegetated sand along beaches and among coastal dunes.

Habitat loss on the Outer Coastal Plain is more permanent than in the Upper Coastal Plain. Conversion of coastal dunes and marshes for commercial development is irreversible. Construction of tall, steep-sided dunes and vegetative stabilization of those dunes to protect infrastructure prevents natural processes from shaping the landscape and the vegetative communities that evolve on that landscape.

ALTERATIONS TO HYDROLOGY

In addition to the loss of vast acreages of wetlands, substantial alterations have occurred in the South Atlantic Coastal Plain's hydrology. The changes are a result of channel dredging for navigation and access to marshes; drainage ditches; degradation of aquatic systems from excessive sedimentation, contaminants, and urban development; changes in managed stream flows from flood control and hydroelectric power generation reservoirs; river channel modifications; flood control levees; and deforestation.

The natural hydrology of a region is directly responsible for the connectedness of wetlands and indirectly responsible for the complexity and diversity of habitats through its effects on topography and soils. Natural resource managers recognize the importance of dynamic hydrology to wetlands and waterfowl-habitat relationships (Fredrickson and Heitmeyer 1988).

Instead of natural hydrology, large-scale, man-made hydrological alterations have changed the spatial and temporal patterns of flooding throughout the entire South Atlantic Coastal Plain. In addition, these alterations have modified both the extent and duration of annual seasonal as well as daily flooding. The alteration of the annual flooding regime has had a tremendous effect on the interior forested wetlands and their associated wetland-dependent species. Changes in daily flooding regimes by drainage ditches and closing inlets through coastal barrier islands accelerate erosion on the ditch banks and throughout the marshes. The changed flooding regimes also decrease the exposure of intertidal areas that would be available with normal lunar tidal cycles. According to Mitsch and Gosselink (1993), restoration of wetland functions is especially difficult because the wetlands depend on a dynamic interface of hydrologic regimes to maintain water, vegetation, and animal complexes and processes.

The dredging of navigation channels also generates a spoil material that must be disposed. If the material is fine-textured, it may not be suitable for placement on the closest potential site, such as beaches. On beaches the material must be a coarse substrate for invertebrate populations and shorebird and turtle nesting.

SILTATION OF AQUATIC ECOSYSTEMS

Deforestation and hydrologic alteration have degraded aquatic systems, including lakes, rivers, sloughs, and bayous. Clearing of bottomland hardwood forests has led to an accelerated accumulation of sediments and contaminants in aquatic systems. Sediment now fills many water bodies, greatly reducing their surface area and depth. Concurrently, the non-point source runoff of excess nutrients and contaminants is threatening the area's remaining aquatic resources. The Service lists six species of aquatic organisms as threatened and twelve species as endangered in North Carolina (Table 2).

Hydrologic alterations have basically eliminated the geomorphologic processes that created sandbars, oxbow lakes, sloughs, and river meander scars. Consequently, the protection, conservation, and restoration of aquatic resources are of added importance in light of the alterations associated with navigation and flood control.

PROLIFERATION OF INVASIVE AQUATIC PLANTS

Compounding the problems faced by aquatic systems is the growing threat from invasive aquatic vegetation. Static water levels caused by the lack of annual flooding and reduced water depths resulting from excessive sedimentation have created conditions favorable for the establishment and proliferation of several species of invasive aquatic plants. Additionally, the introduction of exotic (nonnative) vegetation capable of aggressive growth is further threatening the viability of aquatic systems. These invasive aquatic species threaten the natural aquatic vegetation important to aquatic systems, and choke waterways to a degree that often prevents recreational use. Common reed (*Phragmites australis*) is the most dominant of these plants on the Outer Banks and the refuge, and has a negative impact on the marshes in the area. Alligator weed (*Alternanthera philoxeroides*) is an ever-increasing invasive aquatic plant in eastern North Carolina. It can severely impede the natural surface flow of water with its web-like growth in narrow bodies of water.

CONSERVATION PRIORITIES

The declines in the area of the South Atlantic Coastal Plain's bottomland hardwood forests and their associated fish and wildlife resources have prompted the Service to designate this forest type as an area of special concern. These areas are of particular concern as habitat for neotropical migratory songbirds that only breed in the interior of large forested areas. They also provide habitat for fish-eating raptors that require forested habitat close to water in which to perch and from which to fish. The forests protect the aquatic habitat for interjurisdictional fish and other aquatic organisms. Much of the development has been for crop production, and these areas have potential for restoration when crop prices do not justify the maintenance of intensive drainage systems required to maintain production. Many government habitat restoration programs focus on bottomland hardwood forests.

In the Outer Coastal Plain, the loss of marsh, dune, and beach habitat continues unabated. Although wetland protection laws regulate development in the marshes, the public's desire to live and recreate in dune and beach habitats is steadily growing, and development continues to alter these areas. The potential for restoring these habitats is lower than it is for bottomland hardwood forests because the habitat loss is due to land use conversions to residential and commercial development. Conservationists must mitigate habitat loss by intensive management through restoration or use of a variety of habitat enhancement techniques involving various plantings, mechanical manipulation, prescribed fire, or water management.

A collaborative effort involving private, state, and federal conservation partners is now underway to implement a variety of tools to restore the functions and values of wetlands in the South Atlantic Coastal Plain. The goal is to prioritize and manage wetlands to most effectively maintain and possibly restore the biological diversity in the South Atlantic Coastal Plain. Through cooperative efforts, apportioning resources, and the focusing of available programs, conservationists can improve the South Atlantic Coastal Plain's biological diversity.

Conservationists have initiated several coordinated efforts to set priorities and establish focus areas to overcome the impacts of hydrologic changes and habitat fragmentation. Conservation organizations and agencies established a cooperative private–state–federal partnership known as the North American Waterfowl Management Plan, Atlantic Coast Joint Venture in 1988, to help provide sufficient wintering waterfowl habitat throughout the Atlantic Coastal Plain.

The initial Atlantic Coast Joint Venture effort for waterfowl has expanded to also establish breeding bird objectives for shorebirds and neotropical migratory birds. Partners in Flight has developed bird conservation plans to focus a number of private, state, and federal restoration programs into specific areas in an effort to provide maximum program benefits for neotropical migratory birds.

One of the biggest challenges to the management and restoration efforts underway in the South Atlantic Coastal Plain, and one that affects refuges in particular, is the need to meet long-term management objectives that address comprehensive ecosystem needs. These needs include those of wintering migratory waterfowl, neotropical migratory birds, shorebirds, large mammals, and other wide-ranging species. Often management for one species or species group conflicts with the management objectives for another species or species group. The tendency is to pursue short-term priorities that frequently change as scientific knowledge expands and interests in special resources shift. Biologists must exercise caution to prevent the start-up of management and restoration actions that are difficult to reverse and fail to meet the long-term, comprehensive management needs of the ecosystem or a specific area within the ecosystem. An example might be a tendency to totally manage Pea Island Refuge in an effort to provide habitat for many species of waterfowl that require managed herbaceous wetlands. Such an approach may overlook the critical habitat needs of neotropical migratory songbirds that prefer a shrubby habitat.

Active management of wetlands, moist-soil areas, and croplands on both public and private land is necessary to meet the habitat goals of the Atlantic Coast Joint Venture (Reinecke and Baxter 1996). The management (i.e., vegetation manipulation and hydrology restoration) compensates for the spatial and temporal habitat changes that deforestation and hydrologic alterations have caused throughout the South Atlantic Coastal Plain. When appropriately managed, Pea Island Refuge will make a substantial contribution to meeting the objectives of the Atlantic Coast Joint Venture. Setting habitat and species objectives from the perspective of the South Atlantic Coastal Plain is advantageous because it looks at the big picture and enables managers to plan and provide habitat for a diversity of species throughout their range.

CHALLENGES

In order for Pea Island Refuge to meet its multiple objectives of national, regional, and local scope, ranging from impoundment and marsh management to providing for public use, the Service must seek resources above current levels. Securing resources to successfully address historical wetland, beach, and dune alterations and hydrological functions is the refuge's biggest challenge. In the interim, as the needed resources become available, the refuge must concentrate on its highest priorities without committing irreversible actions that would preclude future implementation of the desired management programs.

PHYSICAL ENVIRONMENT

CLIMATE

Because the flow of air over North Carolina is predominantly from west to east, the continental influence is much greater than the ocean or marine influence. Therefore, the state experiences a fairly large variation in temperature from winter to summer.

The Gulf Stream current flows only a short distance off the North Carolina coast. One might think this "river" of warm water would have a profound effect on the climate, which is true to a degree. Temperatures on the coast are typically warmer in winter months and cooler during summer months than mainland Dare County due to the temperature of the surrounding waters.

Low pressure areas sometimes reform along the coast as "Cape Hatteras lows" and then move north along the coast. Winter's low-pressure storms are usually more intense because of the large north-to-south contrasts. The winter storms bring prolonged periods of steady rain and are responsible for most of the winter precipitation. The forms of precipitation in spring begin to change from these steady rains to occasional thunderstorms. The Gulf of Mexico's warm, moist air produces warm, humid weather throughout the summer. Rainfall comes from occasional thunderstorms. Autumn, North Carolina's driest season, is to many people the most pleasant with its many clear, warm days and cool nights with little rain. This weather usually lasts until November. Winter is cool and has brief occasional cold spells. Snowfall is not common.

The average annual precipitation is 56.99 inches. Rainfall is evenly distributed throughout the year; the average monthly rainfall ranges from 3.43 inches in April to 5.98 inches in August. The average seasonal snowfall is about 1.9 inches. The record snowfall was 8.2 inches at Hatteras in December 1989. Twelve inches fell on the Outer Banks on January 23, 2003. Twenty-five inches is the record at Elizabeth City, North Carolina.

Of the total annual precipitation, about 27 inches usually falls in May through September. The growing season for most crops is within this period. Thunderstorms occur on about 43 days each year. Every few years, a hurricane or tropical storm crosses the county, bringing one to three days of intensive rainfall.

The average relative humidity in mid-afternoon is about 65 percent. Humidity is higher at night, and the average at dawn is about 80 percent. The sun shines on 55 percent of winter days. The prevailing wind is from the southwest. Average wind speed is highest, 13 miles per hour, in spring.

The average daily maximum temperature at the Cape Hatteras weather station from 1971-2000 was 69.9 degrees Fahrenheit, and the average daily minimum is 55.6 degrees.

In January the average temperature is 46.1 degrees, the average daily maximum is 53.6 degrees, and the average daily minimum temperature is 38.6 degrees. The lowest temperature on record, which occurred at Cape Hatteras on January 21, l985, is 6 degrees. In July the average temperature is 79.2 degrees, the average daily maximum temperature is 85.4 degrees, and the average daily minimum temperature is 72.9 degrees. The highest recorded temperature, which occurred on July 10, 1992, was 96 degrees.

The average last freezing temperature in spring is March 16. The average first freezing temperature in the fall is December 7. The average growing season is 265 days.

GEOLOGY

The Outer Banks are part of the Coastal Plain of North Carolina that stretches from the Piedmont Plateau in the west to the continental shelf in the east. Water covered this area during the Tertiary period and early Pleistocene epoch more than 730,000 years ago. The coast later emerged during the first ice age, but with the melting of the continental ice sheets was again submerged.

During the Wisconsin glacial maximum approximately 25,000 years ago, the sea was between 250 and 450 feet below its present level. It seems that the barrier islands of the Outer Banks were formed since the melting of the Wisconsin ice sheet, and have generally been in their current position for the last 4,000 to 5,000 years. Although there is no general agreement as to how the barrier islands were initially created, they may have existed in one form or another near the edge of the current continental shelf during low stands of sea level, and then migrated back and forth across the Coastal Plain with fluctuating sea levels.

The Outer Banks are being constantly modified as a rule. Generally, the barrier islands are long, narrow islands standing only a few feet above sea level. The islands vary in width from about 600 feet to nearly 3 miles, and are separated from the mainland by shallow sounds as much as 28 miles wide. The barrier islands are slowly moving westward, primarily due to a lack of sediment supply and a rise in sea level. The sea level is rising at approximately two feet per century. When it was established in 1938, Pea Island Refuge was 5,915 acres in size. Today, likely due to erosion and natural barrier island processes, the size is approximately 5,000 acres.

This consistent pattern of migration is only one of the dynamic features associated with the barrier islands. The sediments that make up the islands are composed mainly of sand, and are therefore subject to constant alteration by both wind and water (i.e., via waves, currents and flooding). Wind is constantly moving and reshaping the dune features on the islands. Historical documents indicate that such major dunes engulfed dwellings and roads in the past, and the only practical response to this threat was to move such features out of harm's way.

The more common dune feature is the beach dune. These are found just behind the beach line and offer some measure of protection to the land surfaces behind. But unless they are stabilized, beach dunes will also migrate and fluctuate, exposing interior areas to storms and wind. During the 1930s, the Civilian Conservation Corps augmented and stabilized the entire beach dune line of the Outer Banks (Stick 1958; Pilkey et al. 1998). The project trucked sand where the beach dunes had eroded and bulldozers shaped the fill into dunes (Ted Mew, personal communication). Workers stabilized the dunes with sand fences and planted stabilizing vegetation. The program offered artificial protection from overwash and inlet formation to many exposed areas of the islands, including the refuge.

Oregon Inlet at the north edge of Pea Island formed during a northeastern storm in 1846, at the same time that Hatteras Inlet formed to the south. The fishing vessel *Oregon* was lost at the new inlet, and from that point on the inlet has been called Oregon Inlet. Oregon Inlet migrated southward at a rate of 23 meters/year and landward, or westward, at 5 meters/year between 1849 and 1975 (Inman and Dolan 1989). With it, two lighthouse structures were lost. Today, the Bodie Island Lighthouse sits near where the northern extremity of Oregon Inlet once was.

Due to migration, local officials and fishermen began their effort for channel stabilization in the 1940s to ensure a safe route of passage through Oregon Inlet. In 1950, Congress authorized the Corps of Engineers to dredge a 400-foot-wide by 14-foot-deep channel through the Inlet, but the actual dredging did not begin until 1962. This dredging has been ongoing sporadically since that time.

In 1963, the Bonner Bridge over the Oregon Inlet was opened to traffic. Because of erosion on the southern side of the Inlet, a permit was issued to the North Carolina Department of Transportation in 1989 to install a terminal groin on the north end of Pea Island Refuge. Since that time, the Inlet's southern shoreline has remained relatively stable, while the northern shore and the tidal channels within the Inlet have continued to fluctuate in response to coastal processes. The Corps of Engineers has dredged Oregon Inlet for navigational passage for more than 30 years, with approximately 0.6–1.2 million cubic yards of sediment removed annually.

At least 13 inlets have existed between the Virginia state line and Cape Hatteras since historic maps were recorded. Various inlets existed at or near Oregon Inlet from 1585 to 1770 and then again since 1846 with the current inlet. New Inlet, located on the Pea Island Refuge, was open from the 1730s until 1922, when it closed naturally. An attempt to open the inlet artificially in 1925 failed. A hurricane in 1933 reopened the inlet, but it again closed on its own in 1945. The remaining bridge structures found in the shallow sound waters of this area were constructed at that time. A third inlet known as Loggerhead Inlet also may have been in the area of the refuge during the mid- to late-1800s.

The Outer Banks of North Carolina have the highest wave energies striking the Atlantic coast in the southeastern United States. The long-term average annual oceanfront erosion rates for the refuge, as defined by the North Carolina Division of Coastal Management, range from 2 to 16 feet per year. Erosion rates are greatest at the southern boundary of the refuge near Rodanthe and at two points roughly 4 and 6 miles south of Oregon Inlet. Accretion locally occurs approximately 2 miles south of the old Headquarters buildings and stretches for about a mile. Boss and Hoffman (2000a) attribute part of the high erosion rates on Pea Island to the fairly narrow and steep shoreface that allows higher wave energies to reach the beach, and to the lack of sand in the offshore trough to naturally replenish the beaches; they also state that the presence of the bathymetric trough impedes cross-shore transport of sediment to the beaches. Platt Shoals may also reflect and refract incoming waves such that the wave energy is concentrated in certain areas and comparatively defused in others, which may explain the variability in erosion rates within the refuge (Boss and Hoffman 2000a).

There are six "hot spots" of perpetual overwash and erosion along Hatteras and Ocracoke islands. These hot spots threaten North Carolina Highway 12 in three places within the refuge: the Canal Zone Hotspot located 0.75 miles south of Oregon Inlet; the Sandbag Area Hotspot located 3.4 miles south of Oregon Inlet; and the "S" Curves Hotspot, which extends from the south refuge boundary at Rodanthe to about 1 mile north. The State of North Carolina has relocated Highway 12 several times, both within and outside the refuge, as a result of these natural hazards. Many of the hot spots appear to be controlled by the underlying geology, which recent research suggests consists of paleofluvial channels of the Pamlico Creek drainage basin during lower sea levels. This basin emptied into the Neuse/Pamlico system to the southwest of Cape Hatteras. These channels and their valleys were then filled in with estuarine sediments (i.e., mud, peat) as sea level rose (Riggs et al. 1995). North of Oregon Inlet, the Roanoke/Albemarle river basin drained to the east and underlies the current Nags Head–Kitty Hawk area. These soft mud deposits tend to erode slower than sand and gravel sediments (Riggs et al. 1995).

Pea Island would be an overwash-dominated island if left to completely natural processes. Starting with the extensive dune building in the 1930s with the Civilian Conservation Corps and Works Progress Administration, however, man has stabilized the island. Since that time, dune building with sand fences, bulldozers, and vegetation has stabilized the island and held it in place. Overwash is a natural coastal process that adds elevation to central parts of the island and to the sound-side shoreline. The North Carolina Department of Transportation continually removes storm overwash deposits from the roadway of North Carolina Highway 12, and rebuilds artificial dunes between the highway and the beach. Thus, the lack of natural sediment redistribution hinders the island's migration during a time of rising sea level. The oceanfront beaches are narrower than they would naturally be, and the interior and sound shorelines of the island are starved of sediment. The artificial dunes are not in their natural position, composed of their natural stratigraphy and sedimentology, or of natural shapes and sizes.

The sediments composing these barrier islands were deposited in a marine or near-marine environment. Silt and clay may be mixed with sand to form heterogeneous beds of low permeability. The beaches of the Outer Banks are composed mostly of sand but also may have outcrops of mud, peat, pea gravel, shells, or tree stumps, depending on the underlying geology. Sands and gravels dominate areas that once were inlets. Old stream or river channels from periods of lower sea level will have some pea gravel as well as mud from estuaries that filled them as sea level rose. Peat and tree stumps indicate old forests or marshes that the island has since migrated or rolled over. Likewise, oyster or clamshells, as well as shells stained black, are from marsh deposits that are now cropping out on the beach or the shoreface (the underwater portion of the beach). Pea gravel content may vary between 20 and 60 percent on the local beach surface, while shells may compose up to 25 percent of the surface sediments (Carroll 1999). (Much of this has already been documented above.)

No new sediment is being delivered to these barrier islands from either the rivers or eroding headlands, because the rivers discharge into estuaries. The Albemarle and Pamlico sounds separate the flows that would deliver sediment from the beaches. Various geologists, including Riggs et al. (1995) and Pilkey et al. (1998), have called them "sediment starved." The underlying geologic framework of old inlet sands and gravels, fluvial channel sands and gravels, and marsh peats and estuarine muds are supplying a limited amount of sediment to the oceanfront beaches when the island migrates over itself and recycles its sediments.

MINERALS

Sand is the only mineral resource occurring in economic quantities. There are no sand pits in the vicinity of the refuge. Because sand has become a very desirable material due to erosion, there have been several instances of persons removing sand from the refuge without authorization to use on personal projects outside the refuge boundary. Also, the North Carolina Department of Transportation has mined sand from behind the terminal groin to use for dune construction within the refuge.

SOILS

Soil types identified on the refuge are Carteret sand, Corolla fine sand, Duckston fine sands, and Newhan fine sands, and a complex of Corolla and Duckston fine sands (USDA Soil Conservation Service 1992). The soils with an asterisk are listed as hydric in "Hydric Soils of the United States" (USDA Soil Conservation Service 1985). Hydric soils are "soils that in their undrained condition are saturated, flooded, or ponded long enough during the growing season to develop anaerobic conditions that favor the growth and regeneration of hydrophytic (water-loving) vegetation" (USDA Soil Conservation Service 1985) (Figure 3).

Most of the refuge is Carteret sand, a soil with 80 inches or more of sand. It floods regularly to a depth of up to 3 feet with tidal fluctuations and has a water table from the surface to 1 foot below the surface. Carteret soils support freshwater and brackish herbaceous marsh vegetation.

Duckston fine sands occur on the eastern edge of the Carteret soils. They have 8 inches of fine sand over 72 inches of sand. Duckston soils have rapid permeability above the water table. They are poorly drained with water tables from the surface to 1 foot below the surface. They flood more than once every 2 years, but only for 2 to 7 days. Duckston soils support shrub and herbaceous vegetation adapted to poor drainage.

Corolla fine sand and Newhan fine sand are well-drained soils that occur under the dunes on the eastern edge of the refuge. Corolla fine sand occurs on the backsides of dunes and has 3 inches of fine sand over sandy subsoil. The water table is 1-1/2 to 3 feet below the surface. The herbaceous dune vegetation on Corolla soils is adapted to good drainage, but not necessarily tolerant of extremely droughty conditions. Corolla soils are also excellent soils for building construction, but are poor filters for septic systems. Newhan fine sand occurs on the tops of dunes and has 80 inches of fine sand over sandy subsoil. The water table is more than 6 feet below the surface. Newhan soils also support herbaceous vegetation that is the most drought-tolerant and salt-tolerant. They are also excellent soils for building construction, but are poor filters for septic systems.

HYDROLOGY

Ground water provides the freshwater resources for the area. Studies have shown that the groundwater reservoir consists of two types of aquifers: a water table aquifer that extends from the land surface to the first confining beds of silt and clay, and a confined or semi-confined aquifer

Figure 3. Characteristics of soils of Pea Island National Wildlife Refuge

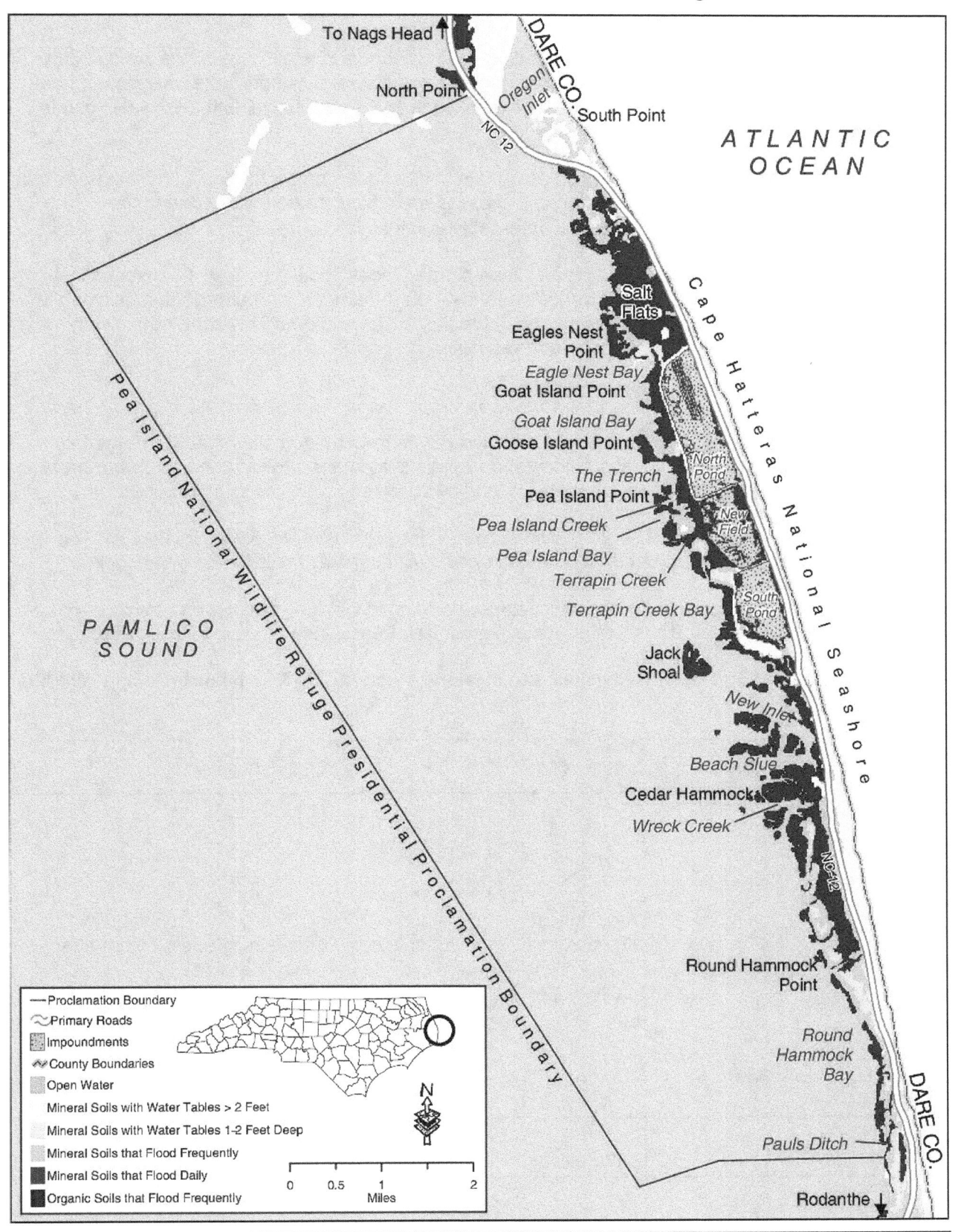

beneath and between the silt and clay beds. The water table aquifer ranges in thickness from 10 to 50 feet and averages 15 feet. The water table itself averages 3 feet above mean sea level.

Maintenance of the fresh ground water depends on the amount of rainfall. Due to the sandy nature of the soils, rainfall enters the water table aquifer with little or no surface runoff. After the ground has become saturated, some runoff occurs in roadside ditches and small intermittent freshwater ponds during periods of intensive rainfall.

The deeper confined aquifers are as much as 30 feet thick and are below the first confining beds that range in thickness from 5 to 20 feet. Exact thicknesses are difficult to determine due to the gradational nature of sediments below the water table aquifer.

The fresh ground water is best described as a lens-shaped mass floating on top of denser salt water. The amount of fresh water in this lens varies depending on the amount of recharge and discharge. Between the fresh water and salt water a zone of brackish water occurs. This zone periodically changes due to flooding, tidal movement, and rainfall.

WATER QUALITY

There are six National Pollution Discharge Elimination System-permitted sites that discharge into waters adjacent to the refuge. One is a domestic sewage system for a town; one is a harbor project; two are domestic water supply treatment plants; and two are seafood-processing facilities.

The state's list of impaired waters due to fecal coliform includes portions of Roanoke, Croatan, and Pamlico sounds. Technical conditions do not exist to develop total maximum daily loads for the water bodies.

The state has classified the water bodies and streams according to their water quality and the uses that quality supports. The classifications for the waters surrounding Pea Island Refuge are listed in Table 3.

Table 3. Classifications of water bodies and streams surrounding Pea Island National Wildlife Refuge

Water Body or Stream	Classification	Best Uses
Pamlico Sound Oregon Inlet Eagle Nest Bay Goat Island Bay The Trench Pea Island Creek Pea Island Bay Terrapin Creek Bay Terrapin Creek Beach Slue Wreck Creek Round Hammock Bay Pauls Ditch	SA – Highest Quality Saltwater HQW – High Quality Water	Commercial shellfishing and all other tidal saltwater uses
Atlantic Ocean	SB – Moderate Quality Saltwater	All recreation

AIR QUALITY

The area closest to the refuge that an environmental agency monitors is the Virginia Beach–Norfolk, Virginia, metropolitan area. The Environmental Protection Agency monitors carbon monoxide, nitrogen dioxide, ozone, sulfur dioxide, and particulates in Norfolk, Virginia Beach, Hampton, Newport News, Suffolk, and Chesapeake. Despite the large population with the industry, traffic, and power plants, the area has exceeded only ozone level standards in 2002. Monitoring has indicated unhealthy levels only twice and unhealthy levels for sensitive groups only thirteen times.

Prescribed burning on the refuge has the potential to have an impact on air quality. The State of North Carolina specifies that prescribed fires purposely set to marshes (for marsh management practices acceptable to the North Carolina Division of Forestry and the Environmental Management Commission) are permissible if not prohibited by ordinances and regulations of governmental entities having jurisdiction. The regulation also includes a disclaimer that addresses certain potential liabilities of burning even though permissible.

VISUAL RESOURCES

Visitors have recognized Pea Island National Wildlife Refuge for its outstanding and diversified visual resources that have been a draw for persons of all ages, backgrounds, and interests since its establishment. A 13-mile stretch of North Carolina Highway 12 runs directly through the refuge and is part of the North Carolina Scenic Byway System; it is also the primary route from the mainland to the historic Cape Hatteras Lighthouse. Cape Hatteras National Seashore, a national recreation area that extends from Nags Head to Ocracoke Island, surrounds the refuge and overlays portions of the same land.

The refuge's location between sound and ocean provides unique opportunities for visitors to view both sunrise and sunset over water. A photo blind enables birding enthusiasts to capture the many species of birds identified on the refuge without disturbing them in their natural environment. Walking trails, raised platforms, and platforms overlooking impoundments offer further opportunities for viewers to appreciate the small mammalian and feathered species dependent upon the refuge for their habitat and survival. The 13 miles of sand dunes create a barrier between ocean and beachfront and the marsh, shrub thickets, tidal ponds, freshwater ponds, and nesting areas. Refuge waters within the sound are a haven for the tens of thousands of migratory birds that use the Atlantic Flyway each season. Islands with sea oats, wax myrtle thickets, salt meadow cord grass, and other vegetation dot the sound.

BIOLOGICAL ENVIRONMENT

HABITATS

Pea Island National Wildlife Refuge is situated on a typical southeastern United States barrier island system with ocean beach, dune, brackish ponds, and marsh communities dissected by tidal creeks containing submerged aquatic vegetation (Figures 4 and 5). The refuge's plant communities have been affected by human development activities over time. Some of these activities occurred before the Service established the refuge and some have occurred since. The most notable products of those activities today are artificial dunes, North Carolina Highway 12, the Herbert C. Bonner Bridge, and three impoundments.

Although natural dunes occur, the Civilian Conservation Corps first constructed some oceanfront dunes in the 1930s and, since then, agencies have vegetated and maintained them for various reasons. The primary reason for dune maintenance on the refuge today is protection of North Carolina Highway 12.

Figure 4. Vegetative habitat types of Pea Island National Wildlife Refuge

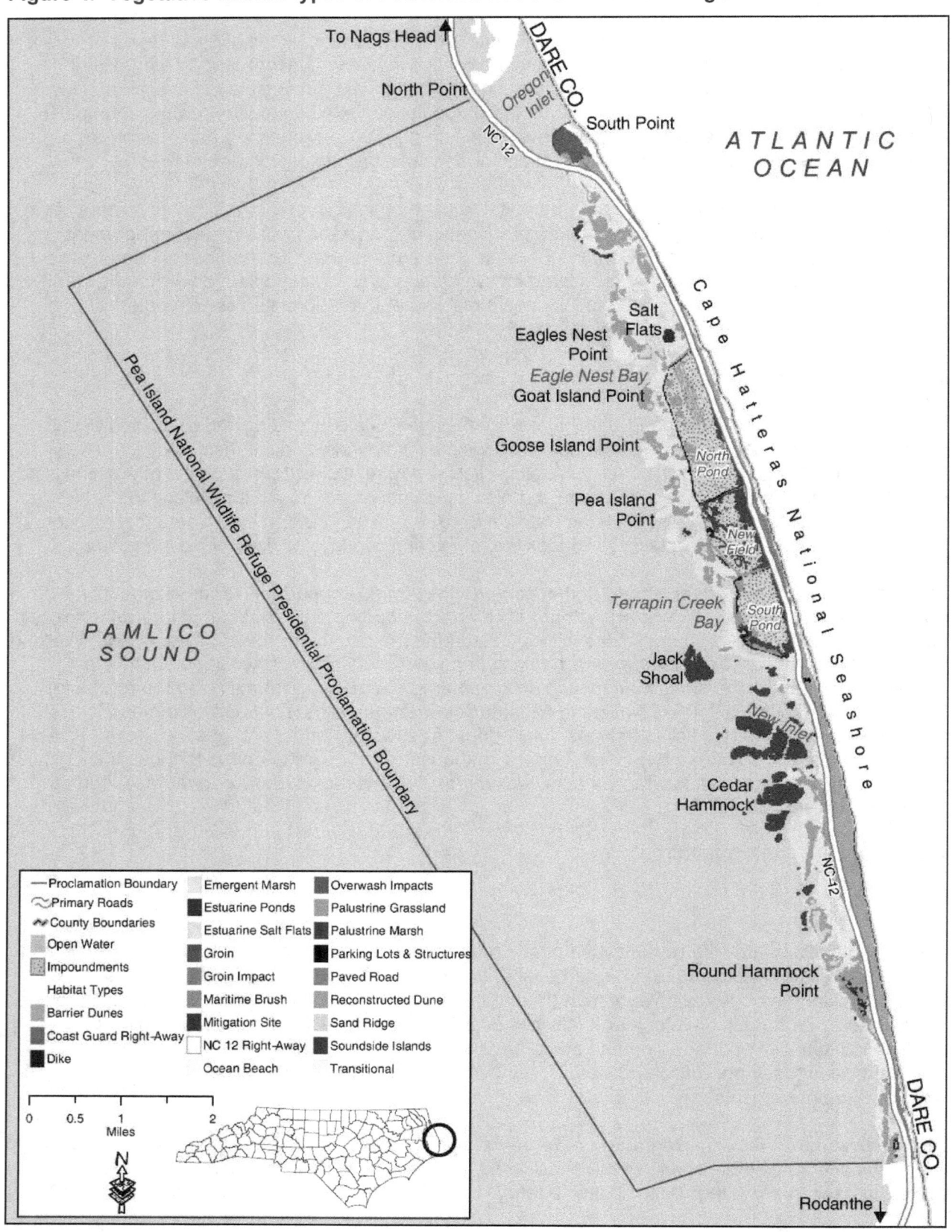

Figure 5. Cross-section of vegetative habitat types of coastal barrier islands

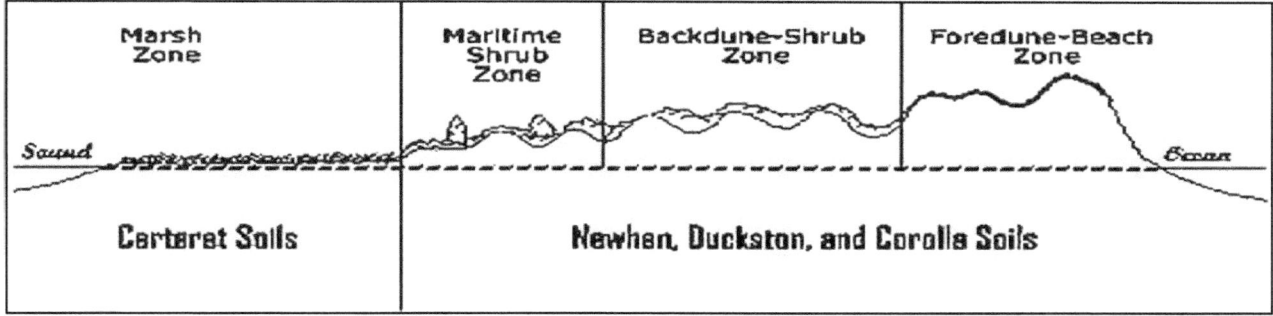

Although a sand trail pre-dated the refuge, the state did not pave what is now North Carolina Highway 12 until the 1950s, and the state has relocated much of it westward since its initial construction.

The Service constructed three man-made impoundments in the late 1950s and 1960s to enhance habitat quality for migratory waterfowl. The plant communities today reflect succession since the late 1930s, with some areas being subjected to ocean overwash, agricultural practices, and prescribed fire. More recently, prescribed fire has substantially altered plant communities and successional stages on most of the refuge. The community descriptions in this document are not complete species lists.

Ocean Beach Community

Lower Beach. This is the exposed portion of the beach between the mean high tide and mean low tide lines. It is the unvegetated portion of the beach subject to diurnal tidal flooding. Substrate consists of unconsolidated sand and variable shell fragment content. This is a dynamic community subject to the effects of tidal swash twice daily.

Upper Beach. This is that portion of the beach above the mean high tide line up to the toe-of-slope for the frontal dune or berm. The substrate consists of unconsolidated sand and shell fragments and is constantly changing due to wind and tidal surges during storm events. Vegetation is sparse, characterized by a small number of mostly succulent species adapted to regular disturbance: Sea rocket (Cakile edentula; Cakile harperi), seabeach sandmat (Chamaesyce spp.), and seabeach knotweed (Polygonum glaucum). Although biologists have not located it on the refuge, the federally threatened seabeach amaranth (Amaranthus pumilus) could occur in this community. This community is subject to the dynamics of coastal processes including frequent tidal inundation and wind disturbance. Landward of the Upper Beach community is a Barrier Dune ecosystem.

Barrier Dune Community

Dune Grass. The Dune Grass Community occurs immediately landward of the Upper Beach community and is subject to exposure to salt spray and abrasive, wind-blown sand. These communities are excessively drained due to the nature of the substrate and are subject to frequent shifting unless stabilized through artificial means. Artificial dune building by sand fencing and dense planting of grasses has led to the development of a high continuous line of dunes which concentrates the effects of storm waves on the beach, increasing erosion rates. Vegetative composition and plant community structure is highly correlated with exposure to salt in the environment, either in aerosol form or by ocean overwash. Generally, plant species found on the ocean side of the dunes are more tolerant to salt and the abrasive effects of wind-blown sand. The Dune Grass community transitions into a Wet or Dry Maritime Grassland, Maritime Shrub, Maritime Forest, or various combinations on the landward side of the barrier dune.

Common plants in this community are sea oats (*Uniola paniculata*), which grow from sturdy rhizomes that help to stabilize shifting sands. Other plants in this community may include American beach grass (*Ammophila breviligulata*), Atlantic coastal panic grass (*Panicum amarum*), seaside bluestem (*Schizachyrium scoparium*), trailing wild bean (*Strophostyles helvula*), seaside croton (*Croton punctatus*), and gaillardia (*Gaillardia pulchella*). Plant species of federal concern, such as dune bluecurls (*Trichostema spp.*) and the federally threatened seabeach amaranth, may also occur in this community, but neither has been documented on the refuge.

Grasslands

Maritime Dry Grassland. This community occurs on low, stable dunes and sand ridges. It also occurs in overwash terraces behind or between dunes in areas subject to inundation by the ocean or partial burial due to wind-blown sand. Frequently, this community transitions into the dune grass community on the ocean side. The dominance of saltmeadow grass (*Spartina patens*) readily distinguishes maritime dry grassland from the dune grass community. Under natural conditions this community is influenced by salt spray that retards shrub invasion. Where dunes are naturally protected or have been artificially stabilized, these grasslands can succeed into maritime shrub and possibly to maritime forest with sufficient time. In contrast, the maritime dry grassland may transition from maritime shrub or maritime forest in areas where there is loss of dune protection. In addition to saltmeadow cordgrass, this community may have a moderate to dense herbaceous cover of species such as seaside goldenrod (*Solidago sempervirens*), marsh pink (*Sabatia stellaris*), seaside greenbrier (*Smilax auriculata*), and gaillardia (*Gaillardia pulchella*). It is not uncommon to find some sparse woody vegetation such as yaupon (*Ilex vomitoria*) and yucca (*Yucca spp.*).

Maritime Wet Grassland. This community occurs on dune swales, sand flats, and sand-filled marsh where the water table is near the surface. Typically, this community type is seasonally or permanently staturated, but lacks surface flooding throughout most of the year. The community may be subject to infrequent overwash.

Dense, herbaceous vegetation dominates this community, with a mix of wetland and mesic species such as saltmeadow grass (*Spartina patens*), bald spikerush (*Fimbristylis spadicea*), three-square bulrush (*Scirpus americancus*), or duneslack muhly (*Muhlenbergia filipes*). Seaside pennywort (*Hydrocotyle bonariensis*), small whitetop sedge (*Rhynchospora colorata*), common foxtail grass, (*Setaria geniculata*), and common broom sedge (*Andropogon virginicus*) may also occur and can sometimes be very common in patches.

Through exposure to some salt spray, occasional (but infrequent) overwash, and saturated soil conditions, succession does not occur quickly in this community type. With dune accretion through overwash or aeolian deposition, the community type could transition into dry grassland or maritime shrub. The lack of standing water for most of the year distinguishes this community from the *Interdune Pond community*. Its higher diversity and occurrence on wetter sites distinguishes it from the Maritime Dry Grassland community.

Shrub Communities

Maritime Shrub. The Maritime Shrub community occurs in a wide range of conditions from excessively to poorly drained soils in areas protected from salt spray and flooding by salt water. These conditions may occur on stabilized sand ridges, in dune swales, and on sand flats. Depending upon successional stage, there may be substantial variation in the plant community. In earlier successional stages it has a dense growth of shrubs, mostly wax myrtle (*Morella cerifera*), red cedar (*Juniperus virginiana*), Southern red cedar (*Juniperus silicicola*.), saltmeadow bush (*Baccharis halimifolia*), yaupon (*Ilex vomitoria*), greenbrier (*Smilax spp.*), blackberry (*Rubus spp.*), and poison ivy (*Toxicodendron radicans*). Stunted live oak (*Quercus virginiana*) dominates older communities. Artificial dune construction increases protection from overwash on sand flats and from salt spray, allowing shrubs to invade. The maritme shrub community can undergo succession into Maritime Evergreen Forest with increased protection.

The prevalence of shrubby, woody plant species distinguishes this community from maritime grasslands and dune grass communities. The relatively low canopy and a lower occurrence of live oak distinguish it from the maritime evergreen forest community. It is distinguishable from the Salt Shrub community due to the predominance of wax myrtle and presence of species such as yaupon, live oak, and greenbrier.

Salt Shrub. The Salt Shrub community occurs along higher margins and other slightly higher areas in salt and brackish marshes. The plant species diversity found in the community is somewhat variable and is positively correlated with the frequency and amount of saltwater flooding. Most salt shrub communities have an open to closed shrub canopy, typically consisting of saltmeadow bush (*Baccharis halimiflora*), marsh elder (*Iva fructescens*), seaside oxeye (*Borrichia frutescens*), wax myrtle (*Morella cerifera*), and southern red cedar (*Juniperus silicicola*), as well as inclusions of marsh vegetation.

The salt shrub community is similar to the maritime shrub community, but is distinguished by the dominance of the species listed above and the absence of species not tolerant of salt, as well as its physical location. The salt shrub community may grade into salt or brackish marsh as areas become wetter. In contrast, the community can grade into maritime shrub, maritime forest, or grassland communities with lower salinity or sand deposition.

Marsh

Salt Marsh. This community occurs on the margins of sounds, estuaries, and other coastal waters. Salt marsh occurs on the landward side of barrier island systems in areas under tidal influence. Although the community is not dependent upon diurnal tide cycles, it does require periodic flooding by water with a moderate salinity level. Smooth cordgrass (*Spartina alterniflora*) dominates the salt marsh community. Although overall plant species diversity is low, black needlerush (*Juncus roemerianus*), salt grass (*Distichlis spicata*), or saltmeadow grass (*Spartina patens*) dominates areas that are slightly higher in elevation. Other plant species may include seashore mallow (*Kosteletskya virginica*), Virginia saltwort (*Salicornia virginica*), rose mallow (*Hibiscus moscheutus*), and bald spikerush or fimbry (*Fimbristylis spadicea*). Although the salt marsh community occurs on the refuge, it is most prevalent in the middle and southern portions of the North Carolina coast.

The salt marsh community may transition into brackish marsh, or it can become an estuarine channel mud flat. It can also undergo a conversion into a salt flat or salt shrub community, depending upon changes in environmental conditions.

The refuge staff manages the salt marshes with prescribed fire at a 3- to 5-year frequency to maintain herbaceous vegetative cover and suppress succession to woody vegetation.

Brackish Marsh. The brackish marsh community occurs along the margins of sounds and estuaries in areas not subjected to regular flooding by salt water. Often referred to as "high marsh," this community is subjected to irregular flooding mostly from wind tides along the Outer Banks. Salinity in the brackish marsh is generally low due to the distance from a saltwater source and freshwater inflow, but can be mid-range for brief periods. If a brackish marsh occurs in an area subjected to regular flooding with low salinity water, mineral deposition can result in mud flats. Black needlerush (*Juncus roemerianus*) dominates the vegetation in the brackish marsh community, but patches of saltmeadow grass (*Spartina patens*) and salt grass (*Distichlis spicata*) are common. Less common are patches of big cordgrass (*Spartina cynosuroides*) and sawgrass (*Cladium jamaiciense*). As salinity increases, this community can grade into salt marsh or, if salinity decreases, freshwater marsh. This community is most prevalent in the middle and northern portions of the North Carolina coast.

The refuge staff manages the brackish marshes with prescribed fire at a 3- to 5-year frequency to maintain herbaceous vegetative cover and suppress succession to woody vegetation.

Salt Flat. The salt flat community occurs in estuarine areas subjected to irregular flooding by salt water. It occurs in shallow depressions wherein evaporation of the high salinity ocean water concentrates salt. Sparse cover and low diversity characterize its plant density and species composition. In vegetated areas, dominant species may include halophytic herbs such as saltmeadow glasswort (*Salicornia virginica*), Bigelow's saltwort (*S. bigelovii*), jointed saltwort (*S. maritima*), rarely sea blite (*Suaeda linearis*), sand spurrey (*Spergularia marina*), and orach (*Atriplex patula*). Saltmarsh cordgrass (*Spartina alterniflora*), salt grass (*Distichlis spicata*), and seaside oxeye (*Borrichia frustecens*) occur in marginal zones. The centers of these communities are often completely barren of vegetation.

These communities tend to be relatively small and occur within the salt marsh community. Primary differences between the salt flat and salt marsh communities include the dominance of vegetation with high salt tolerance and lower overall vegetative cover in the salt flat community. The salt flat community can change or shift location depending upon change in environmental conditions, such as a change in water circulation, salinity, or sand deposition. The salt flat community may transition into either salt or brackish marsh.

Exposed Overwash Flats. The exposed overwash flats are marine flats, not otherwise considered part of the current beach. These flats are direct results of overwash during storm events. These flats are the unvegetated, sandy areas adjacent to beaches and inlets that can have high shell content. At low tide, rich overwash from previous storms or other events are exposed. Due to the lack of vegetation, this habitat type is attractive to several species of shorebirds and colonial nesting birds as nesting habitat and is the most likely place for the occurrence of seabeach amaranth. This community will transition into a dune grass community as natural dunes begin to form with accumulation of various types of debris.

Managed Wetlands. These are manmade impoundments with borrow canals around the perimeter that may include open water, moist soil, exposed sand/mud flats, and emergent vegetation with varying amounts and management regimes. Pea Island National Wildlife Refuge has three impoundments: 390-acre North Pond, 192-acre New Field Pond, and 208-acre South Pond. Plant communities within the impoundments include maritime wet grassland, maritime shrub, salt marsh, brackish marsh, and open water. Open water areas typically have a bottom substrate dominated by sago pondweed (*Potamogeton pectinata*), wigeon grass (*Ruppia maritime*), and muskgrass (*Chara spp.*). Horned pondweed (*Zannichellia palustris*) has been identified on occasion. The refuge staff manages this wetland community primarily for wintering waterfowl and spring shorebird migration.

The staff manages the areas by draining water in the spring to create mudflats for shorebirds and allow annual seed-bearing plants, maintaining it at a low elevation through the late summer shorebird migration, and allowing them to fill or pumping water to fill them for waterfowl migration in the fall.

The staff fills the impoundments by opening the water control structures when the tide is appropriate to fill or drain them whenever possible. The impoundments are burned, mowed, and/or disked as needed to suppress succession to perennial herbaceous and woody plants.

WILDLIFE

Appendix VI provides a complete list of wildlife species that occur on the refuge. Table 4 lists the species of management concern that occur on the refuge.

Birds

Birds are the most common and evident land vertebrates along the Outer Banks. Because the environment is predominantly maritime, the large and conspicuous water and marsh birds are especially well represented. Approximately 265 species of birds regularly visit the refuge, with about 50 additional species considered accidental visitors.

The area is roughly at the midpoint of the Atlantic Flyway and is a much used and valuable feeding and resting area for numerous species of wintering waterfowl. Snow geese, tundra swans, coots, and more than 25 species of ducks winter here. In addition to waterfowl, large numbers of shorebirds, colonial nesting birds, gulls, terns, ibises, hawks, owls, and numerous species of passerine birds frequent the area. During the spring and fall, large numbers of raptors, especially accipiters and falcons, use the Outer Banks as a migration corridor. Other birds such as warblers, shorebirds, colonial nesting birds, gulls, terns, herons, and egrets also follow the barrier islands during migration.

Avian species composition changes throughout the year since most are migratory. Peak shorebird spring migration occurs in early to mid-May, with a less defined fall migration beginning in late July and extending through September in some years. The populations of migratory waterfowl peak during the months of November through February.

In summer, dunlins, dowitchers, plovers, sandpipers, royal terns, least terns, black skimmers, American oystercatchers, yellowlegs, willets, black-necked stilts, laughing gulls, and numerous other shorebird species are observed. Many wading birds such as glossy ibises; snowy and great egrets; little blue, tri-colored, green, and black-crowned night herons; American avocets; and others are also present. An interesting variety of songbirds is present throughout the year.

Osprey and brown pelicans are very common. Although they were species of special concern in past years, they have made a remarkable comeback.

Several species of shorebirds and colonial nesting birds have been found nesting along the open beaches of the area. The black skimmer, least tern, common tern, and gull-billed tern nest in the cobble and overwash areas of the beach above high tide. From one to four American oystercatchers nest on the refuge beach each year. All of these birds are recognized species of various levels of concern in a recent Fish and Wildlife Service publication entitled, "Birds of Conservation Concern 2002." Degradation or loss of breeding habitat is the primary cause for concern with all of these species.

Mammals

Of the 47 species of mammals that occur in the lower coastal plain of North Carolina, 21 native terrestrial mammals, 8 marine mammals, and the feral cat are recorded for the Outer Banks. The most common land mammals are the cottontail rabbit, raccoon, and mink. Semi-aquatic furbearers

Table 4. Species of Management Concern at the Pea Island National Wildlife Refuge

Species	Status	Brackish Marsh	Maritime Shrub	Beach, Dune, Grass / Dry Grassland	Managed Wetlands (Moist Soil Units)
Piping Plover	FL			X	
Loggerhead Sea Turtle	FL			X	
Green Sea Turtle	FL			X	
Bald Eagle	FL	X			
Seabeach Amaranth	FL			X	
Saltmarsh Sharp-tailed Sparrow	FSC	X			
Seaside Sparrow	FSC	X			
Black Rail	FSC	X			
Yellow Rail	FSC	X			
King Rail	FSC	X			
Sedge Wren	FSC	X			X
Prairie Warbler	FSC		X		
Yellow-throated Warbler	FSC		X		
Northern Parula	FSC		X		
Red Knot	FSC			X	
Wilson's Plover	FSC			X	
Least Tern	FSC			X	
Black Skimmer	FSC			X	
American Oystercatcher	FSC			X	
Canada Goose	SMC				X
Snow Goose	SMC				X
Tundra Swan	SMC				X
American Black Duck	SMC	X			X
Gadwall	SMC	X			X
Mallard	SMC				X
American Widgeon	SMC				X
Blue-winged Teal	SMC				X
Green-winged Teal	SMC				X
Ruddy Duck	SMC				X
Ringneck Duck	SMC				X
Northern Pintail	SMC				X
Greater Scaup	SMC				X
Lesser Scaup	SMC				X
Gull-billed Tern	SMC			X	
Common Tern	SMC			X	
(FL=Federally-listed, FSC=Federal Species of Concern, SMC=Species of Management Concern on Pea Island NWR)					

such as the muskrat, nutria, and river otter are common. White-tailed deer numbers have been increasing in recent years. Marine species, including various species of whales, dolphins, and porpoises, are seen at rare intervals in the nearshore ocean waters.

Reptiles and Amphibians

There are 20 species of reptiles recorded on the barrier islands. Sea turtles include the loggerhead and the green, and they are present only during the nesting season. The relatively few permanent freshwater ponds produce a correspondingly small number of amphibian species.

Fish

Many species of important invertebrates and fish are found in the waters surrounding the islands. The marshes and tidal creeks serve as nursery grounds fish such as spot, croaker, red drum, striped and white mullet, Atlantic menhaden, and several species of flounder. Striped bass, bluefish, and spotted sea trout are also present. Productive shellfish beds are found throughout the surrounding waters. Clams and scallops are found in the grass and softer mud bottoms, and crab and shrimp are found on the bottom. Oysters are found in the shallow sound areas.

INSECTS AND DISEASES

The gypsy moth is now well established as far south as northeastern North Carolina. The North Carolina Division of Plant Industry and USDA Forest Service closely monitor gypsy moth populations using pheromone traps located throughout the Dare County mainland and barrier islands, including refuge lands. When they detect large-scale outbreaks, they use integrated pest management techniques to suppress the outbreak, but not necessarily eliminate the species from the area. Although the refuge is within the quarantine area of northeastern North Carolina, there have not been any outbreaks of the gypsy moth requiring treatment other than on Roanoke Island.

EXOTIC ORGANISMS

At the present time biologists know little about exotic organisms on the refuge. Unknown individuals introduced the ring-necked pheasant to the barrier islands and a viable population existed until the mid-1990s. A few birds remain on the refuge and were sighted in the spring of 2004. There are feral cats on the refuge, but their numbers and the extent of their impact on wildlife are unknown. Other possible species include nutria, phragmites, alligator weed, and beach vitex.

THREATENED AND ENDANGERED SPECIES

Four federally listed species occur in the area. Among them are the piping plover, loggerhead and green sea turtles, and bald eagle (Table 2).

The Service has listed the bald eagle as a federally threatened species and biologists observe them infrequently throughout the year. There have been no nesting attempts on the refuge. Sighting numbers have been increasing in recent years.

The Service has listed the Atlantic Coast and Northern Great Plains populations of the piping plover as a federally threatened, whereas the Great Lakes population is endangered. Between one and three nesting attempts have occurred annually since 1996. Over those 9 years, the plovers have attempted to nest 12 times and have fledged 5 chicks.

Primary federally protected reptiles found using the refuge are the Atlantic loggerhead and green sea turtle. Both species are inhabitants of the open ocean and nest just above the high tide line on the beach. Mating takes place in the water near nesting beaches. Egg-laying occurs most frequently during June thru mid-August.

The refuge is within the known range of the seabeach amaranth and dune bluecurls. The Service has listed the seabeach amaranth as federally threatened, whereas the dune bluecurls is a species of special concern. Biologists have not observed either species on the refuge.

The refuge staff will give the status and habitat requirements of the above species primary consideration during the planning and implementation of management actions.

CULTURAL RESOURCES

The refuge has no documented cultural resource sites. In 1978, the Thunderbird Research Corporation conducted background and archival investigations and field reconnaissance to assess the cultural resources of the Pea Island National Wildlife Refuge. It concluded that, due to the dynamic nature of the geologic forces on the barrier islands, it is unlikely that any archaeological resources have been preserved on the refuge. There was the Pea Island Lifesaving Station in the vicinity of the former refuge headquarters, but the facilities were moved frequently and no archaeological remains were found at that location (Thompson and Gardner 1979). The refuge staff and refuge visitors occasionally find shipwrecks uncovered on the beach, and the staff reports the shipwrecks to the State Historic Preservation Office. The State Historic Preservation Office has not found any of these to be significant.

SOCIOECONOMIC CONDITIONS AND LAND USE

The entire span of Pea Island National Wildlife Refuge lies within Dare County, North Carolina. Recently made more accessible to the mainland by bridges and primarily supported by tourism, coastal Dare County has seen an influx of tourists, visitors, and residents over recent decades. This considerable population growth and development of the barrier islands has brought substantial economic benefit to a region historically rural and impoverished. As a result, the refuge has seen greater recreational and public use due to this increase in visitors. However, the region's natural resources of land and water have suffered increasing demands, often with negative impact. As one of the few remaining tracts of intact natural land, the refuge and, consequently, its management considerations have become even more critical.

Pea Island National Wildlife Refuge and Dare County are in the northeastern part of North Carolina and are bounded by Currituck County to the north, Tyrrell County to the west, and Hyde County to the south. The Alligator River forms the western boundary of the county, which is bound to the north by the Albemarle Sound, to the east by the Atlantic Ocean, and to the south by the Hyde County line dividing the Pamlico Sound.

For many decades, Dare County has been in the forefront of economic growth and development in the State of North Carolina, and historically, unemployment has been lower than the state average. Seven million tourists visit the Outer Banks of Dare, Currituck, and Hyde counties every year. The next closest areas of economic growth and social life are Greenville, North Carolina, 100 miles west of the refuge, and Virginia Beach, Virginia, 100 miles north of the refuge.

Despite the growth on the Outer Banks, Dare County is still predominantly rural, with the largest town being Kill Devil Hills (2000 population: 5,897). Like other rural areas throughout the country, outdoor activities are both popular and necessary. Hunting, recreational fishing, and bird watching are popular pastimes, and commercial fishing is an important element of the local economy. The importance of Pea Island Refuge and its appropriate management is, therefore, easily understood.

HISTORY OF DARE COUNTY

The original residents of the area were Native Americans described as those of the Coastal Algonkian linguistic group at the time of European contact. Northeastern North Carolina was the most southern extent of Coastal Algonkian habitation. One chiefdom was located on the Outer Banks on Hatteras Island (Haag 1958). The Algonkians lived in permanent villages where they could hunt, fish, shellfish, and farm in close proximity to the village. They utilized seasonal villages to follow migrating fish and wildlife populations. They grew corn, beans, sunflower, and squash in small gardens; and hunted deer, bear, alligators, turtles, and a variety of small mammals. Mention of the Algonkians ceased by the mid-eighteenth century (Mathis and Crow 1983).

As early as 1584, English officers spent two months exploring Roanoke Island and its surrounding area. In 1585, Sir Walter Raleigh sent a fleet of seven vessels back to the island in an attempt to establish the first English colony in what is now eastern North Carolina. Fort Raleigh was built on Roanoke Island, but the survivors returned to England the following year. In 1587, Raleigh sent an expedition of 117 people that included women and children to give permanence to the colony. Led by John White, these settlers rebuilt the fort. On August 18, 1587, White's granddaughter, Virginia Dare, was born in the colony—the first English child born in the New World. Later that year, White sailed back to England for supplies, but Spanish hostilities and England's financial hardships delayed his return for three years. Upon arriving back at Roanoke Island in 1590, he found no trace of the colonists. Many theories have been proposed about the fate of those 117 people—called "The Lost Colony"—but the mystery remains unsolved. The area remained unpopulated for more than a half century after the disappearance of the "Lost Colony." Sir John Colleton established the first permanent settlement on Colington Island on the Outer Banks in the winter of 1664–1665. Shipwrecked sailors and settlers from Virginia established the first settlements. These settlers made an effort to grow tobacco, to grow grapes for a winery, and to raise hogs. The only real profit was from oil extracted from beached whales. Raising livestock on the grasslands of the dunes became an important occupation. The only agriculture was in small gardens (Stick 1958).

In the early 1700s, pirates moved into the area to prey on ships that passed too close to the treacherous shoreline. The most famous of these pirates, Blackbeard, made his headquarters on the Outer Banks. His death in 1718 brought an end to piracy. Around 1726, residents built windmills to grind grain on Roanoke Island and the Outer Banks. The residents made a living from farming, fishing, hunting, and beachcombing (U.S. Department of the Interior 1981).

Modern tourists first found the Outer Banks of Dare County at Nags Head in the 1830s when planters from the inland counties came to escape the hot humid summer. Cottages and the Nags Head Hotel became a home to visitors. The hotel was the scene of nightly dinners and dances. A railway was built for transportation to the beach (Outer Banks Chamber of Commerce 2003).

In the early 1800s, the Atlantic Ocean earned the name "Graveyard of the Atlantic" as numerous vessels sunk. During the Civil War, Union forces captured Fort Hatteras and Roanoke Island to secure access to North Carolina by sea. The Union ironclad ship, USS Monitor, sank in a gale off Cape Hatteras on December 30, 1862 (Outer Banks Chamber of Commerce 2003).

In 1870, the state assembly established Dare County, (named for Virginia Dare), from parts of Hyde, Currituck, and Tyrrell Counties. During this time, most opportunities for work were in the U.S. Coast Guard as lighthouse operators or weather station employees. The improvements of inlets and advances in navigation and transportation allowed commercial fishing to become an important part of the economy (Stick 1958).

On December 17, 1903, Wilbur and Orville Wright made the first successful power-driven airplane flight from Kill Devil Hill near Kitty Hawk on the Outer Banks. German submarines filled the waters off the North Carolina coast during World War I and II. Since World War II, tourism replaced hunting and fishing as the principal industry (Outer Banks Chamber of Commerce 2003).

The rivers and sounds were once the major transportation avenues in the area. As the area grew and the railroad arrived, boat traffic declined. In the twentieth century with the popularity of automobiles, the state developed a network of highways connecting the county to all areas of the eastern United States. The state replaced a drawbridge across the Croatan Sound on U.S. Highway 64 at Manns Harbor in 2002 with a high-rise bridge so motorists could bypass downtown Manteo on their way to the Outer Banks. The state is widening U.S. Highway 64 to four lanes that will connect the area to Interstate 95 and the Outer Banks. There are small local airports in Manteo and Frisco; regional airports in Greenville; and an international airport in Norfolk, Virginia. Amtrak provides passenger rail service as far east as Rocky Mount.

LAND USE IN DARE COUNTY

Logging and farming have seldom been important sources of income in Dare County due to the deep, sandy soils of the dunes, the saturated soils of the marshes on the Outer Banks, and the wetlands with deep organic soils on the mainland. The forest and marsh plant communities have always provided hunting opportunities, however, and the marshes are important nursery areas for fish. The beaches, dunes, wildlife, and fishing opportunities on the Outer Banks are major attractions to tourists for their summer vacations.

There is limited residential construction in the marshes, pocosins, and forested wetlands of the county. The largest development has been on the northern end of the coastal barrier islands known as the Outer Banks from Hatteras Village to Corolla.

Before the Civil War, farmers cultivated up to 5,000 acres of corn and tobacco on mainland Dare County in a settlement known as Beechlands, near Milltail Creek. They also grazed cattle on 25,000 acres of marsh. The Dare County Lumber Company harvested enough timber on 168,000 acres of mainland Dare County to set up a settlement called Buffalo City, which eventually went bankrupt. Both areas are now part of the Alligator River National Wildlife Refuge.

Today, Dare County is 57 percent forested (142,212 acres) and 3 percent farmland (4,961 acres). From 1992 to 1997, the land in farms decreased 30 percent from 7,046 acres to 4,961 acres; the average size of the farms decreased 45 percent from 1,007 acres to 551 acres; the number of full-time farm operators remained the same at 6; the total market value of agricultural products sold increased 34 percent from $554,000 to $836,000; and the average market value of agricultural products sold per farm increased 17 percent from $79,114 to $92,923 (Table 5).

Table 5. Dare County agricultural statistics from 1997

Number of Farms	9
Acres in Farms	4,961
Average Size of Farms (Acres)	551
Market Value of Land Per Farm	$55,033
Market Value of Land Per Acre	$1,007
Market Value of Equipment Per Farm	$75,877
Total Cropland (Acres)	4,265
Market Value of All Products Sold	$836,000
Market Value of Products Sold Per Farm	$92,923
Operators with Farm as Principal Occupation	6
Operators with Anther Occupation as Principal Occupation	3
Land in Soybeans (Acres)	3,516

Source: USDA Census of Agriculture, 1997

Soybeans are the most important crop in Dare County. Production has increased substantially between 1992 and 1997 (Table 6) (U.S. Department of Agriculture 1997).

Table 6. Commodity production in Dare County in 1992 and 1997

Commodity	1997 Production	1992 Production	1997-1992 Change
Soybeans (acres)	3,516	2,736	Increased 29%
Wheat (acres)	0	1,652	

Source: USDA Census of Agriculture, 1997

DEMOGRAPHICS IN DARE COUNTY

Dare County is primarily rural with a total estimated population of 29,967 in 2000 (U.S. Department of Commerce, Bureau of the Census 2000a) (Table 7). The county population increased 32 percent between 1990 and 2000. Kill Devil Hills is the largest town with a population of 5,897.

The population is 94.7 percent White, 2.7 percent Black, 2.2 percent Hispanic, 0.4 percent Asian, and 0.3 percent Native American (U.S. Department of Commerce, Bureau of the Census 2000a). In 2000, the median family income was $35,258, about the same as the state average of $35,320. The poverty rate was 8.1 percent of the population, well below the state average of 12.6 percent (U.S. Department of Commerce, Bureau of the Census 2000a). The unemployment rate in May 2002, was 3.0 percent, well below the State of North Carolina's unemployment rate of 6.7 percent (North Carolina Employment Security Commission 2002).

The percentage of high school graduates in the population older than 25 years old is 60 percent; the percentage of college graduates is 16 percent. The state averages are 56 percent for high school and 14 percent for college (U.S. Department of Commerce, Bureau of the Census 2000a). Home ownership rate is 74.5 percent, above the state average rate of 69.4 percent. There are 2.34 persons per household in Dare County, slightly below the state average of 2.49 (Table 7).

EMPLOYMENT IN DARE COUNTY

The hotel and food service and retail trade industries are the largest employer in Dare County, employing 3,028 and 3,022 of 12,543 employees with an annual payroll of $281.6 million in 2000 (U.S. Department of Commerce, Bureau of the Census 2000b). This is due in large part to the tourist industry on the Outer Banks (North Carolina Employment Security Commission 1999).

OUTDOOR RECREATION

Fish and wildlife resources have had a profound effect on recreation in the area. Dare County has always had an abundance of fish and game, due to its diversity of lands and waters. Early in the twentieth century, sportsmen established clubs to protect game and wildlife. Later, as part of a comprehensive wildlife management program, the Service established Pea Island National Wildlife Refuge to conserve and restore habitat for native wildlife and migratory birds.

Recreation in the area is also based on the water in the ocean, sounds, rivers, and lakes. Swimming in the ocean and sunbathing on the beach are the anchors of recreation on the Outer Banks. Boat ramps provide access to the river and sound. Numerous outfitters provide boats and guided tours. The North Carolina Coastal Plain Paddle Trails Guide lists trails through the Pea Island and Alligator River Refuges (North Carolina Division of Parks and Recreation 2001). Many vendors sell and rent canoes, kayaks, sailboats, surfboards, and sailboards. There are numerous opportunities to fish in the surf, from piers, in small boats in the sounds and streams, and from large boats in the ocean.

In 2000, the sectors employing the largest numbers of persons were in decreasing order as follows: hotel and food service, retail trade, construction, real estate, wholesale trade, professional services, administrative support, and health care, manufacturing, and finance (U.S. Department of Commerce, Bureau of the Census 2000b).

A variety of federal, state, and local government agencies and non-governmental organizations provide environmental education and interpretation opportunities. These include the National Park Service at Cape Hatteras National Seashore; the State of North Carolina at Jockey's Ridge State Park and the State Aquarium; the town of Manteo at Roanoke Island Festival Park; and The Nature Conservancy at Nags Head Woods.

Many of the festivals in the area are focused on natural resources, including Wings over Water throughout the county and Wildfest in Manteo. At least one fishing tournament is held every month from May to November. The Nature Conservancy at Nags Head Woods holds weeklong ecocamps throughout the summer.

Table 7. Economic and population data for northeastern North Carolina counties.

County	Average Income[1]	Poverty Rate (%)[1]	2004 Average Unemployment Rate (%)[2]	2000 Population[1]	Population Trend
N. Carolina	$35,320	12.6	6.1	8 million	+21% since 1990
County in the Vicinity of the Pea Island National Wildlife Refuge					
Dare	$35,258	8.1	7.6	29,967	+32% since 1990
Other Northeastern North Carolina Counties					
Beaufort	$28,614	17.4	9.0	44,958	+6% since 1990
Bertie	$22,816	12.6	9.3	19,773	Same as 1990
Camden	$35,423	12.2	4.0	6,885	+16% since 1990
Carteret	$34,348	11.8	6.5	59,383	+13% since 1990
Chowan	$27,900	18.7	4.0	14,526	+7% since 1990
Craven	$33,214	13.8	4.7	91,436	+12% since 1990
Currituck	$36,287	10.8	3.6	18,190	+32% since 1990
Gates	$30,087	15.4	2.6	10,516	Same as 1900
Halifax	$24,471	23.6	9.3	57,370	Same as 1950
Hertford	$23,724	23.1	4.0	22,601	Same as 1960
Hyde	$23,568	24.8	10.9	5,826	-37% since 1900
Martin	$26,058	20.1	8.4	25,593	Same as 1940
Northampton	$24,218	23.1	7.9	22,086	Same as 1980
Pamlico	$28,629	16.8	4.9	12,934	+14% since 1990
Pasquotank	$29,305	19.0	3.6	34,897	+11% since 1990
Perquimens	$26,489	19.5	3.3	11,368	Same as 1920
Tyrrell	$21,616	25.7	7.5	4,149	-17% since 1900
Washington	$27,726	20.5	8.3	13,723	Same as 1960

1 U.S. Census Bureau, 2000 Census of the United States

2 North Carolina Economic Security Commission, December, 2004

OUTDOOR RECREATION ECONOMICS

Fish and wildlife are the focus of the refuge, but they are also important to the local economy. First, a considerable commercial fishery is present in ocean, lakes, and sounds. Striped bass, red drum, flounder, speckled trout, croakers, blue crabs, and gray trout are the major species harvested. Second, hunting and fishing are economically important to local businesses, both directly as the local population spends money, and indirectly as an attraction that draws sportsmen from outside the county.

Unfortunately, a general lack of regard for the conservation of fish and wildlife resources, combined with the channel dredging and wetland clearing and draining, has led to the loss of valuable fishery spawning grounds and the loss of habitat for many wildlife species. In the attempt to protect and restore some of these resources, Pea Island National Wildlife Refuge serves an important role, not only by providing habitat for a diversity of plant and wildlife species, but also as a place where people can go to enjoy these resources either through observation, photography, education, or interpretation; or more directly through fishing.

No studies have been performed to estimate the economic impact of outdoor recreation on Pea Island Refuge. However, the Fish and Wildlife Service surveyed participants in wildlife-dependent recreation in North Carolina in 2001. The survey documented an average expenditure of $69 per day by anglers, $74 per day by hunters, and $199 per day by wildlife observers and photographers (U.S. Fish and Wildlife Service 2001).

The Partnership for the Sounds sponsored a study of the economic impact of its facilities. The study demonstrated that the average visitor spent $108 per visit, with a range of $63.70 to $332.55 per day (Vogelsang 2001). A similar study of visitors at Chincoteague National Wildlife Refuge in Virginia also showed a range of expenditures from $62 to $101 per day (U.S. Environmental Protection Agency 1997).

A study commissioned by the State of New Jersey demonstrated that the average visitor to the shorebird migration spent $130 per day (New Jersey Department of Environmental Protection 2000). Birdwatchers on eight national wildlife refuges in New Jersey reported a range of expenditures from $25 to $41 per day (Kerlinger 1994).

Ecotourists on Dauphin Island, Alabama, spent an average of $60 per visitor per day (Kerlinger 1999).

Birdwatchers from the local area on High Island, Texas, reported an average expenditure of $46 per day, and nonresidents reported $693 per trip (Eubanks et al. 1993). The average visitor to the Great Texas Coastal Birding Trail spent $78 per day (Eubanks and Stoll 1999).

Studies at the Santa Ana National Wildlife Refuge in south Texas demonstrated a range of expenditures from $88 to $145 per day on nature-based tourist activities. The Laguna Atascosa National Wildlife Refuge in south Texas reported a range of $83 to $117 per day (U.S. Environmental Protection Agency 1997).

Birdwatchers to the Salton Sea National Wildlife Refuge in California spent an average of $57 per day (National Audubon Society 1998).

With improved facilities and staffing, Pea Island Refuge can continue to serve as an important commodity in the economic life of the community. Ecotourism, fishing, wildlife observation and photography, and environmental interpretation are increasingly being seen as a desirable industry. As the population increases and the number of places left to enjoy wildlife decreases, the refuge may become even more important to the local community. It can benefit the community directly by providing recreational opportunities for the local population, and indirectly by attracting tourists from outside the parish to generate additional dollars to the local economy.

TOURISM

Seven million tourists visit the Outer Banks of Dare, Currituck, and Hyde counties every year. Tourism in the area is based on the outdoor recreation opportunities described above and the cultural attractions in the area. Roanoke Island, on which Manteo is located, was the birthplace of Virginia Dare, the first English child born in America. The state legislature named the county in her honor. The county seat in Manteo has a historic district featuring old homes and limited development along the streams and the sound. Manteo also features the Roanoke Island Festival Park with a historic visitor's center and a replica of the Queen Elizabeth II; the Elizabethan Gardens managed by the National Park Service as a replica of a formal English garden; and Fort Raleigh National Historic Site, the site of the first settlement.

Other cultural attractions include the National Park Service's Wright Brothers Memorial, Bodie Island Lighthouse, and Cape Hatteras Lighthouse; the North Carolina Maritime Museum; the Frisco Native American Museum; and the Chicamocomico Lifesaving Station.

Cultural resources form the basis of many events that attract tourists. Thes include the historical workshops, lectures, and programs at the North Carolina Maritime Museum; tours of historic homes and their gardens; readings of books on historical themes; Virginia Dare's Birthday; National Aviation Day, and Week at the Wright Brothers Memorial; Freedman's Colony Celebration at Festival Park; and an Antique Fair at Festival Park.Pea Island National Wildlife Refuge could serve as an additional attraction to tourists visiting the area at least seasonally.

TRANSPORTATION

In its early days, residents of the area relied on water transportation. The rivers and streams that crisscross the county served as a means for transportation, trade, and communication between almost every community in the area. Some of the important waterways in the area were the Albemarle, Pamlico, Croatan, and Roanoke Sounds and the Alligator River. While today these waterways are no longer necessary for most of the transportation needs within the county, they are still important as sources of income and for recreation.

Ferry transportation began to the area that is now Pea Island in the mid-1920s when Captain J.B. Tillet established a tug and barge service across Oregon Inlet. In 1934, the North Carolina Highway Commission recognized the importance of this service to residents and began subsidizing Tillet's business. In 1942, full reimbursement by the state began and Tillet eliminated the tolls. This continued until 1950 when Tillet sold his business to the state. Before 1951, Pea Island had only a sand pathway traversing the refuge. The Service authorized a specific road easement for the State of North Carolina in October 1951 and the state constructed a clay-surface road. The state initially paved the road that is now North Carolina Highway 12 in the mid-1950s and ferry service ceased with the opening of the Herbert C. Bonner Bridge on November 20, 1963.

U.S. Highway 64 runs east and west through the middle of the area and connects population centers in central North Carolina and Interstate 95 to the Outer Banks. U.S. Highways 158 and 168 run north and south through the center of the area and connect Dare County with population centers in southeastern Virginia. A number of smaller roads connect the various communities in the area.

Visitors can reach Pea Island National Wildlife Refuge via North Carolina Highway 12. Refuge dike roads are not open to vehicular traffic. Road access is a constraint on vehicular access, but not necessarily on public use. Travel by foot or boat is limited only by a user's willingness to exert the manpower.

CULTURAL ENVIRONMENT

Dare County is a rural county in predominantly rural northeastern North Carolina. Cultural opportunities in the immediate area are limited to the history-based facilities outlined in the tourism section; theaters at local high schools and parks; music at local fairs, festivals, and nightclubs; and art at local fairs, festivals, and 20 small galleries. There has been a summer-long production of "The Lost Colony" annually since 1936 at the Fort Raleigh National Historic Site commemorating the first English settlers on Roanoke Island. Greenville, North Carolina, and East Carolina University, located 100 miles west of the refuge, offer the nearest opportunities for large theatrical or musical performances. Norfolk, Virginia, located 100 miles to the north, has the area's largest art museums and venues for performing arts with national touring collections and companies.

/REFUGE ADMINISTRATION AND MANAGEMENT

LAND PROTECTION AND CONSERVATION

The refuge covers approximately 5,000 acres (reduced by erosion from the original 5,915 acres). Its acquisition history is summarized in Table 8. Figure 6 shows the refuge's approved acquisition boundary.

Table 8. Acquisition history of Pea Island National Wildlife Refuge

YEAR	NUMBER OF TRACTS	ACRES	COST	COST ACRE	TOTAL ACREAGE	TOTAL COST
1937	1	1,539.36	$8,466.48	$5.50	1,539.36	$8,466.48
1938	4	4,247.42	$26,935.38	46.34	5,786.78	$35,401.86
1959	3	47.12	$5,000.00	$106.11	5,834.20	$40,401.86
Total	8	5,834.20	$40,401.86			

VISITOR SERVICES

The refuge is an important link to the other natural areas that together make these experiences possible. Carefully selected and managed staff, programs, and facilities provide the wildlife-dependent environmental education, interpretation, and recreation opportunities the refuge's visitors expect. A few commercial businesses have interests in guiding canoeing and kayaking tours and angling adventures.

Hunting

Currently, the Service does not permit hunting on the refuge. Careful evaluation has failed to identify any game species on the refuge that could support a hunt without impacting the primary wildlife management programs that are focused on waterfowl and other migratory birds.

Figure 6. Approved acquisition boundary, Pea Island National Wildlife Refuge

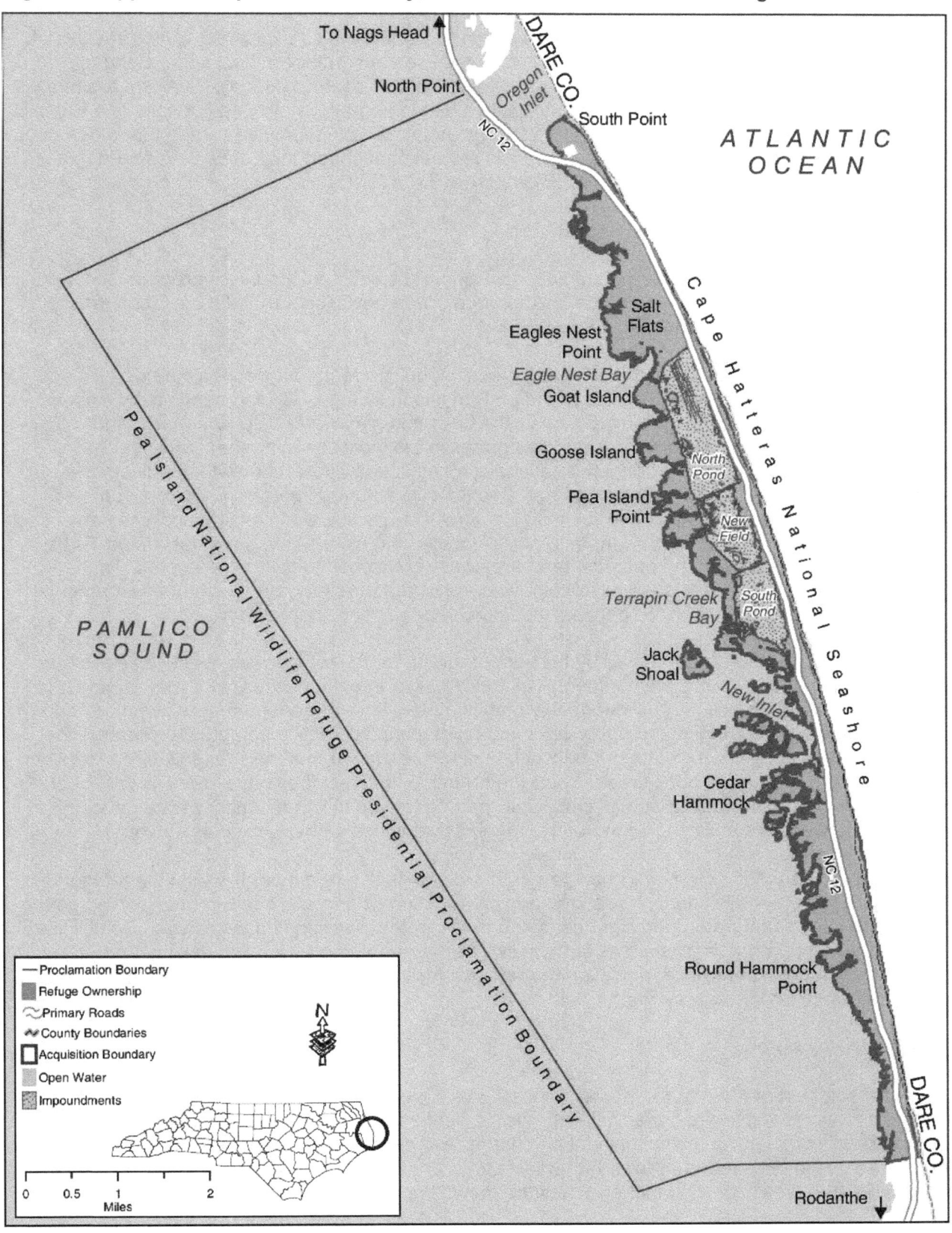

Fishing

Pea Island National Wildlife Refuge is located within one of the top five saltwater fishing capitals of the United States. Surf fishermen can readily find secluded and private fishing spots along the refuge's 13-mile oceanfront. Red drum, striped bass, spotted seatrout, and flounder are the most popular species sought. Boat ramps are available to launch boats, kayaks, and canoes into Pamlico Sound, and the refuge offers special permits for nighttime surf fishing. Once a year, the refuge opens North Pond to crabbing, providing a unique family recreational opportunity while also ensuring a proper balance of creatures in this important waterway.

Environmental Education and Interpretation

The refuge's trained professional personnel and well-organized intern/volunteer program offers public programs on migratory birds, wading birds, shorebirds, waterfowl, loggerhead turtles, and the piping plover, as well as their habitats and nesting habits.

Opportunities to participate in self-guiding experiences, guided tours, educational nature talks and walks and programs are available year-round on Pea Island Refuge. Guided canoe tours enable visitors to inspect and appreciate more closely the bays and backwater trails and marshlands. The refuge offers children's programs, outreach programs in the local school system, and special seminars and conferences, including the nationally recognized Wings over Water Festival, on a regular and continuing basis. The refuge has an extensive volunteer program. Not only do these volunteers present educational opportunities to others, they participate in experiential programs, such as the Turtle Patrol, which enables them to patrol, locate, and identify sea turtle nests, and Turtle Watch, which affords them the opportunity to escort newly hatched turtles to the ocean. These programs, plus specially designed internships and the workamper program, provide environmental education and appreciation to the participants that can be passed on to others.

The Visitor Center, built and manned by the support group for the refuge, has quality displays that give experienced and novice environmentalists more insight into the necessity for maintaining and sustaining wildlife refuges. A knowledgeable staff is able to answer general nature questions and provide additional information through videos and an ongoing interactive computer program. The Visitor Center also offers a plethora of educational and interpretive materials for sale. Teachers and librarians have lauded the book selections at the refuge as the best they have seen. A variety of educational/interpretive books and toys specially geared toward children continues the refuge's dedication towards establishing sound educational opportunities at the earliest age levels.

The ocean and sounds, which are not a part of the refuge itself, are accessible from the refuge for most types of water-dependent recreation, ranging from surf fishing and shelling to fly-fishing on the sound side. Personal watercraft is not permitted in the waters surrounding the refuge. Nonwildlife-dependent recreational uses, such as surfing, swimming, sunbathing, bicycling, hiking, and picnicking, occur on the refuge; however, the refuge's facilities and programming are not designed to specifically support these activities.

Wildlife Observation

As a strategic part of the Atlantic Flyway, the refuge's opportunities to observe migratory birds, as well as shore and water birds, are limitless. Visitor Center volunteers are eager to point out recent and unusual sightings, lend binoculars at no charge, and provide assistance in helping new hobbyists enjoy their experience to the fullest. Two wildlife trails are associated with the North Pond, a brackish impoundment. A service road that encircles the pond is open to the public for wildlife observation.

Raised observation platforms, spotting scopes, and interpretive signs are provided along the route. The limited human interruption of this natural resource enables visitors to view the waterfowl, songbirds, turtles, and other wildlife native to the island.

Wildlife Photography

Pea Island National Wildlife Refuge is a photographer's paradise. Between the ocean, beachfront, dunes, and impoundments, which draw tens of thousands of migratory birds, photographers have unlimited opportunities for wildlife photography. Its unique location, situated where sunrises occur over the ocean and sunsets over the sound, enables camera enthusiasts to shoot natural beauty from one end of the day to the other. A photo blind, observation decks, oceanfront vistas, and canoe tours through the bays and marshes promote and encourage the noninvasive wildlife photography that is popular with the general public.

Universal Access

Pea Island Refuge gives special attention to ensuring that visitors with disabilities can visit the refuge for pleasure, education, interpretation, and wildlife observation opportunities. The Visitor Center offers a special indoor bird watching area for those who do not want to take a trail around the impoundment. A portion of the impoundment trail is level and accessible by wheelchair, and a wheelchair is available at no charge for those who request it. The North Pond Wildlife Trail is universally accessible.

Public Involvement

The refuge offers nearly limitless involvement for the public on either a volunteer or spectator basis. Steady, reliable volunteers operate the Visitor Center. The refuge offers special educational opportunities to the scores of local residents and visitors who volunteer for these unique experiences. Sea turtle watch and patrol programs not only provide assistance for the threatened loggerhead and endangered green turtle, but also enable refuge staff to educate the public on the habits and habitats of these wildlife species. Tern and pelican banding and counts also enable the sharing of expertise and equipment in exchange for further educational opportunities and participation in avian protection and record-keeping. Volunteers and staff share their information with beach visitors who may otherwise have no interest, concern, or knowledge in protecting threatened and endangered species. The Coastal Wildlife Refuge Society, a nonprofit local organization, was established to provide support for continued maintenance of the refuge and its educational programs, and to recruit volunteers for continuation of this process.

The refuge's intern program provides unique experiences for college students and graduates geared towards careers in the environmental sciences. The program also provides additional volunteer services to maintain the high standards of the refuge. A work camping program, bartering a campsite and utilities in exchange for work hours, enables the refuge to take advantage of a wide spectrum of individual experiences and expertise that enhance the refuge. Each of these programs instills a sense of pride and public stewardship among the volunteers, ensures them of their role in ownership of the land, and heightens awareness about the critical need for protecting the human/natural interactions.

PERSONNEL, OPERATIONS, AND MAINTENANCE

Personnel

The staff of the Alligator River National Wildlife Refuge manages Pea Island National Wildlife Refuge from its office in Manteo. Alligator River Refuge uses 6.3 full-time equivalent positions (5.4 non-fire and 0.9 fire) of its 23 positions at Pea Island Refuge. One park ranger (0.9 full-time equivalent position) is stationed on the refuge. The staff conducts extensive environmental education and interpretation programs with the assistance of 25,000 volunteer-hours every year. The refuge complex's current staff is listed in Table 9.

Operations

The staff manages the refuge marshes with prescribed fire and manages the impoundments and moist-soil units with water management, prescribed fire, and tillage. The refuge controls common reed (*Phragmites australis*) in both the marshes and moist-soil units. The staff and volunteers monitor waterfowl, shorebirds, colonial nesting birds, wading birds, and sea turtles. They also maintain the facilities that support the public use program, as well as the levees and pumps that enable management of the impoundments and moist-soil units.

REFUGE INFRASTRUCTURE

Roads and Trails

The refuge has an established half-mile-long wildlife trail on the levee of the south shoreline of the impoundment known as North Pond. This trail, called the North Pond Wildlife Trail, is universally accessible and features several overlooks and one wildlife observation platform. Pedestrians may also walk around the entire impoundment on a 4-mile service road. There is a second, shorter wildlife trail on the north end of North Pond called the Salt Flats Wildlife Trail. The service road is open to bicycles; however, the designated trails are not. The North Pond Wildlife Trail area is part of a series of trails among the eleven refuges and one fish hatchery in eastern North Carolina. This series of trails was established in honor of the late television news commentator Charles Kuralt, for the recognition he brought to the National Wildlife Refuge System. Figure 7 shows the locations of the refuge's roads and trails.

Only the refuge staff has vehicular access to the remainder of the refuge roads. These roads are used by the staff to conduct wildlife surveys and maintain the marshes, impoundments, levees, and pumps.

Utility Corridors and Distribution

The Cape Hatteras Electric Membership Cooperative has a power transmission right-of-way across refuge lands. The right-of-way is 13 miles long by 50 feet wide and covers 79 acres of land in the backdune area parallel to North Carolina Highway 12. Permits to relocate the power lines have been approved on several occasions due to encroachment by the ocean. The last relocation was completed in 2004.

Table 9. Staff of the Alligator River and Pea Island National Wildlife Refuges in 2005

Position	Status	Percent of Time on Pea Island
Management Staff		
Refuge Manager, GS-0485-14	PFT	60
Deputy Refuge Manager, GS-0485-13	PFT	40
Assistant Refuge Manager, GS-0485-12	PFT	25
Administrative Officer, GS-0341-09	PFT	25
Office Assistant, GS-0303-07	PPT	25
Forestry Technician, GS-0462-07	PFT	10
Biological Staff		
Wildlife Biologist, GS-0486-12	PFT	60
General Biologist, GS-0401-07	PFT	50
Interpretive Staff		
Park Ranger (Interpretation), GS-0025-12	PFT	60
Park Ranger (Interpretation), GS-0025-09	PFT	90
Park Ranger (Interpretation), GS-0025-07	TERM	90

Position	Status	Percent of Time on Pea Island
Law Enforcement Staff		
Park Ranger (Law Enforcement), GS-0025-09	PFT	30
Maintenance Staff		
Engineering Equipment. Operator Supervisor, WS-5716-09	PFT	25
Engineering Equipment Operator, WG-5716-10	PFT	10
Engineering Equipment Operator, WG-5716-09	PFT	10
Engineering Equipment Operator, WG-5716-08	PFT	10
Automotive Worker, WG-5823-08	PFT	10
Fire Management Program		
Fire Management Officer, GS-0460-12	PFT	10
Fire Management Officer (Wildland Urban Interface), GS-0401-11	PFT	10
Fire Management Specialist, GS-0401-09	PFT	10
Forestry Technician, (Fire) GS-0462-08	PFT	10
Forestry Technician (Fire), GS-0462-06	PFT	10
Forestry Technician, (Fire) GS-0462-06	PFT	10

Position	Status	Percent of Time on Pea Island
Forestry Technician (Fire) GS-0462-07	PFT	10
Engineering Equipment Operator, (Fire) WG-5716-08	PFT	10
Engineering Equipment Operator, (Fire) WG-5716-08	PFT	10
Red Wolf Program		
Wildlife Biologist, GS-0486-13	PFT	0
Wildlife Biologist, GS-0486-09	PFT	0
Wildlife Biologist, GS-0486-11	PFT	0
Wildlife Biologist, GS-0486-09	PFT	0
Wildlife Biologist, GS-0486-07	TERM	0
Bio. Science Tech., GS-0404-07	PFT	0
Office Assistant, GS-0303-07	TERM	0
PFT = Permanent Full Time employee TERM = Term Employee (up to four years)		

Communication Systems

The refuge communications system currently consists of mobile radios with a base station located at Alligator River National Wildlife Refuge on mainland Dare County. The staff uses cellular phones for communication between the field and office.

Waste Collection and Disposal

The National Park Service constructed the restroom facilities located in the Visitor Center parking lot in 1983. They are responsible for daily cleaning and overall operation of the facility.

Volunteers transfer general trash to dumpsters located at the refuge office and Visitor Center, which are emptied by Dare County for a fee. The North Carolina Department of Transportation is responsible for removing trash from the North Carolina Highway 12 right-of-way. Septic systems treat sanitary waste from the office, intern quarters, Visitor Center restrooms, and workamper pads.

Figure 7. Current visitor facilities at Pea Island National Wildlife Refuge

Figure 7. Current visitor facilities at Pea Island National Wildlife Refuge

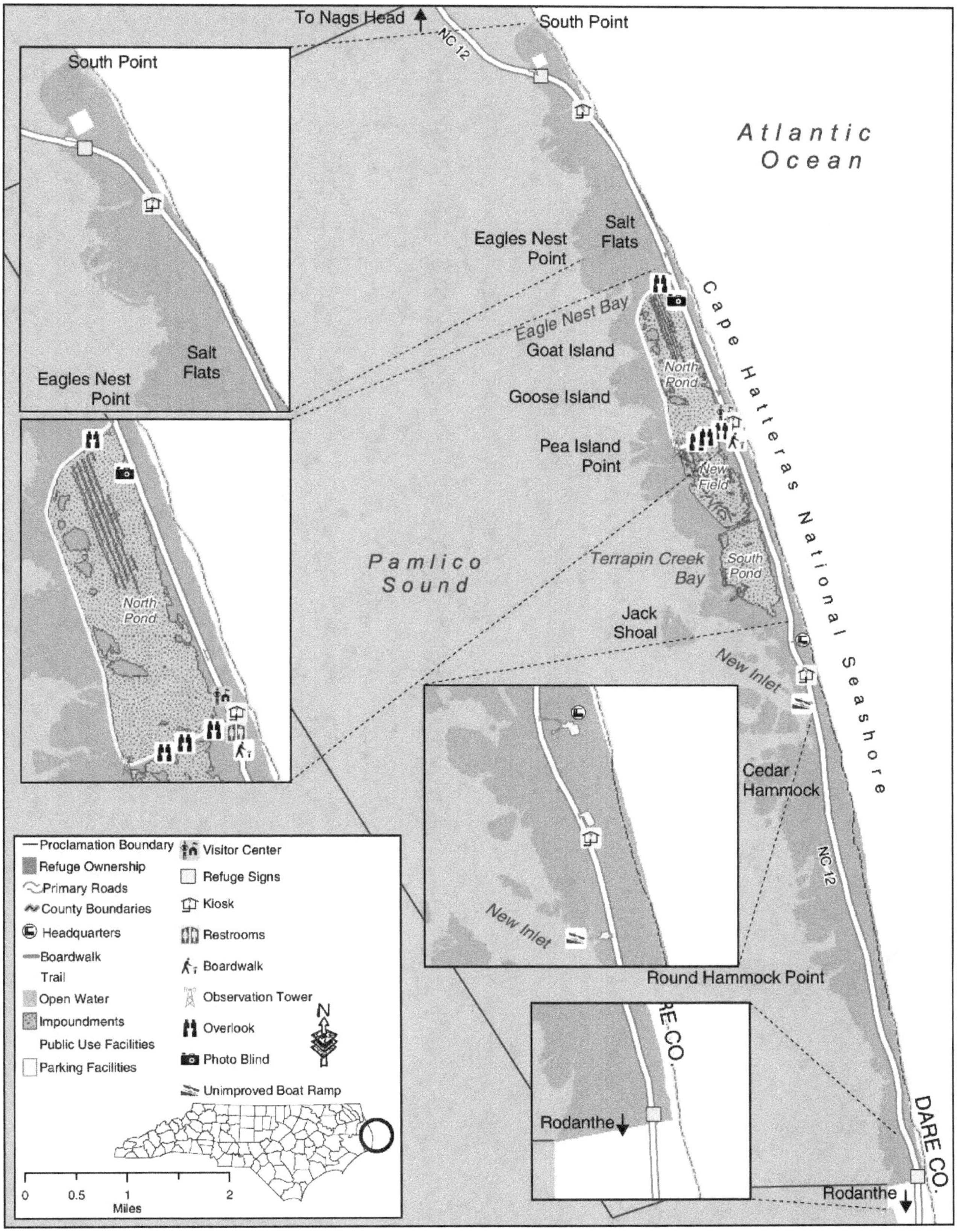

III. Plan Development

PUBLIC INVOLVEMENT AND THE PLANNING PROCESS

At initial planning meetings, the refuge and planning staff discussed strategies for completing the plan, identified the issues and concerns, and compiled a mailing list of likely interested government agencies, non-governmental organizations, businesses, and local citizens. The Service invited these agencies, organizations, businesses, and citizens to participate in four public scoping meetings on June 26 and 27, 2000, in Rodanthe and Manteo, North Carolina. The staff introduced the attendees to the refuge and its planning process, and asked them to identify their issues and concerns. The staff published announcements giving the locations, dates, and times for the public meetings in the *Federal Register* and legal notices in local newspapers. The staff also sent the announcements as press releases to local newspapers and as public service announcements to television and radio stations. The planning staff placed fifty posters announcing the meetings in local post offices, local government buildings, and stores.

The Service expanded the planning team's identified issues and concerns to include those generated by the agencies, organizations, businesses, and citizens from the local community. These issues and concerns formed the basis for the development and comparison of the objectives in the different alternatives described in this environmental assessment.

The alternatives were subjects of discussion at a second round of four public meetings held on September 25 and 26, 2000, in Rodanthe and Manteo, North Carolina. The planning staff again published announcements giving the locations, dates, and times for the public meetings, as well as legal notices in local newspapers. They also sent press releases to local newspapers and public service announcements to television and radio stations. The staff placed seventy-five posters announcing the meetings in local post offices, local government buildings, and stores.

At the second round of public meetings, members of the public expressed concern that the three alternatives being considered did not represent a wide enough range of alternatives. The refuge staff developed Alternatives 4 and 5 in response to those concerns. Alternative 4 assumes that natural forces will dominate the landscape from the north end of North Pond to Oregon Inlet. Alternative 5 assumes that, except for the impoundments and administrative sites (e.g., buildings and their parking lots), natural forces will dominate throughout the refuge.

SUMMARY OF ISSUES, CONCERNS, AND OPPORTUNITIES

The input of local citizens and public agencies, the team members' knowledge of the area, and the resource needs identified by the refuge staff and biological review team all contributed to the issues and concerns addressed in the plan. The Fish and Wildlife Service assembled a planning team to evaluate the resource needs. The team then developed a list of goals, objectives, and strategies to shape the management of the refuge for the next 15 years.

These issues provided the basis for developing the refuge's alternative management objectives and strategies. These issues also played a role in determining the desired conditions for the refuge and were considered in the preparation of the long-term comprehensive conservation plan. The issues and concerns are described below. They are of local, regional, and national significance and reflect similar issues that were, in part, identified by the public at the planning meetings.

HYDROLOGY

Alteration of Coastal Processes: The dunes on Pea Island Refuge were originally low, broad dunes with relatively flat slopes. In the 1930s, the Civilian Conservation Corps enhanced the dunes, making them higher and steeper to protect the road on the backside of the dunes. These dunes destroyed unvegetated habitats that existed on the original dunes and prohibited the western migration of the dunes. The North Carolina Department of Transportation maintains North Carolina Highway 12 through the refuge by removing sand from the road surface and placing it on the dunes, maintaining their steep slopes. The construction of the groin in 1989-90 to protect the Bonner Bridge over the Oregon Inlet alters the normal flow of sand off shore that replenishes the beaches. Ocean overwash that would occur on an unaltered inlet spit would maintain early successional habitats suitable for beach nesting birds. The groin prevents this kind of overwash. The Army Corps of Engineers maintains the Oregon Inlet navigation channel by dredging. Their dredge disposal activities can alter the quantity and quality of sand for the nearshore environment and refuge beaches that alter invertebrate populations that are the prey for shorebirds and some nearshore fish.

FISH AND WILDLIFE POPULATIONS

The refuge staff and the public at the scoping meetings contributed ideas for the fish and wildlife population issues. In addition, staff of the Fish and Wildlife Service and cooperating agencies and organizations conducted a biological review of Pea Island National Wildlife Refuge in 1999 and 2000, as part of the comprehensive conservation planning process. They identified objectives and strategies needed to protect wildlife populations and meet the minimum feeding and nesting habitat requirements of waterfowl, shorebirds, colonial nesting birds, and neotropical migratory birds.

Threatened and Endangered Species: Recovery and protection of threatened and endangered plants and animals are important responsibilities delegated to the Service and its national wildlife refuges. Eight threatened or endangered animals use (or could use) Pea Island Refuge: the piping plover (federally threatened Atlantic Coast and Northern Great Plains populations and endangered Great Lakes populations); bald eagle (federally threatened); loggerhead sea turtle (federally threatened); leatherback sea turtle (federally endangered); hawksbill sea turtle (federally endangered); green sea turtle (federally threatened); Kemp's ridley sea turtle (federally endangered); and seabeach amaranth (federally endangered).

Loggerhead sea turtles are the most prevalent federally listed species on the refuge. An average of 10 females typically nests successfully on the refuge every year. There was a record high of 37 nests in 1994 and a record low of 1 nest in 2004. Although less common, green sea turtles use Pea Island Refuge beaches for nesting on occasion.

Prior to 1996, no historic data existed documenting the nesting of piping plovers on the refuge except one nest in the 1960s on a newly constructed finger island in North Pond. Historically, the refuge had wide beaches, low flat naturally formed dunes, and overwash fans. Prior to construction of artificial dunes in the 1930s, it is presumed that piping plovers nested on overwash areas and beaches on the refuge. Construction of the dune system in the 1930s, maintenance of North Carolina Highway 12, and erosion of the beaches have degraded or removed nesting habitat.

Construction of the terminal groin in the early 1990s to protect the Bonner Bridge resulted in sand deposition on the ocean side of the groin. After sand mining by the North Carolina Department of Transportation in 1995, the first plover nest occurred in 1996. Since that time, plovers have nested on an irregular basis in the area behind the groin. There have been no other nesting attempts elsewhere on the refuge since 1996.

Nests are susceptible to predation and pedestrian trampling and do not always produce young despite being posted as closed and patrolled. Symbolic fencing is used to protect nests. Piping plovers forage on refuge beaches throughout the year.

Bald eagles have historically nested on lands adjacent to the Pamlico Sound, but the refuge does not provide adequate nesting habitat. They do nest on the mainland in Dare County and adjacent counties and travel over the shorelines and refuge impoundments for foraging.

Waterfowl: Management of refuge impoundments and marshes for waterfowl is important for meeting the refuge's purpose. The waterfowl objectives help guide water management actions on the refuge. In order to meet the waterfowl objectives, the refuge must maintain the impoundments to meet waterfowl habitat needs and provide sufficient sanctuary areas to provide undisturbed resting and feeding areas for waterfowl.

Shorebirds and Colonial Nesting Birds: Management of refuge impoundments, beaches, and flats for shorebirds and colonial nesting birds is important for meeting the refuge's purpose. The shorebird objectives help guide operation and management actions on the refuge. The refuge must maintain the impoundments to meet the habitat needs of shorebirds and colonial nesting birds, especially during the fall and spring migrations, and provide sufficient sanctuary areas that provide undisturbed resting and feeding areas for shorebirds and colonial nesting birds.

Neotropical Migratory Birds: Neotropical migratory birds are a species group of special management concern. Providing habitat (i.e., brackish marshes, grasslands, and maritime shrub) for these birds is a refuge objective. Strategic marsh management compatible with the refuge's waterfowl habitat objectives contributes to the maritime shrub needs of neotropical migratory birds.

HABITAT MANAGEMENT

The staff and the public at the scoping meetings contributed ideas for the fish and wildlife population issues. In addition, staff of the Fish and Wildlife Service and cooperating agencies and organizations conducted a biological review of Pea Island National Wildlife Refuge in 1999 and 2000 as part of the comprehensive conservation planning process. They identified objectives and strategies needed to meet the minimum feeding and nesting habitat requirements of waterfowl, shorebirds, colonial nesting birds, and neotropical migratory birds.

Impoundment Management: The staff manages impoundments for moist-soil vegetation and submerged aquatic vegetation for waterfowl habitat, and mud flats for shorebird habitat. Providing quality habitat requires water management using water control structures and pumps; vegetation management with disking, prescribed burning, and mowing; and monitoring of water levels, vegetation, and invertebrates.

Marsh Management: The staff manages marshes for perennial emergent vegetation and salt flats for waterfowl, wading birds, shorebirds, and colonial nesting birds, and habitat for neotropical migratory songbirds. Providing quality habitat requires prescribed burning and control of invasive species such as common reed (*Phragmites australis*).

Maritime Shrub Management: The staff manages woody shrub, trees, and vines for certain colonial nesting birds and as neotropical migratory songbird habitat. Providing quality habitat requires little management other than allowing natural succession and, on occasion, limited prescribed burning and control of invasive species such as common reed (*Phragmites australis*).

VISITOR SERVICES (PUBLIC USE)

Pea Island National Wildlife Refuge offers five of the six priority wildlife-dependent recreational opportunities identified in the National Wildlife Refuge System Improvement Act of 1997. Wildlife observation and photography, along with educational and interpretive programs, attract thousands of visitors annually to the refuge. Fishing is popular along the 13 miles of refuge beach and is allowed within the North Pond impoundment one day a year during the annual crabbing rodeo. Hunting is not authorized on the refuge at this time.

Wildlife Observation and Photography: Pea Island National Wildlife Refuge has consistently been called a "birders' paradise" due to its mid-way location along the Atlantic Flyway and the numerous migratory visitors and overwintering avian species. Especially in peak migration seasons but also throughout the year, the refuge welcomes thousands of avid birdwatchers, nature lovers, and fortunate passers-by. The majority of these visitors simply observe the migration, aided by the refuge's universally accessible boardwalks and spotting scopes. Some make use of the refuge's photo blind and observation platforms.

Environmental Education and Interpretation: With numerous visitors to the beach during the summer months, the refuge provides an array of public tours and educational/interpretive programs to educate visitors about the refuge and the diversity and significance of its wildlife and habitat. Due to the limitations of an inadequately small staff, the refuge relies heavily on a network of local volunteers, student interns, and workampers for the implementation of this public outreach. Year-round, the refuge staff and a dedicated group of volunteers work to highlight the importance of the refuge and the work of the Fish and Wildlife Service.

Fishing: The refuge attracts several thousand anglers annually, primarily in the surf and in the area surrounding Bonner Bridge. Existing parking lots on the refuge are limited, especially since the damage resulting from Hurricane Isabel in September 2003; therefore, many anglers park on the side of North Carolina Highway 12 to access the beach. Historically, pedestrian traffic created nearly 80 foot paths over the artificial dunes. Many of these paths no longer exist, but access is permitted at basically any point along the highway. The refuge permits night access for fishing outside of the sea turtle nesting season.

Hunting: Currently, no hunting is permitted on Pea Island National Wildlife Refuge. Migratory bird hunting is prohibited by Presidential Proclamation on the refuge and on 25,700 acres of adjacent Pamlico Sound waters. Hunting and fishing are integral parts of the rural North Carolina culture. Waterfowl hunting is currently permitted within the adjacent Cape Hatteras National Seashore on Bodie Island. It is not surprising that there is considerable state and local interest in providing hunting opportunities. Any future hunting opportunities on the refuge will be dependent upon providing safe, quality experiences that are compatible with refuge purposes.

RESOURCE PROTECTION

Cultural Resources: There have been limited archaeological investigations within the refuge. A cultural resources and impact area assessment conducted in 1979 concluded that there were numerous hunt clubs on the refuge as well as the Pea Island Lifesaving Station, but that there were no significant archaeological remains on the refuge. The assessment recommended that no further work be done (Thompson and Gardner 1979). The staff must conduct management activities so as to avoid compromising sensitive sites.

Land Acquisition: There is a 10-acre inholding owned by the State of North Carolina on the northern end of the refuge surrounding the old Oregon Inlet Coast Guard Station. Acquiring this inholding would secure the Service's ability to protect all refuge resources. The Service does not, however, wish to purchase the Coast Guard Station itself nor be responsible for its upkeep.

Law Enforcement and Refuge Regulation: The staff enforces applicable laws and regulations through the use of one full-time law enforcement officer who covers both Pea Island and Alligator River Refuges. The officer has obligations over more than 158,000 acres and the extensive territory limits his ability to perform his functions. His other workload limits the amount of time he can devote to the monitoring of permits and the enforcement of permit conditions. During the summer months, it is important to have more of a law enforcement presence on Pea Island Refuge due to the large number of visitors to the beach and Visitor Center areas.

Other: There are other threats to refuge resources that require closer monitoring and management. Pest plants and animals and wildlife diseases are concerns of which the refuge should be paying closer attention.

Required dredging for channel maintenance results in the need for disposal of sand removed from Oregon Inlet. The placement of that dredged material on refuge beaches by the Army Corps of Engineers requires a permit that mandates monitoring in the disposal areas to ensure sand compatibility. The inlet would naturally bypass a higher volume of sand to the refuge beach if the groin that protects the bridge were not present. Placing the dredge material on the beaches partially compensates for the interception of sand by the groin, but the grain size of the dredged material is not always compatible with invertebrate survival on the beaches. The refuge staff must monitor the grain size and the placement of the dredged material closely.

Scheduled and post-storm maintenance of the North Carolina Highway 12 right-of-way also poses threats to refuge resources. This activity requires close coordination with the state and frequent monitoring.

GENERAL ADMINISTRATION

Funding and Staffing: Pea Island National Wildlife Refuge is currently unfunded and unstaffed and relies on personnel officially stationed at Alligator River National Wildlife Refuge to conduct all work. By utilizing an extensive volunteer workforce, the refuge is able to provide some environmental education, interpretation, and wildlife observation opportunities.

Wilderness Review: Refuge planning policy requires a wilderness review as part of the comprehensive conservation planning process. The Wilderness Act of 1964 defines a wilderness area as an area of federal land that retains its primeval character and influence, without permanent improvements or human inhabitation, and is managed so as to preserve its natural conditions and which 1) generally appears to have been influenced primarily by the forces of nature, with the imprint of man's work substantially unnoticeable; 2) has outstanding opportunities for solitude or primitive and unconfined types of recreation; 3) has at least 5,000 contiguous roadless acres or is of sufficient size to make practicable its preservation and use in an unimpeded condition; or is a roadless island, regardless of size; 4) does not substantially exhibit the effects of logging, farming, grazing, or other extensive development or alteration of the landscape, or its wilderness character could be restored through appropriate management at the time of review; and 5) may contain ecological, geological, or other features of scientific, educational, scenic, or historic value.

In 1974 the Service submitted a Final Environmental Impact Statement (FES-75-92) that proposed wilderness designation for several roadless islands on Pea Island National Wildlife Refuge. Wilderness designation was recommended for all islands on the Pamlico Sound side of the refuge, encompassing approximately 180 acres. These areas consist of salt marsh with each island being dominated by needlerush with marsh elder scattered throughout. However, the Service never forwarded the recommendation to Congress. The refuge is currently managing the islands as if they were wilderness areas until the Service forwards the recommendation to Congress and Congress either approves or denies the recommendation.

During this comprehensive planning process, the lands within Pea Island National Wildlife Refuge were reviewed for their suitability in meeting the criteria for wilderness, as defined by the Wilderness Act of 1964. No lands in the refuge, other than the areas already recommended, were found to meet these criteria. Therefore, the suitability of refuge lands for wilderness designation is not further analyzed in this plan.

IV. Management Direction

INTRODUCTION

Under the preferred alternative, the Service would protect, maintain, restore, and enhance refuge lands for resident wildlife, waterfowl, migratory nongame birds, and threatened and endangered species. Refuge staff would initiate extensive wildlife and plant census and inventory activities to develop the baseline biological information needed to implement management programs on the refuge.

The refuge would direct all management actions towards achieving the refuge's primary purposes: (1) preserving nesting and migratory habitat for neotropical migratory songbirds; and (2) helping to meet the habitat conservation goals of the North American Waterfowl Management Plan. In addition, the staff would manage the refuge to contribute to other national, regional, and state goals for protecting and restoring populations of wildlife.

The Service would implement active habitat management through forest management and moist-soil unit management designed to provide a historically diverse complex of habitats that meets the foraging, resting, and breeding requirements for a variety of species.

Under this alternative, the refuge would continue to seek acquisition of all inholdings from willing sellers within the present acquisition boundary. The primary purpose for this acquisition would be to provide a system of coastal marshes, pocosins, and forested habitats of sufficient size and carrying capacity to reach regional objectives associated with area-sensitive neotropical birds, anadromous fish, colonial nesting birds, forest-associated waterfowl, and wetland forest landscapes. Lands acquired as part of the refuge would be made available to the public for compatible wildlife-dependent recreation and environmental education.

During the 15-year life of this plan, the refuge staff would develop and implement a habitat management plan, designed to maintain the present spatially and specifically diverse mosaic of habitats with little negative effect to wildlife objectives.

The Service would provide opportunities for quality wildlife-dependent recreation activities. The refuge would maintain the interior and exterior access roads to provide all-weather vehicular access to a broad segment of the public. The staff would permit hiking to support wildlife-dependent recreation to the extent that these opportunities do not substantially interfere with or detract from the achievement of wildlife conservation. They would provide wildlife observation sites and platforms; interpretive trails, boardwalks, and kiosks; and restrooms at specific sites to allow for fully accessible environmental education and interpretation programs. The plan provides for quality fishing and hunting programs, consistent with sound biological principles with sufficient focus on migratory bird needs for resting, loafing, feeding, and courting requirements. The Service would permit fishing along the banks of streams and ditches and from boats. The staff would continue to implement an environmental education plan, incorporating an aggressive and proactive promotion of both on- and off-site programs.

VISION

The vision for the refuge is as follows:

Pea Island National Wildlife Refuge in North Carolina is an example of a historic mid-Atlantic coastal barrier island in a relatively undisturbed condition. Features including North Carolina Highway 12, the

---

Herbert C. Bonner Bridge, a terminal groin, and utility lines affect natural processes and will partially determine future pressures on refuge resources.

Wildlife viewing will increase in popularity as thousands of birds and unique, rare and threatened wild creatures continue to seek sanctuary on this barrier island refuge. Refuge staff and partners will be increasingly diligent in the conservation and management of fish, wildlife, and plant species and their habitats in the face of rising human impacts.

The refuge will encourage visitors to participate in compatible wildlife-dependent recreational activities. Working with others, Pea Island National Wildlife Refuge will adaptively manage natural resources and create in this wild place a legacy of barrier island fish, wildlife, and plants for future visitors to experience and enjoy.

GOALS

FISH AND WILDLIFE POPULATIONS: Protect, maintain, and enhance healthy and viable populations of indigenous migratory birds, wildlife, fish, and plants including federal and state threatened and endangered species.

HABITAT: Restore, maintain, and enhance the health and biodiversity of barrier island upland and wetland habitats to ensure optimum ecological productivity.

PUBLIC USE: Provide the public with safe, quality wildlife-dependent recreational and educational opportunities that focus on barrier island wildlife and habitats of the refuge. Continue to participate in local efforts to sustain economic health through nature-based tourism.

RESOURCE PROTECTION: Protect refuge resources by limiting the adverse impacts of human activities and development.

ADMINISTRATION: Acquire and manage adequate funding, human resources, facilities, equipment, and infrastructure to accomplish all refuge goals.

OBJECTIVES, STRATEGIES, AND PROJECTS

The goals, objectives, and strategies addressed below are the Service's response to the issues, concerns, and needs expressed by the planning team, the refuge staff, and the public. These goals, objectives, and strategies reflect the Service's commitment to achieve the mandates of the National Wildlife Refuge System Improvement Act of 1997; the mission of the National Wildlife Refuge System; the North American Waterfowl Management Plan; and the purpose and vision for Pea Island National Wildlife Refuge. Depending upon the availability of funds and staff, the Service intends to accomplish these goals, objectives, and strategies during the next 15 years.

FISH AND WILDLIFE POPULATIONS

Goal: Protect, maintain, and enhance healthy and viable populations of indigenous migratory birds, wildlife, fish, and plants including federal and state threatened and endangered species.

Fish

Objective: Manage refuge resources continuously to protect species of fish and other marine and estuarine species in estuarine nurseries and adjacent waters.

Discussion: This objective improves on the status quo by providing for the surveying and monitoring of fish species in the estuarine ponds and impoundments. There are fish and other aquatic species on the refuge, but there are substantial aquatic resources in the Atlantic Ocean, Pamlico Sound, and other bays and inlets surrounding the refuge. The flooded edges of the marshes on the refuge and shallow water adjacent to the marshes are important fish nursery areas. Proper land management on the refuge is critical to the maintenance of water quality in those nursery areas.

Strategies:

- Assist with and/or conduct studies and investigations to the extent possible.

- Survey and monitor fish species in the estuarine ponds and impoundments every three years.

Invertebrates

Objective: Document presence or absence of invertebrate species as they are identified.

Discussion: This objective is the same as the status quo. Invertebrates are important food for shorebirds and colonial nesting birds and indicators of water quality. This alternative provides for the documentation of presence of species, but not detailed surveys of the refuge.

Strategy:

- Assist in conducting studies and investigations to the extent possible.

Land Birds

Objective: Provide resting, nesting, and foraging habitat continuously for about 100 species of land birds.

Discussion: This objective is an improvement on the status quo by providing for conducting ground surveys and studies. The traditional emphasis on the refuge has been on waterfowl, shorebirds, colonial nesting birds, and wading birds. There is good habitat on the refuge for land birds that utilize coastal dunes, shrublands, and marshes for nesting, resting, and foraging. This alternative adds the staff to perform the surveys and studies and investigations.

Strategies:

- Assist with and/or conduct banding activities as requested or directed.

- Assist with and/or conduct studies and investigations, as requested.

- Conduct 36 ground surveys annually of all land birds (3 times monthly).

Mammals

Objective: Monitor mammal populations as opportunities present themselves.

Discussion: This objective is an improvement on the status quo by providing for conducting surveys of land and semi-aquatic species. There is good habitat on the refuge for mammals that utilize coastal dunes, shrublands, and marshes for nesting, resting, and foraging. This alternative adds the staff to perform the surveys.

Strategies:

- Monitor and collect data continuously from stranded marine mammals.

- Survey and monitor land and semi-aquatic mammal populations annually.

- Evaluate mammalian predator populations for management actions.

- Evaluate the potential of game species to be harvested by hunting.

- Review and revise species lists as necessary.

Piping Plovers

Objective: Protect and monitor use of nesting, foraging, and wintering habitat by piping plovers.

Discussion: This objective is the same as the status quo. Three populations of piping plover, one endangered (Great Lakes) and two threatened (Atlantic Coast and Northern Great Plains), use the refuge. The birds nest on sand without any vegetation and shallow pools of water nearby. In a natural system, this habitat would occur in areas where the ocean washed over gaps in the dunes. On the refuge, this habitat occurs behind the groin along the northern edge of the refuge that is the southern shore of Oregon Inlet. Sand accumulates behind the groin and creates the exposed sand where the birds nest. The refuge staff must periodically remove sand to create the depressions in which water collects. Disturbance of birds and destruction of eggs by pedestrians and predators killing chicks are threats to the plovers.

Strategies:

- Monitor piping plover activities to document nesting success at least twice weekly during nesting.

- Post active nesting areas and close them to all access.

- Protect nests from predators (e.g., raccoons and feral cats) as needed.

Reptiles and Amphibians

Objective: Monitor reptile and amphibian populations as opportunities present themselves.

Discussion: This objective improves on the status quo by providing for the documentation of the presence of reptiles and amphibians. There is limited habitat on the refuge for reptiles and amphibians that utilize coastal dunes, shrublands, and marshes for nesting, resting, and foraging. This alternative adds the staff to perform the surveys.

Strategies:

- Document presence or absence of reptiles and amphibians as they are identified.

- Assist in conducting studies and investigations to the extent possible.

Sea Turtles

Objective: Protect and monitor sea turtle nesting activities.

Discussion: This objective is the same as the status quo. The refuge has an average of ten nesting sea turtles (primarily the threatened Loggerhead Sea Turtle) each year in summer. The turtles hatch in the early fall. Refuge volunteers and staff patrol the beach during the nesting season and mark the nest locations. They monitor the nest locations when hatching should occur and make sure the hatchlings get to the ocean.

Strategies:

- Document the nests established during each nesting season.

- Protect nesting habitat from human disturbance.

- Protect hatchling sea turtle crawls to the ocean during each nesting season.

- Monitor and collect data from stranded (dead) sea turtles.

Shorebirds and Colonial Nesting Birds

Objective: Provide forage and resting habitat in impoundments for 6,000 shorebirds and colonial nesting birds during spring migration and 3,000 shorebirds and colonial nesting habitat during the fall migration. Protect nesting habitat for 1,000 shorebirds and colonial nesting birds during spring migration.

Discussion: This objective improves on the status quo by providing habitat for 3,000 birds in the fall by managing the water levels in impoundments to create mudflats so they can feed on invertebrates. This alternative also provides for monitoring shorebirds and colonial nesting birds (e.g., terns, skimmers, oystercatchers, and other species) that utilize the refuge for nesting and foraging. Many species nest on the beach or in the dunes where visitors fish or observe or photograph wildlife. Refuge staff monitors these areas and erects fences to protect the nests, birds, and hatchlings. Birds use the beach as well as the mudflats in the impoundments to forage for invertebrates. Providing the habitat in the impoundments requires the removal of water from the impoundments after waterfowl migration season to create mudflats where they can probe for the invertebrates with their bills.

Strategies:

- Assist with and/or conduct banding activities as directed.

- Assist with and/or conduct studies and investigations to the extent possible.

- Conduct about 36 ground surveys annually (3 times monthly).

- Conduct surveys to monitor nesting and fledging activities as necessary.

Marsh and Wading Birds

Objective: Protect habitat for 500 marsh and wading birds. Provide habitat for about 200 marsh and wading birds.

Discussion: This objective is the same as the status quo. There is good habitat on the refuge for marsh and wading birds (e.g., rails, egrets, herons, and others) in marshes, ditches, and impoundments. The staff surveys marsh and wading birds from the ground at the same time as they survey other birds.

Strategies:

- Assist with and/or conduct banding activities as directed. Assist with and/or conduct studies and investigations to the extent possible.

- Conduct a total of 36 ground surveys of all marsh and wading birds annually (3 times monthly).

Waterfowl

Objective: Provide wintering habitat for 3,000 snow geese, 500 tundra swans, 100 migratory Canada geese, and 5,000 dabbling ducks annually. Protect wintering habitat for 1,500 North Atlantic and Atlantic population Canada geese, 1,500 dabbling ducks, and 1,000 diving ducks annually. Document the use of habitat by waterfowl.

Discussion: This objective is the same as the status quo. The Service established the refuge for waterfowl habitat. The "peas" on the refuge were trailing wild beans (*Strophostyles helvula*), reseeding annual plants that trailed in the backdune areas where perennial vegetation was sparse. Snow geese migrated south through the refuge just as the "peas" were maturing. The "peas" are scarce now, but the Service manages impoundments for waterfowl and they inhabit the inlets and sounds surrounding the refuge. The staff surveys the waterfowl from the air and the ground.

Strategies:

- Assist with and/or conduct banding activities as directed.

- Assist with and/or conduct studies and investigations to the extent possible.

- Conduct about 36 ground surveys annually (3 times monthly).

- Conduct about 14 aerial surveys bi-monthly from September to March.

- Conduct productivity surveys for tundra swans and snow geese each winter as requested.

- Conduct brood surveys yearly to determine which species are breeding.

HABITAT

Goal: Restore, maintain, and enhance the health and biodiversity of barrier island upland and wetland habitats to ensure optimum ecological productivity.

Barrier Dune, Groin Flats, and Overwash Areas

Objective: Provide about 450 acres of artificial and natural barrier dune habitat for a variety of birds and other wildlife continually by allowing biogeophysical processes to occur to the extent possible. Manage portions of about 40 acres of groin flats periodically for piping plover and other shorebird nesting/foraging habitat. Allow biogeophysical processes to dominate on about 70 acres of reconstructed dunes along North Carolina Highway 12 wherever practicable and possible.

Discussion: This objective is the same as the status quo. The majority of these areas are manmade habitats. The Civilian Conservation Corps constructed the high, steep-sided dunes to protect the road and the North Carolina Department of Transportation removes sand from the highway where it is close to the dunes and the ocean and places it back on the dunes maintaining their artificial profile. The area behind the groin on the northern end of the refuge accumulates sand regularly enough that it remains unvegetated. This area is good piping plover habitat, but the staff must excavate it regularly to maintain depressions where water can accumulate for the plovers.

Strategies:

- Evaluate, regulate, and monitor North Carolina Department of Transportation dune reconstruction projects regularly on about 70 acres along North Carolina Highway 12.

- Evaluate, regulate, and monitor sand transport projects of non-Service agencies regularly to limit impacts.

- Conduct surveys, studies, and inventories as necessary.

- Analyze and quantify data using geographic information systems as necessary.

Estuarine Salt Flats and Ponds

Objective: Provide 135 acres of salt flats for shorebirds, colonial nesting birds, waterfowl, and other wildlife continuously by allowing biogeophysical processes to dominate where possible. Provide 40 acres of estuarine ponds for wading birds, shorebirds, colonial nesting birds, waterfowl, and other wildlife continuously by allowing biogeophysical processes to dominate where possible.

Discussion: This objective is the same as the status quo. These areas are good habitats for wildlife without any active management. The staff monitors them as necessary.

Strategies:

- Conduct surveys, studies, and inventories as necessary.

- Analyze and quantify data using geographic information systems as necessary.

Impoundments

Objective: Manage about 790 acres of impoundments for submerged aquatic vegetation production in South Pond. Provide about 500 acres of mud/sand flat habitat in impoundments annually for shorebird foraging/loafing during spring migration. Provide about 200 acres of mud/sand flat habitat in impoundments for shorebird foraging/loafing during fall migration. Maintain a minimum of 40 acres of open water within the impoundments annually as year-round resting/feeding areas for waterfowl, shorebirds, colonial nesting birds, wading birds, and other wildlife and fish. Provide and maintain about 200 acres of moist-soil vegetation and palustrine marsh in impoundments annually for marsh birds, waterfowl, and other wildlife. Provide about 85 acres of maritime scrub/shrub islands in impoundments annually for land birds and wading birds. Maintain and improve structural integrity and provide about 50 acres of shrub and grassland habitat annually (in appropriate balance) on impoundment dikes for land birds, passerines, and waterfowl.

Discussion: This objective improves on the status quo by providing more acreage for submerged aquatic vegetation (500 to 750), mud/sand flats in the spring (300 to 500), and mud/sand flats in the fall (100 to 200). These types provide more habitats for waterfowl and shorebirds. The refuge impoundments attract a wide range of migratory birds and other types of wildlife. The staff orients most management towards waterfowl, shorebirds, and wading birds, but land birds and mammals utilize the maritime scrub/shrub islands and grasslands within the impoundments. Invertebrates are the prey base for the foraging shorebirds in the spring and fall. Reptiles and amphibians also thrive in the impoundments.

Strategies:

- Manage for submerged aquatic vegetation by improving water level management in South Pond and increasing monitoring efforts of management effectiveness.

- Manage mud and sand flats by monitoring the effects of water level management.

- Manage for moist-soil vegetation through water level management and vegetation controls.

- Manage scrub/shrub habitats by allowing natural processes to dominate.

Grasslands and Sand Ridges

Objective: Provide 27 acres of predominantly palustrine grassland for a variety of birds and other wildlife annually. Manipulate 50 transitional acres of grassland/shrub community and 183 acres of sand ridges to increase grassland coverage for a variety of birds and other wildlife.

Discussion: This objective improves on the status quo by providing for surveys, studies, and inventories of the area. These upland grassland communities provide unique habitat on the refuge in that they are herbaceous areas that are neither upland dunes nor brackish marshes. The dunes to the east protect them from the wind; the marshes to the west are too wet for many of the species that utilize them. This alternative adds the staff to perform the surveys.

- Maintain the area in a perennial herbaceous successional stage.

- Conduct surveys, studies, and inventories as necessary.

- Analyze and quantify data using geographic information systems as necessary.

Maritime Scrub/Shrub

Objective: Manage, monitor, and maintain 565 acres of maritime scrub/shrub habitat for land birds and other wildlife annually.

Discussion: This objective improves on the status quo by providing for surveys, studies, and inventories of the area. These woody plant communities provide unique habitat on the refuge in that they are the only woody vegetation on the 5,000-acre refuge. The vertical structure of the branching provides sites for land birds to nest and escape from predators; many species bear fruit to feed the land birds and other wildlife species. This alternative adds the staff to perform the surveys.

Strategies:

- Conduct scientifically valid surveys, studies, and inventories as necessary.

- Analyze and quantify data using geographic information systems as necessary.

Salt Marsh

Objective: Manage, monitor, and provide about 1,375 acres of emergent salt marsh for a variety of birds and other wildlife. Cooperate with regulatory agencies that monitor about 30 acres of mitigation marsh to determine mitigation success. Manage 30-acre mitigation marsh as emergent marsh when mitigation criteria are fully met to the satisfaction of the Corps of Engineers. Protect about 180 acres of emergent marsh soundside islands continuously as candidate wilderness for a variety of marsh birds and other wildlife.

Discussion: This objective improves on the status quo by providing for surveys, studies, and inventories of the area. These herbaceous plant communities are the dominant habitat on the refuge and support waterfowl, wading birds, marshbirds, and many other wildlife species. The dense vegetation is especially important to the secretive marsh birds such as rails. This alternative adds the staff to perform the surveys.

Strategies:

- Manage barrier island marshes with prescribed fire or another technique that controls succession and maintains a diverse vegetative community.

- Manage soundside islands by allowing natural processes to dominate.

- Conduct surveys, studies, and inventories as necessary.

- Analyze and quantify data using geographic information systems as necessary.

Soundside Islands (Proposed Wilderness Areas)

Objective: Monitor and protect about 180 acres of islands continuously as candidate wilderness for a variety of shorebirds, water birds, and other wildlife.

Discussion: This objective is the same as the status quo. The marshes on the islands are the dominant habitat on the refuge and support waterfowl, wading birds, marshbirds, and many other wildlife species. The dense vegetation is especially important to the secretive marsh birds, such as rails and soras.

Strategy:

- Manage by allowing natural processes to dominate.

Threatened and Endangered Plant Species

Objective: Protect threatened and endangered plant species and associated habitats as identified.

Discussion: This objective is the same as the status quo. The federally threatened seabeach amaranth (*Amaranthus pumilus*) and the plant species of federal concern, such as dune bluecurls (*Trichostema spp.*), may occur in this community, but neither has been documented on the refuge. The eroding beach and steep dune slopes minimize the potential that they will establish a population.

Strategies:

- Train staff in identification of seabeach amaranth and dune bluecurls.

- Encourage staff to remain vigilant of the plants and follow up on potential sightings.

PUBLIC USE

Goal: Provide the public with safe, quality wildlife-dependent recreational and educational opportunities that focus on barrier island wildlife and habitats of the refuge. Continue to participate in local efforts to sustain economic health through nature-based tourism.

Commercial Ecotours

Objective: Provide quality and diverse ecotour programs by issuing four permits per year for two paddling ecotours per day per site per permit.

Discussion: This objective improves the status quo by increasing the total number of permits issued (from two to four per year) while decreasing the total number of ecotours that each permittee conducts (from a maximum of five per day to two per day per site).

Strategies:

- Review applications for permits for paddling ecotours and grant permits to the most qualified applicants.

- Consider applications for permits for other ecotour opportunities.

- Provide training and information to permitees to ensure that visitors are aware of the refuge and its mission.

Environmental Education

Objective: Increase environmental education opportunities for 3,000 students on-site per year and 2,000 students off-site per year to meet the current demand.

Discussion: This objective improves on the status quo by proposing a 100 percent increase in participation on and off the refuge. There is currently a demand for programs in excess of what the staff and volunteers can provide. Volunteers and staff conduct a wide variety of environmental education programs, especially during the summer tourist season. This alternative proposes to add staff and volunteers to conduct the programs.

Strategies:

- Utilize permanent staff and volunteers to design, plan, and conduct programs.

- Conduct 300 programs on the refuge and 5 programs off the refuge in schools and at the facilities of other agencies and organizations.

- Advertise the availability of programs with fliers, print media, and the web site.

Fishing

Objective: Provide access opportunities for 50,000 fishing visits annually.

Discussion: This objective is the same as the status quo. The refuge is well known among saltwater anglers as an excellent surf fishing location. The public has pedestrian access to the beach across the dunes from parking areas and boating access to the sound. The refuge has provided access to the refuge for surf fishing at night outside of the turtle nesting season.

Strategies:

- Work with partners to improve information about beach fishing access (up to 150 vehicles at oceanside parking lots, not including road shoulders).

- Improve information about access for sound fishing (20 vehicles at New Inlet and up to 100 vehicles at Bonner Bridge).

- Continue to provide self-issuing permits for night fishing for up to 2,000 persons annually.

- Plan and implement two fishing events; one 3-hour crabbing and fishing rodeo for 200 to 300 people each June and explore the potential of other fishing events.

Hunting

Objective: Provide opportunities for up to 24 hunting use days annually.

Discussion: This objective provides more opportunities than the status quo. There is a Proclamation boundary around the refuge that prohibits migratory bird hunting. The narrow width of the refuge makes hunting with some types of firearms questionable from a safety standpoint. Hunting with shotguns can be done safely in many areas of the refuge. An archery hunt for deer has potential if the population is high enough to support it. Other species, such as rabbits or quail and Canada geese, could be considered if populations would support a hunt.

Strategy:

- Evaluate the potential of white-tailed deer and other wildlife to be harvested by hunting.

Interpretation

Objective: Improve interpretive programming and facilities to meet the current demand by annually providing interpretation opportunities for 1,400,000 visitors, including staff/volunteer-conducted talks for 2,000 visitors, tours for 800 visitors, and demonstrations for 800 visitors; 60,000 on-refuge Visitor Center visits; 150,000 kiosk visits; and 1,200,000 visits on interpretive trails.

Discussion: This objective improves on the status quo by proposing a 20 percent increase in visitation for interpretation over the status quo from 1.1 million to 1.4 million. There is currently a demand for interpretive programs in excess of what the staff and volunteers can provide. The refuge is located in an area that attracts 7 million tourists each year and has a tremendous opportunity to educate the public through interpretation. The volunteer workforce is an important asset to deliver the interpretive programs and maintain the interpretive facilities.

Strategies:

- Utilize permanent staff and volunteers to design, plan, and conduct programs.

- Conduct 40 programs for 2,000 visitors, 40 tours for 800 visitors, and 40 demonstrations for 800 visitors.

- Staff the Visitor Center 60 hours per week.

- Advertise the availability of programs with fliers, print media, and the web site.

- Maintain kiosks to accommodate 150,000 visitors and trails to accommodate 1.2 million visitors.

Nonwildlife-dependent Recreational Public Uses

Objective: Evaluate nonwildlife-dependent recreational uses on a weekly and case-by-case basis; regulate 750,000 visits for recreational uses such as beachcombing, sunbathing, surfing, hiking, jogging, swimming, kite-flying, boating, and biking where compatible; or regulate the number of visits for certain tolerated uses to limit impacts; or prohibit visits for recreational uses that are not compatible.

Discussion: This objective proposes to improve on the status quo by actively enforcing refuge regulations with a recently hired law enforcement officer. The refuge is located in a heavily used tourist area and within the Cape Hatteras National Seashore. Visitors are not necessarily aware of the subtle differences between permitted recreational uses on the refuge and the National Seashore. There is a practical limit as to how much signage the refuge can erect and how effective the signage is, and how many of the non wildlife-dependent recreational uses refuge staff can prevent. The staff must prohibit noncompatible uses and enforce regulations efficiently.

Strategies:

- Utilize management and biological staff to evaluate requests for uses.

- Enforce regulations with full time and dual function officers.

Outreach

Objective: Increase and improve communication with media, conservation organizations, elected officials, local communities, and other potential supporters to reach 10 million people annually.

Discussion: This objective proposes to double the size of the refuge's outreach audience from 5 to 10 million. The refuge is located in an area that attracts 7 million tourists each year and has several large urban centers within a few hundred miles. The refuge staff has excellent relationships with local media outlets and an excellent web site.

Strategies:

- Provide basic and detailed refuge information on programs, resources, management, and regulations with printed material, through contact with the media, and on the Internet.

- Maintain proactive monthly schedule of Service programs and activities at the refuge headquarters and Visitor Center, on kiosks, and on the Internet.

Refuge Support

Objective: Work formally with the Coastal Wildlife Refuge Society and informally with other groups and agencies to provide approximately $150,000 annually to support refuge programs and facilities.

Discussion: This objective is the same as the status quo. The refuge has the Coastal Wildlife Refuge Society as its "Friends" group that raises funds for the refuge, applies for grants to conduct programs on the refuge, and recruits and coordinates volunteers.

Strategies:

- Meet with the Coastal Wildlife Refuge Society at its regular meetings.

- Maintain contact with officers and members between regular meetings.

- Communicate the needs of the refuge for funds and volunteer staffing to the Coastal Wildlife Refuge Society.

- Identify refuge needs for additional organizational support and activity.

- Develop additional support groups as needed.

Special Events

Objective: Plan, coordinate, and execute two major and four minor quality special events annually in eastern North Carolina for 7,500 people.

Discussion: This objective proposes a 50 percent increase from current level of participation in special events. The refuge currently participates in Wings over Water, a nature-based recreation festival, each autumn; a Crabbing and Fishing Rodeo each June; and Wildfest, a family-oriented nature-based festival each autumn. There are opportunities to engage the public at more special events that will educate them and provide nature-based recreation opportunities. This alternative provides for additional staff to assist the wildlife interpretive specialist plan and execute the events.

Strategies:

- Establish and maintain relationships with other agencies and organizations to conduct special events.

- Publicize events with fliers and personal contacts, in the print media, and on the Internet.

Visitor Protection

Objective: Identify safety hazards and ensure the safety of visitors by eliminating hazards; control access into hazardous areas; and inform visitors of potential hazards.

Discussion: This objective is the same as status quo. It improves visitor protection by providing for patrols by the refuge law enforcement officer frequently enough to warn visitors of hazards. This alternative provides for additional staff to identify hazards and react to them appropriately.

Strategies:

- Maintain an awareness of potential safety hazards and inform the proper staff when hazards are reported or discovered.

- Notify the public of safety hazards with signs and printed material.

- Conduct law enforcement patrols on a regular basis.

Volunteer Coordination

Objective: Support and enhance designated refuge programs by recruiting, training, and coordinating volunteers to donate 30,000 hours of service annually.

Discussion: This objective provides for a 20 percent increase over current levels of volunteer hours. The refuge depends heavily on volunteers to conduct its public use, biological, and maintenance programs. Volunteers come from the local community, colleges, and great distances (as workampers). The refuge provides housing and a food stipend for college interns and camper pads and hookups for workampers. Volunteers staff the Visitor Center, conduct public use programs, monitor sea turtle nesting and hatching, and maintain the buildings, grounds, and public use facilities. The refuge only has one permanent full-time staff person assigned to the refuge. This alternative provides for additional staff to coordinate volunteers more effectively.

Strategies:

- Recruit volunteers from the local community, conservation and youth organizations, universities, work kamper news, and the Internet.

- Utilize the public use staff to coordinate the volunteers.

- Utilize the appropriate staff to train and supervise volunteers engaged in support of the public use, biological, and maintenance programs.

Wildlife Observation

Objective: Provide 100-120 quality guided observation tours annually averaging 8 people each to meet current demand. Provide observation facilities for 1,200,000 visits.

Discussion: This objective provides for a 20 percent increase in visitors participating in wildlife observation over current levels. Refuge visitors have access to the refuge beaches, dunes, and marshes from a number of parking lots, a trail around North Pond, and an observation blind at the north end of North Pond. This alternative provides for additional staff to maintain the facilities better.

Strategies:

- Utilize permanent staff and volunteers to design, plan, and conduct programs.

- Advertise the availability of programs with fliers, print media, and the web site.

- Maintain facilities that support wildlife observation.

- Identify and provide additional quality/low impact wildlife observation opportunities.

Wildlife Photography

Objective: Provide quality opportunities and facilities for wildlife photography sufficient for 300,000 visits annually.

Discussion: This objective is the same as the status quo. A substantial proportion of refuge visitors photograph wildlife as part of their refuge experience. Refuge visitors have access to the refuge beaches, dunes, and marshes from a number of parking lots, a trail around North Pond, and photography blind at the north end of North Pond. This alternative provides for additional staff to maintain the facilities better.

Strategies:

- Utilize permanent staff and volunteers to design, plan, and conduct programs.

- Advertise the availability of programs with fliers, print media, and the web site.

- Maintain facilities that support wildlife photography.

- Identify and provide additional quality/low impact wildlife photography opportunities.

RESOURCE PROTECTION

Goal: Protect refuge resources by limiting the adverse impacts of human activities and development.

Communication Towers

Objective: Limit impacts to refuge resources from existing and proposed communication towers.

Discussion: The plan is the same as the current level of management. Communication towers pose threats to migrating birds as they fly at night and strike the towers, often in large flocks. There is only one tower on the refuge, but there are great demands to erect more towers in the rapidly developing area in which the refuge is located. This plan provides for additional staff to assist with reviewing permits and coordinating with the United States Navy on the operation of its tower.

Strategies:

- Limit impacts to refuge resources by coordinating with the United States Navy on development and maintenance of its communication tower.

- Minimize impacts to refuge resources by providing review and comment on all other communication tower projects that are proposed.

- Avoid adverse impacts to refuge resources by developing special use conditions consistent with Fish and Wildlife Service guidelines for communication tower construction and maintenance proposals.

Cultural Resources

Objective: Avoid all impacts to cultural resources on the refuge.

Discussion: The plan is the same as the current level of management. The Historic Preservation Act mandates that the Service protect cultural resources on the refuge. A consultant performed a cultural resources study of the refuge in 1978. The refuge is a very active area geologically. Although there have been buildings and shipwrecks on the refuge lands, the study concluded that the dynamic nature of the geologic processes has destroyed evidence of their existence. The State Historic Preservation Office has not deemed any of the recently discovered resources significant. The staff will refer all land-disturbing activities to the Service's Regional Archaeologist.

Strategies:

- Avoid all impacts to cultural resources by evaluating all proposed external projects and coordinating with the Service's Regional Archaeologist within 30 days of receiving a proposal.

- Avoid all impacts to cultural resources by coordinating all internal projects with the Service's Regional Archaeologist within 30 days of receiving funds.

- Manage and limit impacts to identified cultural resources annually by restricting access to or regulating activities in cultural resource areas.

- Provide access to cultural resources training to the management and law enforcement staff.

Inholdings

Objective: Maintain contact with the North Carolina Aquarium on the use, management, and potential future development of the 10-acre inholding.

Discussion: The plan is the same as the current level of management. There was a Coast Guard Station on the northern end of Pea Island National Wildlife Refuge. The Coast Guard abandoned the station and transferred it to the State of North Carolina. The North Carolina Aquarium administers the property, but has not developed it or utilized it for programs. If the Aquarium develops the property or wishes to dispose of it, the refuge staff must be aware of its plans.

Strategies:

- Enhance refuge resources and programs by coordinating specific inholder activities on a case-by-case basis.

- Limit impacts to refuge resources annually by developing special use conditions for permitted inholder activities on the refuge.

Interagency Coordination

Objective: Facilitate and enhance refuge programs and protect refuge resources by coordinating with local, state, federal, public, and private agencies at least 20 times annually formally and informally.

Discussion: The plan is the same as the current level of management. The management of Pea Island Refuge requires an extraordinary amount of coordination because the refuge is located within a national seashore, has a state highway running through it, has an active Corps of Engineers dredging project, is within a larger tourist area that attracts 7 million visitors annually, and is in an area subject to destructive natural forces. The plan provides for additional staff to coordinate with other agencies and organizations.

Strategies:

- Represent the Service throughout the year at a minimum of 20 local meetings, 15 state meetings, 5 national meetings, 10 public meetings, and 5 meetings with private organizations.

- Enhance public use programs and facilities by formally coordinating with the National Park Service annually through regular meetings and other forms of contact.

- Enhance refuge programs and resources by developing cooperative agreements with other local, state, and federal agencies annually.

- Review and revise existing cooperative agreements annually.

Land Protection

Objective: Acquire the state-owned 10-acre inholding surrounding the Oregon Inlet Coast Guard Station within the approved refuge acquisition boundary if it becomes available.

Discussion: This objective is the same as the status quo. There was a Coast Guard Station on the northern end of Pea Island National Wildlife Refuge. The Coast Guard abandoned the station and transferred it to the State of North Carolina. The North Carolina Aquarium administers the property, but has not developed it or utilized it for programs. If the Aquarium wishes to dispose of it, the Service will acquire it. This alternative provides for additional staff that will maintain contact with the North Carolina Aquarium.

Strategy:

- Maintain contact with the North Carolina Aquarium regarding the availability of the 10-acre inholding.

Law Enforcement

Objective: Ensure public safety and protect refuge resources continuously by encouraging voluntary compliance and enforcing refuge regulations as necessary.

Discussion: This objective provides for more proactive enforcement than the status quo. It improves law enforcement by providing for patrols frequent enough to establish a presence and signage that encourages voluntary compliance.

Strategies:

- Patrol frequently enough to establish a presence for law enforcement on the refuge.

- Provide assistance to and coordinate with appropriate local, state, and federal law enforcement agencies to ensure compliance with local, state, and federal laws.

Navigable Waters

Objective: Consult with the National Park Service and the State of North Carolina to establish a cooperative management agreement to regulate certain activities within selected waters.

Discussion: This objective pursues the agreement more proactively than the status quo. There are state waters under the jurisdiction of North Carolina and waters over which the National Park Service has jurisdiction that are bays and inlets surrounded on three sides by refuge land. There are illegal activities that occur on those waters that threaten refuge habitat and fish and wildlife populations.

The State of North Carolina and the National Park Service have limited resources to enforce existing regulations on those waters. Under this alternative, the Service would actively pursue co-management of those waters.

Strategy:

- Coordinate selection of waters with Fish and Wildlife Service coordinating refuge manager.

Permits

Objective: Limit impacts to or enhance refuge resources by evaluating approximately 40 use proposals annually on a case-by-case basis.

Discussion: This objective increases the capacity for permit review from 30 proposals in the status quo to 40 proposals. Visitors and researchers apply for permits to engage in recreation activities or perform research on the refuge. The staff reviews the permits, and establishes and enforces conditions under which applicants may engage in the activity. This alternative adds staff to assist in permit review and development and monitoring of permit conditions.

Strategy:

- Protect refuge resources annually by developing special conditions for those permitted uses that are compatible.

Pest Animals

Objective: Limit impacts to refuge resources by monitoring, controlling, or eradicating pest animals as necessary.

Discussion: This objective is the same as the status quo. Pest animals, particularly feral cats, are a threat to wildlife populations. There is no active control program at this time.

Strategies:

- Encourage all staff and volunteers to maintain vigilance while observing wildlife in the course of their routine duties and report pest animals to the appropriate authorities.

- Develop a Nuisance and Exotic Animal Control Plan.

Pest Plants

Objective: Improve native plant communities and limit impacts on approximately 25 acres by monitoring, controlling, or eradicating pest plants as necessary.

Discussion: This objective is the same as the status quo. Pest plants, particularly common reed (*Phragmites australis*), are a threat to the natural vegetative communities on the refuge. The refuge staff is currently managing common reed with herbicides and pest plants in the vicinity of the Visitor's Center with mowing and hand weeding.

Strategies:

- Monitor pest plants and record their location in an electronic format.

- Develop a Nuisance and Exotic Pest Control Plan.

- Control pest plants with mechanical or chemical measures.

Rights-of-Way (Highway and Utility)

Objective: Limit impacts to refuge resources by coordinating on the development and maintenance of rights-of-way.

Discussion: This objective is the same as the status quo. The State of North Carolina and the Cape Hatteras Electric Cooperative have rights-of-way through the refuge. These rights-of-way are subject to conditions that ensure compatibility with the refuge purposes. The staff reviews proposals to move those rights-of-way and acquire new rights-of-way.

Strategies:

- Minimize impacts to refuge resources by providing review and comment on all other right-of-way projects that are proposed.

- Avoid adverse impacts to refuge resources by developing terms and conditions to ensure the compatibility of right-of-way construction and maintenance proposals.

Sand Management

Objective: Limit impacts to refuge resources by managing sand removal and placement on the refuge annually, and by monitoring biogeophysical shoreline processes four times a year and after storm events.

Discussion: This objective is the same as the status quo. The North Carolina Department of Transportation removes sand from North Carolina Highway 12 that blows from the beaches and dunes east of the highway. The Corps of Engineers dredges sand from Oregon Inlet on the north end of the refuge and disposes compatible sand on the refuge's beaches. The refuge staff maintains a relationship with both agencies, reviews applications for permits to move sand, and establishes and enforces conditions under which they may move sand. Of critical concern is the compatibility of sand placed on refuge beaches for shorebird foraging habitat.

Strategy:

- Protect habitat for shorebirds, sea turtles, and other species by analyzing sand budget data and biota annually.

Water Quality

Objective: Monitor water quality on a weekly basis by measuring salinities at up to nine collection points west of North Carolina Highway 12.

Discussion: This objective is the same as the status quo. Measuring the salinities keeps the staff aware of salinity levels in the impoundments on the refuge and the Pamlico Sound immediately west of the refuge.

Strategies:

- Train staff and volunteers to measure salinity.

- Record the data in an electronic format.

- Analyze the data and adapt management accordingly.

Wilderness Areas

Objective: Allow natural processes to dominate on the candidate wilderness islands annually.

Discussion: This objective is the same as the status quo. There are 180 acres of candidate wilderness islands in the Pamlico Sound. The staff is allowing natural processes to dominate on these islands. Members of the public and researchers present proposals to engage in recreation or perform research on the islands.

Strategies:

- Avoid impacts to candidate wilderness islands by reviewing and evaluating two to three proposed development projects per year.

- Review and evaluate proposals for additional protection designations as directed.

Wildlife Disease Control and Prevention

Objective: Limit impacts to refuge resources from wildlife diseases as necessary.

Discussion: This objective is the same as the status quo. There have not been any significant incidences of wildlife disease on the refuge.

Strategies:

- Observe wildlife on the refuge during routine monitoring, note any disease symptoms, and report them to the appropriate authorities.

- Encourage all staff and volunteers to maintain vigilance while observing wildlife in the course of their routine duties and report disease symptoms to the appropriate authorities.

- Follow up on visitors' observations of potential disease symptoms.

- Coordinate with local, state, and federal agencies to monitor and control wildlife disease.

Goal: Acquire and manage adequate funding, human resources, facilities, equipment, and infrastructure to accomplish all refuge goals.

Capital Property Management

Objective: Use increased level of funding and staffing to effectively operate, maintain, and dispose of capital property; acquire minimum equipment necessary to support refuge programs.

Discussion: This objective improves on the status quo by providing for the acquisition of the minimum amount of equipment to support the refuge programs. The refuge is currently reasonably well equipped, but replacement schedules are not adequate to avoid major repairs of critical equipment.

Strategies:

- Conduct one capital property inventory annually.

- Evaluate operating condition of capital property.

- Maintain and upgrade property to ensure safety of staff and general public.

Financial Management

Objective: Manage budget and develop and administer contracts in accordance with Fish and Wildlife Service policy.

Discussion: This objective improves on the status quo by providing a new refuge operations specialist at Pea Island National Wildlife Refuge to assist with financial management. The management and administrative staff at Alligator River National Wildlife Refuge currently manage the finances of Pea Island National Wildlife Refuge.

Strategies:

- Develop annual and long-term budgets.

- Develop and execute contracts.

- Process travel vouchers.

- Maintain Refuge Operating Needs System (RONS) and Maintenance Management System (MMS) databases by adding new needs and deleting funded projects.

- Apply for flex-funding and other grants.

Office Space

Objective: Provide and maintain a safe adequate office, parking facilities, and utilities for the planned size of the staff.

Discussion: This objective improves on the status quo by providing for new offices at Pea Island National Wildlife Refuge for the staff located there and at Alligator River National Wildlife Refuge for the staff that serves Pea Island National Wildlife Refuge. The Service has evaluated the facilities and determined that they are near the end of their useful life. Computerization, an increasing volunteer workforce (currently 25,000 hours per year), and a planned increase in staff at Pea Island Refuge mandate a new facility designed for the planned level of use. The rented office space in Manteo, where most of the currently shared staff is located, is cramped with inadequate parking for the staff's personal or government vehicles and visitors' vehicles. There is no parking space for equipment that requires trips to the Alligator River Refuge shop for repair.

Strategies:

- Replace 1960s office, shop, garage, and residence.

- Provide Service-owned Manteo office space and parking facilities for optimum staff levels by building a refuge headquarters/Visitor Center.

- Provide fuel, office supplies, and utilities for refuge operations and staff.

Personnel

Objective: Manage personnel in accordance with Fish and Wildlife Service policy.

Discussion: This objective improves on the status quo by providing a new refuge operations specialist at Pea Island National Wildlife Refuge to assist with personnel management. The management and administrative staff at Alligator River National Wildlife Refuge currently manage the personnel of Pea Island National Wildlife Refuge.

Strategies:

- Recognize employee performance annually through the employee incentive program.

- Hire and manage minimum levels of staff to meet refuge objectives at approved full-time equivalent (FTE) levels.

- Provide the minimum 40-hour staff training opportunity for professional, technical, and leadership development goals.

Real Property Management

Objective: Use increased level of funding and staff to effectively maintain buildings, grounds, firebreaks, structures, roads, and other facilities to protect the health and safety of the refuge staff and public.

Discussion: This objective improves on the status quo by providing a new refuge operations specialist at Pea Island Refuge to assist with property management. The management and administrative staff at Alligator River National Wildlife Refuge currently manage the property of Pea Island National Wildlife Refuge.

Strategies:

- Maintain buildings, structures, and other facilities to support refuge programs.

- Evaluate the need for and acquire additional buildings, structures, and other facilities to support refuge programs.

- Conduct one real property inventory annually.

V. Plan Implementation

INTRODUCTION

This chapter outlines the staff and activities that will execute the strategies specified in Chapter IV and the new staff, budget, equipment, and facilities that are needed, see (Tables 10, 11, 12, 13, and14). The priorities assigned to the Refuge Operations Needs System (RONS) and Maintenance Management System (MMS) projects in Appendix VIII determine the priorities of the strategies. There is no direct correlation between a specific position, piece of equipment, or facility and a specific strategy since any one position, piece of equipment, or facility executes more than a single strategy.

PROPOSED PROJECTS

Table 10. Projects supporting wildlife strategies

Strategy	Projects
Personnel Projects	
Conduct surveys, monitoring, studies, and investigations.	Use existing wildlife biologist, biological technician, and forestry technician. Recruit, hire, train new wildlife biologist (RONS 00095).
Protect wildlife.	Existing law enforcement officer.
Manage budget, contracts, personnel, and property.	Use existing refuge manager, deputy manager, assistant manager, and office assistants. Recruit, hire, train new assistant refuge manager (refuge operations specialist) (RONS 97039)
Apply for flexible fund and other grants.	Use existing wildlife biologist. Recruit, hire, train new wildlife biologist (RONS 00095).
Equipment Projects	
Replace equipment to survey and protect wildlife.	Replace John Deere 4240 Tractor (MMS 98014). Replace vehicles (MMS 01030, 02015, 02016, 03006). Replace equipment shared by Alligator River NWR.

Table 11. Projects supporting habitat strategies

Strategy	Projects
Personnel Projects	
Conduct surveys, monitoring, studies, and investigations.	Use existing wildlife biologist, biological technician, and forestry technician. Recruit, hire, train new wildlife biologist (RONS 00095).
Conduct prescribed burning.	Use existing fire management officer, wildlife biologist, forestry technicians, and engineering equipment operators.
Protect habitat.	Use existing law enforcement officer.
Manage budget, contracts, personnel, and property.	Use existing refuge manager, deputy manager, assistant manager, and office assistants. Recruit, hire, train new assistant refuge manager (refuge operations specialist) (RONS 97039).
Apply for flexible fund and other grants.	Use existing wildlife biologist. Recruit, hire, train new wildlife biologist (RONS 00095).
Equipment Projects	
Replace equipment to manage habitat.	Replace John Deere 4240 Tractor (MMS 98014). Replace vehicles (MMS 01030, 02015, 02016, 03006). Replace equipment shared by Alligator River NWR.
Facility Projects	
Replace facilities to manage habitat.	Replace bulkheads, water control structures, and pumping stations (various MMS projects).

Table 12. Projects supporting public use strategies

Strategy	Projects
Personnel Projects	
Plan, design, and conduct programs and outreach.	Use existing park rangers and volunteers. Recruit, hire, train new park ranger (RONS 00099).
Maintain education, interpretation, wildlife observation, and photography facilities.	Use existing volunteers and staff from Alligator River Refuge. Recruit, hire, train new maintenance worker (RONS 00092).
Protect visitors.	Existing law enforcement officer.
Manage budget, contracts, personnel, and property.	Use existing refuge manager, deputy manager, assistant manager, and office assistants. Recruit, hire, train new assistant refuge manager (refuge operations specialist) (RONS 97039).
Apply for flexible fund and other grants.	Use existing park rangers. Recruit, hire, train new park ranger (RONS 00099).
Equipment Projects	
Replace equipment to maintain facilities as necessary.	Replace John Deere 4240 Tractor (MMS 98014). Replace vehicles (MMS 01030, 02015, 02016, 03006). Replace equipment shared by Alligator River Refuge.
Facility Projects	
Replace facilities as necessary.	Replace parking lots, kiosks, office, shop, garage, and residence (various MMS).

Table 13. Projects supporting resource protection strategies

Strategy	Projects
Personnel Projects	
Maintain cooperation with agencies, organizations, and permit holders. Review permits and develop conditions for uses allowed by permits. Monitor pest animals and plants and permitted uses.	Use existing refuge manager, deputy manager, assistant manager, and wildlife biologists. Recruit, hire, train new assistant refuge manager (refuge operations specialist) (RONS 97039) and new wildlife biologist (RONS 00095).
Maintain equipment and facilities.	Use existing volunteers and staff from Alligator River Refuge. Recruit, hire, train new maintenance worker (RONS 00092).
Enforce regulations.	Use existing law enforcement officer.
Manage budget, contracts, personnel, and property.	Use existing refuge manager, deputy manager, assistant manager, and office assistants. Recruit, hire, train new assistant refuge manager (refuge operations specialist) (RONS 97039).
Apply for flexible fund and other grants.	Use existing park rangers. Recruit, hire, train new park ranger (RONS 00099).
Equipment Projects	
Replace equipment as necessary.	Replace John Deere 4240 Tractor (MMS 98014). Replace vehicles (MMS 01030, 02015, 02016, 03006). Replace equipment shared by Alligator River Refuge.
Facility Projects	
Replace facilities as necessary.	Replace parking lots, kiosks, and office (various MMS projects).

Table 14. Projects supporting refuge administration strategies

Strategy	Projects
Personnel Projects	
Manage budget, contracts, personnel, and property.	Use existing refuge manager, deputy manager, assistant manager, and office assistants. Recruit, hire, train new assistant refuge manager (refuge operations specialist) (RONS 97039).
Maintain equipment and facilities.	Use existing volunteers and staff from Alligator River Refuge. Recruit, hire, train, new maintenance worker (RONS 00092).
Equipment Projects	
Maintain, repair, and replace equipment as necessary.	Replace John Deere 4240 Tractor (MMS 98014). Replace vehicles (MMS 01030, 02015, 02016, 03006). Replace equipment shared by Alligator River Refuge.
Facility Projects	
Maintain, repair, and replace facilities as necessary.	Replace bulkheads, water control structures, pumping stations, parking lots, kiosks, office, shop, garage, and residence (various MMS projects).

REFUGE ADMINISTRATION

The Service administers Pea Island National Wildlife Refuge from an office in Manteo, North Carolina, 15 miles northwest of the refuge's northern boundary. Construction on the refuge is not practical because almost the entire refuge is wetland or actively eroding sand dunes. The staff stores its refuge equipment on Alligator River National Wildlife Refuge, 25 miles northwest of Pea Island Refuge. The Service uses staff from the Manteo office and the shop at Alligator River Refuge to manage the Pea Island Refuge.

FUNDING AND PERSONNEL

Currently, the Service has approved a staff of 23 permanent positions to serve the Alligator River National Wildlife Refuge Complex (which includes Pea Island Refuge) headquartered in Manteo; the manager has stationed one position from the Alligator River Refuge on Pea Island Refuge. Of the 23 positions, 6.3 full-time equivalents (5.4 non-fire and 0.9 fire) are spent on Pea Island Refuge. Of the 23 positions, 9 are funded for fire management.

To complete the extensive wildlife habitat management and restoration projects and conduct the necessary inventorying, monitoring, and mapping activities, resources are needed to maintain and replace equipment and facilities, perform studies, and provide more staff to administer refuge programs. The proposed public use facilities are shown in Figure 8. The proposed staffing plan (Table 15) outlines a staff of 39 employees (12.25 full-time equivalent positions dedicated to Pea Island Refuge) that would enable the refuge to achieve its objectives and strategies within a reasonable time. The annual cost of implementing the plan (including salaries and benefits) would be $706,100. The cost of replacing equipment and facilities and equipping new employees on Pea Island Refuge would be $3,592,500. The cost of replacing equipment on Alligator River Refuge that supports Pea Island Refuge would be $7,498,000. The rate at which this refuge realizes its full potential to contribute locally, regionally, and nationally to wildlife conservation and appropriate wildlife-dependent recreation and environmental education is totally dependent upon adequate resources.

VOLUNTEERS

The refuge depends on volunteers extensively, especially for its visitor services programs. Volunteers currently contribute 25,000 staff hours; this plan anticipates contributions of 30,000 hours. The refuge utilizes volunteers from the community, college interns, and workkampers. College interns rotate through work assignments in the visitor services, biology, and maintenance programs. The staff recruits workkampers for the skills the refuge needs. The refuge provides quarters for college interns and pads for recreational vehicles for the workkampers.

STEP-DOWN MANAGEMENT PLANS

A comprehensive conservation plan is a strategic plan that guides the direction of the refuge. Before the staff implements some of the strategies and projects, it prepares or updates detailed step-down management plans. To assist in preparing and implementing the step-down plans, the staff often cooperates with federal, state, and local agencies and non-governmental organizations. The staff develops these plans in accordance with the National Environmental Policy Act. The following are examples of step-down plans that may be developed for the refuge:

Biological Inventory/Monitoring Plan (Update): This plan will describe inventory and monitoring techniques and time frames. The staff will inventory plant communities and associations in the refuge

as well as all trust species (e.g., shorebirds, colonial nesting birds, songbirds, neotropical passerines, and waterfowl), listed species (e.g., federal and state threatened, endangered, and species of concern), key resident species, and monitor population trends.

Habitat Management Plan (Update): This plan will describe the overall desired habitat conditions needed to fulfill the refuge's purpose and objectives. The plan will include sections dealing with each habitat on the refuge. The staff will develop procedures, techniques, strategies, and timetables for achieving desired conditions into an overall plan.

Moist Soil/Water Management Plan (Update): This plan will describe the strategies and procedures (timing and duration of flooding and disturbance) for manipulating the refuge's water management units to meet habitat management objectives.

Figure 8. Future visitor facilities at Pea Island National Wildllife Refuge

Figure 8. Future visitor facilities at Pea Island National Wildllife Refuge

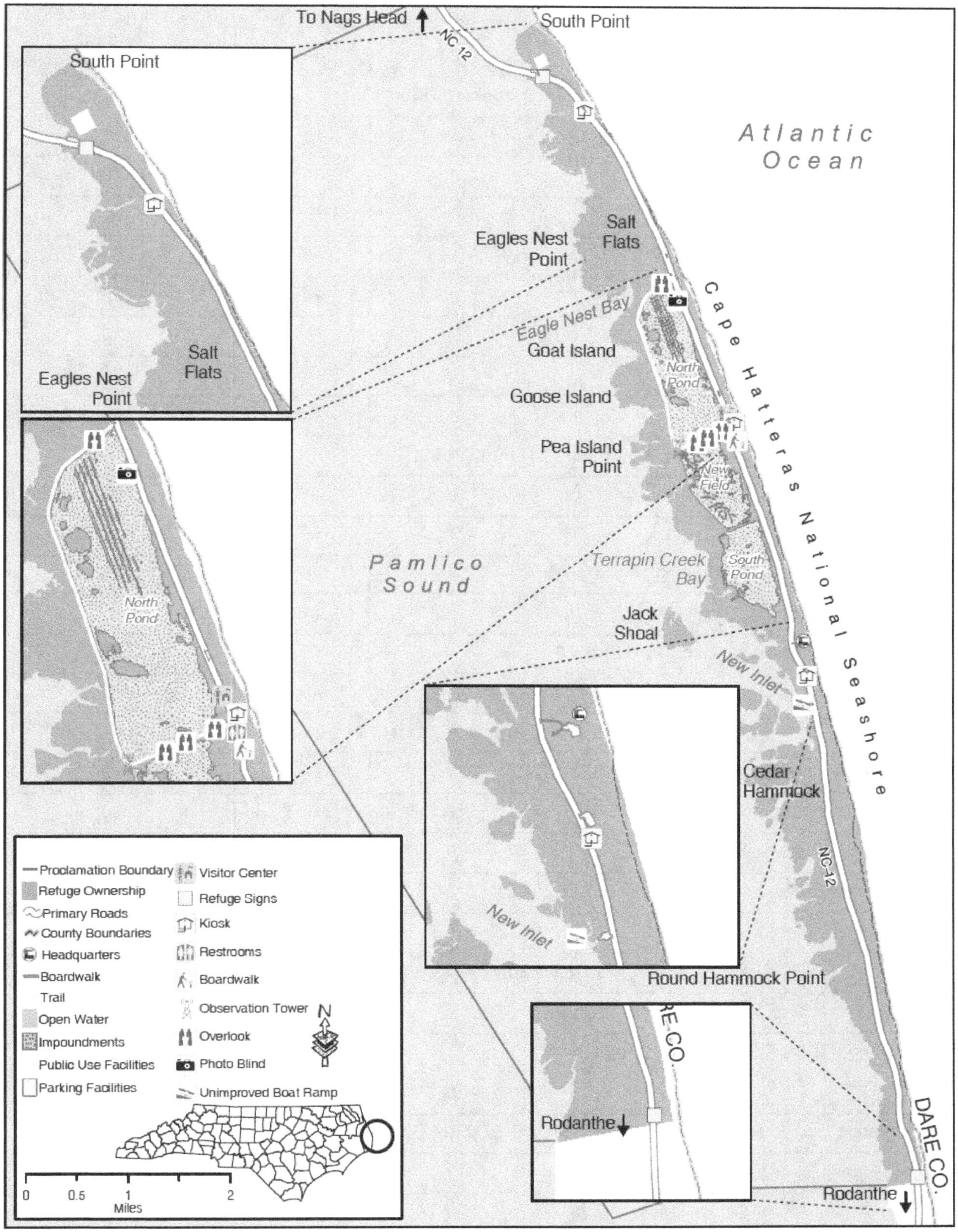

Table 15. Proposed staffing plan for Pea Island National Wildlife Refuge

Position	Status	Percent of Time on Pea Island
Management Staff		
Refuge Manager, GS-0485-14*	PFT	60
Deputy Refuge Manager, GS-0485-13*	PFT	40
Assistant Refuge Manager, GS-0485-12*	PFT	25
Refuge Operations Specialist, GS-0485-09**	PFT	50
Refuge Operations Specialist, GS-0485-07**	PFT	100
Computer Specialist, GS-11**	PFT	10
Administrative Officer, GS-0341-09*	PFT	25
Office Assistant, GS-0303-07*	PPT	25
Biological Staff		
Wildlife Biologist, GS-0486-12*	PFT	60
Forester, GS-0460-11**	PFT	20
Wildlife Biologist, GS-0486-09**	PFT	100
Biologist, GS-0486-07**	PFT	45
Biological Science Technician, GS-0404-07*	PFT	50
Forestry Technician, GS-0462-07*	PFT	10
Interpretive Staff		
Park Ranger (Interpretation), GS-0025-12*	PFT	60
Park Ranger (Interpretation), GS-0025-09*	PFT	90
Park Ranger (Interpretation), GS-0025-09**	PFT	100
Park Ranger (Volunteer Coordinator), GS-0025-09**	PFT	60
Park Ranger (Interpretation), GS-0025-05*	TERM	90
Law Enforcement Staff		
Park Ranger (Law Enforcement), GS-0025-09*	PFT	30
Park Ranger (Law Enforcement), GS-0025-07**	PFT	50
Maintenance Staff		
Engineering Equipment. Operator Supervisor, WS-5716-09*	PFT	25
Mobile Heavy Equipment Mechanic, WG-5716-10**	PFT	10

Position	Status	Percent of Time on Pea Island
Engineering Equipment Operator, WG-5716-10*	PFT	10
Engineering Equipment Operator, WG-5716-09*	PFT	10
Engineering Equipment Operator, WG-5716-08*	PFT	10
Automotive Worker, WG-5823-08*	PFT	10
Maintenance Worker, WG-4749-08**	PFT	100
Maintenance Worker, WG-4749-05**	PFT	0
Fire Management Program		
Fire Management Officer, GS-0460-12*	PFT	10
Fire Management Officer (Wildland Urban Interface), GS-0401-11*	PFT	10
Fire Management Specialist, GS-0401-09*	PFT	10
Forestry Technician, (Fire Program Technician) GS-0462-08*	PFT	10
Forestry Technician, (Fire) GS-0462-08*	PFT	10
Forestry Technician (Fire), GS-0462-06*	PFT	10
Forestry Technician, (Fire) GS-0462-06*	PFT	10
Forestry Technician (Fire) GS-0462-07*	PFT	10
Engineering Equipment Operator, (Fire) WG-5716-08*	PFT	10
Engineering Equipment Operator, (Fire) WG-5716-08*	PFT	10
PFT = Permanent Full Time employee *TERM = Term Employee (up to four years)* ** = Existing Staff, ** = New Staff*		

Marsh Management Plan (Update): This plan will describe strategies for meeting refuge marsh management objectives. Also, the plan will address scrub/shrub habitat management.

Integrated Pest Management Plan (Develop): This plan will address the complex issue of bringing exotic and nuisance plants and animals to a maintenance control level on the refuge. It will cover chemical pesticide use (e.g., aerial and ground application), mechanical eradication, and biological controls. The Nuisance/Exotic Animal and Plant control plans will be sections of this plan.

Nuisance/Exotic Animal Control Plan (Update): This plan (as part of the Integrated Pest Management Plan) will describe survey, removal or control, and monitoring techniques for both terrestrial and aquatic nuisance and exotic animals (vertebrate and invertebrate). The plan will include wild dogs, feral cats, and resident Canada geese.

Nuisance/Exotic Plant Control Plan (Update): This plan (as part of the Integrated Pest Management Plan) will describe survey, removal or control, and monitoring techniques for both terrestrial and aquatic nuisance and exotic plants.

Fire Management Plan (Update): This plan will describe wild and prescribed fire management techniques that the staff will employ on the refuge. Wildfire control descriptions will include initial attack strategies and cooperative agreements with other agencies.

Visitor Services Plan (Develop): This plan will describe the refuge's wildlife-dependent recreation, environmental education, and interpretive programs. It will address specific issues or items, such as access, facility requirements, site plans, and handicapped accessibility. The environmental education, fishing, hunting, and sign plans will be sections of this plan.

Environmental Education Plan (Develop): This plan will reflect the objectives and strategies of the comprehensive conservation plan and address environmental education guidelines following Service standards.

Fishing Plan (Update): This plan (as part of the Visitor Services Plan) will address specific aspects of the refuge's fishing program. It will define season structures, fishing areas, methods, access, handicapped accessibility, facilities needed, and refuge specific regulations.

Sign Plan (Update): This plan (as part of the Visitor Services Plan) will describe the refuge's strategy for informing visitors via signage. It will incorporate Service guidelines.

Law Enforcement Plan (Update): This plan will provide a reference to station policies, procedures, priorities, and programs concerning law enforcement.

MONITORING AND ADAPTIVE MANAGEMENT

The staff will review this comprehensive conservation plan annually to determine the need for revision. A revision will occur if and when substantial information becomes available, such as a change in ecological conditions. The staff will augment this plan by detailed step-down management plans to address the completion of specific strategies in support of the refuge's goals and objectives. Revisions to the plan and the step-down management plans will be subject to public review and compliance with the National Environmental Policy Act.

Appendix I. Glossary

Adaptive Management	A process in which projects are implemented within a framework of scientifically driven experiments to test predictions and assumptions outlined within the comprehensive conservation plan. The analysis of the outcome of project implementation helps managers determine whether current management should continue as is, or whether they should modify it to achieve the desired conditions.
Alternative	Alternatives are different means of accomplishing refuge purposes, goals, and objectives and contributing to the National Wildlife Refuge System. An alternative is a reasonable way to fix the identified problem or satisfy the stated need.
Approved Acquisition Boundary	A project boundary that the Director of the Fish and Wildlife Service approves upon completion of the detailed planning and environmental compliance process.
Biological Diversity	The variety of life and its processes, including the variety of living organisms, the genetic differences among them, and the communities and ecosystems in which they occur. The National Wildlife Refuge System's focus is on indigenous species, biotic communities, and ecological processes.
Biological Integrity	The biotic composition, structure, and functioning at genetic, organism, and community levels comparable with historic conditions including the natural biological processes that shape genomes, organisms, and communities.
Canopy	A layer of foliage; generally the upper-most layer in a forest stand. It can refer to mid- or understory vegetation in multilayered stands. Canopy closure is an estimate of the amount of overhead tree cover (also called canopy cover).
Categorical Exclusion	A category of actions that do not individually or cumulatively have a significant effect on the human environment and have been found to have no such effect in procedures adopted by a federal agency, pursuant to the National Environmental Policy Act of 1969.
CFR	Code of Federal Regulations.

Compatible Use	A wildlife-dependent recreational use or any other use of a refuge that, in the sound professional judgment of the refuge manager, will not materially interfere with, or detract from, the fulfillment of the mission or the purposes of the refuge. A compatibility determination supports the selection of compatible uses and identifies stipulations or limits necessary to ensure compatibility.
Comprehensive Conservation Plan	A document that describes the desired conditions of the refuge; provides long-range guidance and management direction for the refuge manager to accomplish the purposes, goals, and objectives of the refuge; and contributes to the mission of the National Wildlife Refuge System and meets relevant mandates.
Conservation Easement	A legal document that provides specific land-use rights to a secondary party. A perpetual conservation easement usually grants conservation and management rights to a party in perpetuity.
Cooperative Agreement	A simple habitat protection action in which no property rights are acquired. An agreement is usually long-term and either party can modify it. Lands under a cooperative agreement do not necessarily become part of the National Wildlife Refuge System.
Corridor	A route that allows movement of individuals from one region or place to another.
Cover Type	The present vegetation of an area.
Cultural Resources	The remains of sites, structures, or objects used by people of the past.
Cypress and Tupelo Swamp	A vegetation type found in low-lying areas, swales, and open ponds that holds water several months, if not all of the year. Large hollow trees are used as bear den sites.
Deciduous	Pertaining to perennial plants that are leafless for some time during the year.
Ecological Succession	The orderly progression of an area through time in the absence of disturbance from one vegetative community to another.
Ecosystem	A dynamic and interrelating complex of plant and animal communities and their associated nonliving environment.
Ecosystem Management	Management of natural resources using systemwide concepts to ensure that all plants and animals in ecosystems are maintained at viable levels in their native habitats, and that basic ecosystem processes are perpetuated indefinitely.

Environmental Health	The composition, structure, and functioning of soil, water, air, and other abiotic features comparable with historic conditions, including the natural abiotic processes that shape the environment.
Even-aged Forests	Forests that are composed of trees with a time span of less than 20 years between oldest and youngest individuals.
Endangered Species	A plant or animal species listed under the Endangered Species Act that is in danger of extinction throughout all or a significant portion of its range.
Endemic Species	Plants and animals that occur naturally in a certain region and whose distribution is relatively limited to a particular locality.
Environmental Assessment	A concise document, prepared in compliance with the National Environmental Policy Act, that briefly discusses the purpose and need for an action, alternatives to such action, and provides sufficient evidence and analysis of impacts to determine whether to prepare an environmental impact statement or a finding of no significant impact.
Fauna	All the vertebrate or invertebrate animals of an area.
Federal Trust Species	All species in which the Federal Government has primary jurisdiction, including federally listed threatened or endangered species, migratory birds, anadromous fish, and certain marine mammals.
Fee-title	The acquisition of most or all of the rights to a tract of land. There is a total transfer of property rights with the formal conveyance of a title. While a fee title acquisition involves most rights to a property, the seller may reserve certain rights or sell them, including water rights, mineral rights, or use reservations (the ability to continue using the land for a specified time period, or the reminder of the seller's life).
Finding of No Significant Impact	A document prepared in compliance with the National Environmental Policy Act, supported by an environmental assessment, which briefly presents why a federal action will have no significant effect on the human environment and for which the agency will not prepare an environmental impact statement.
Floodplain Woods	Bottomland hardwood forests. Consists of hardwoods (old-growth and midsuccession-aged timber) and cypress/tupelo stands found on low ridges that drain slowly and are subject to flooding. Species include overcup, willow, and water oaks, sweetgum, and green ash. Old-growth trees typically exceed 120 years of age. Red oaks were removed in the 1940s. Midsuccession-logged timber that may need restoration to improve wildlife habitat. Missing several key oak species.

Fragmentation	The process of reducing the size and connectivity of habitat patches. The disruption of extensive habitats into isolated and small patches.
Goal	Descriptive, open-ended, and often broad statements of desired future conditions that convey a purpose but do not define measurable units.
Geographic Information System	A computer system capable of storing and manipulating spatial data.
Ground Story (flora)	Vascular plants less than one meter in height, excluding tree seedlings.
Herbaceous Wetland	An area of land that is annually or seasonally inundated with vegetation consisting primarily of grasses, sedges, rushes, and cattail.
Historic Conditions	The composition, structure, and functioning of ecosystems resulting from natural processes that, based on sound professional judgment, were present prior to substantial human-related changes to the landscape.
Habitat	The place where an organism lives. The existing environmental conditions required by an organism for survival and reproduction.
Indicator Species	A species of plant or animal that is assumed to be sensitive to habitat changes and represents the needs of a larger group of species.
Inholding	Privately owned land inside the boundary of a national wildlife refuge.
Issue	Any unsettled matter that requires a management decision.
Migratory	The seasonal movement from one area to another and back.
Monitoring	The process of collecting information to track changes of selected parameters over time.
National Environmental Policy Act	A federal law that requires all agencies, including the Service, to examine the environmental impacts of their actions, incorporate environmental information, and use public participation in the planning and implementation of all actions. Federal agencies must integrate this Act with other planning requirements, and prepare appropriate policy documents to facilitate better environmental decision-making.
National Wildlife Refuge	A designated area of land, water, or an interest in land or water within the National Wildlife Refuge System.

National Wildlife Refuge System	Various categories of areas administered by the Secretary of the Interior for the conservation of fish and wildlife, including species threatened with extinction; and all lands, waters, and interests therein administered by the Secretary as wildlife refuges, wildlife ranges, game ranges, wildlife management areas, or waterfowl production areas.
Native Species	Species that normally live and thrive in a particular ecosystem.
Neotropical Migratory Bird	A bird species that breeds north of the United States/Mexican border and winters primarily south of that border.
Objective	A concise, quantitative (where possible) target statement of what a plan will achieve. The planners derive objectives from goals and they provide the basis for determining management strategies. Objectives should be attainable and time-specific.
Planning Area	A planning area may include lands outside existing planning unit boundaries that are being studied for inclusion in the unit and/or partnership planning efforts. It may also include watersheds or ecosystems that affect the planning area.
Planning Team	A planning team prepares the comprehensive conservation plan. Planning teams are interdisciplinary in membership and function. A team generally consists of a planning team leader; refuge manager and staff biologists; staff specialists or other representatives of Service programs, ecosystems or regional offices; and state-partnering wildlife agencies as appropriate.
Preferred Alternative	The alternative determined by the decision-maker that best achieves the refuge's purpose, vision, and goals; contributes to the Refuge System mission; addresses the significant issues; and is consistent with principles of sound fish and wildlife management.
Purpose(s) of the Refuge	The purpose(s) specified in or derived from the law, proclamation, executive order, agreement, public land order, donation document, or administrative memorandum establishing, authorizing, or expanding a refuge, refuge unit, or subunit.
Refuge Operating Needs System	A national database that contains the unfunded operational needs of each refuge. Projects included are those required to implement approved plans and meet goals, objectives, and legal mandates.
Seral Forest	A forest in the mature stage of development, usually dominated by large, old trees.
Sink	A habitat in which local mortality exceeds local reproductive success for a given species.

Sink Population	A population in a low-quality habitat in which the birth rate is generally less than the death rate and the population density is maintained by immigrants from source populations.
Source	A habitat in which local reproductive success exceeds local mortality for a given species.
Source Population	A population in a high-quality habitat in which birth rate greatly exceeds death rate and the excess individuals leave as migrants.
Step-down Management Plans	Step-down management plans provide the details necessary to implement management strategies and projects identified in the comprehensive conservation plan.
Strategy	A specific action, tool, or technique or combination of actions, tools, and techniques used to meet unit objectives.
Threatened Species	Species listed under the Endangered Species Act that are likely to become endangered within the foreseeable future throughout all or a significant portion of their range.
Trust Species	Species for which the Fish and Wildlife Service has primary responsibility, including most federally listed threatened and endangered species, anadromous fish once they enter the inland coastal waterways, and migratory birds.
Understory	Any vegetation with canopy below or closer to the ground than canopies of other plants.
Wildlife Corridor	A landscape feature that facilitates the biologically effective transport of animals between larger patches of habitat dedicated to conservation functions. Such corridors may facilitate several kinds of traffic, including frequent foraging movement, seasonal migration, or the once-in-a-lifetime dispersal of juvenile animals. These are transition habitats and need not contain all the habitat elements required by migrants for long-term survival or reproduction.
Wildlife-dependent Recreation	A use of a refuge involving hunting, fishing, wildlife observation, wildlife photography, and environmental education and interpretation. The National Wildlife Refuge System Improvement Act of 1997 specifies that these are the six priority general public uses of the system

Appendix II. References and Literature Cited

Bellrose, F.C. 1976. *Ducks, Geese, and Swans of North America.* Stackhole Books, Harrisburg, Pennsylvania. 544 pp.

Bookhout, T.A. 1994. *Research and Management Techniques for Wildlife and Habitats.* Fifth edition. The Wildlife Society, Bethesda, Maryland. 740 pp.

Boss, S.K. and C.W. Hoffman. 2000a. Relationship of stratigraphy, geomorphology, and sediment texture on coastal erosion, Pea Island, North Carolina. *2000 Geological Society of America, Southeastern Section Meeting, Abstracts with Programs* 32(2): A-7.

Boss, S.K. and C.W. Hoffman. 2000b. Sand Resources of the North Carolina Outer Banks, 4th Interim Report: Assessment of Pea Island Study Area. Draft Report submitted to the Outer Banks Task Force, North Carolina Department of Transportation, February 8, 2000.

Carroll, A. 1999. *Analysis of the Shell Mat of the Northern Outer Banks in Relation to the Underlying Geologic Framework and Relative Strength of the Alongshore Current.* Senior Thesis. Duke University, Division of Earth and Ocean Sciences. 20 pp. + figures.

Cowardin, Lewis M., Virginia Carter, Francis C, Golet and Edward T. LaRoe. 1979. *Classification of Wetlands and Deepwater Habitats of the United States.* Washington, DC: U.S. Fish and Wildlife Service, Office of Biological Services FWS/OBS-79/31. 131 pp.

Dahl, T.E. 2000. *Status and Trends of Wetlands in the Conterminous United States.* U.S. Department of the Interior, Fish and Wildlife Service, Washington, DC. 82 pp.

Eldridge, J. 1992. Management of habitat for breeding and migrating shorebirds in the Midwest. In M.K. Laubhan and D. Hamilton, eds., *Waterfowl Management Handbook.* U.S. Fish and Wildlife Service, Fort Collins, Colorado.

Eubanks, Ted, Paul Kerlinger and R.H. Payne. 1993. High Island, Texas: A case study in avitourism. *Birding* 25(6):415-420.

Eubanks, Ted, and John Stoll. 1999. *Avitourism in Texas: Two Studies of Birders in Texas and Their Potential Support for the Proposed World Birding Center.* Texas Parks and Wildlife, Contract No. 44467.

Fredrickson, L.H. and M.E. Heitmeyer. 1988. Waterfowl use of forested wetlands of the southern United States: an overview. Pages 307-323 in M.W. Weller, ed., *Waterfowl in Winter.* University of Minnesota Press, Minneapolis, Minnesota.

Fredrickson, L.H. and F. A. Reid. 1988. Nutritional value of waterfowl foods. In M.K. Laubhan and D. Hamilton, eds., *Waterfowl Management Handbook.* U.S. Fish and Wildlife Service, Fort Collins, Colorado.

Fredrickson, L.H. 1991. Strategies for water level manipulation in moist soil systems. In M.K. Laubhan and D. Hamilton, eds., *Waterfowl Management Handbook.* U.S. Fish and Wildlife Service, Fort Collins, Colorado.

Frost, C. 1995. Presettlement fire regimes in southeastern marshes, peatlands, and swamps. Pages 39-60 in Susan I. Cerulean and R. Todd Engstrom, eds., *Fire in Wetlands: A Management Perspective.* Proceedings of the Tall Timbers Fire Ecology Conference, No. 19. Tall Timbers Research Station, Tallahassee, Florida.

Frost, C. 1998. Presettlement fire frequency regimes in the United States: a first approximation. Pages 70-81 in Teresa L. Pruden and Leonard A. Brennan, eds., *Fire in Ecosystem Management: Shifting the Paradigm from Suppression to Prescription.* Proceedings of the Tall Timbers Fire Ecology Conference, No. 20. Tall Timbers Research Station, Tallahassee, Florida.

Haag, W.G. 1958. *The Archeology of Coastal North Carolina.* Louisiana State University, Coastal Study Series 2.

Hamel, P.B. 1992. *The Land Manager's Guide to the Birds of the South.* The Nature Conservancy and U.S. Department of Agriculture, Forest Service. Atlanta, Georgia.

Hefner, J.H. and J.D. Brown. 1984. Wetland trends in the southeastern United States. *Wetlands* 4:1-11.

Hunter, W.C., D.N. Pashley and R.E.F. Escano. 1992. Neotropical migratory landbirds species and their habitats of special concern within the Southeast region. Pages 159-169 in D.M. Finch and P.W. Stangel, eds., *Status and Management of Neotropical Migratory Birds.* U.S. Forest Service, General Technical Report RM-229, Fort Collins, Colorado.

Hunter, W.C., L.H. Peoples and J.A. Collazo. 2001. *South Atlantic Coastal Plain Partners in Flight Bird Conservation Plan.* Partners in Flight, www.partnersinflight.org.

Hunter, W.C. 2004. Southeastern Coastal Plains – Caribbean Regional Shorebird Plan, U.S. Shorebird Conservation Plan.

Inman, D.L., and R. Dolan. 1989. The Outer Banks of North Carolina: budget of sediment and inlet dynamics along a migrating barrier system. *Journal of Coastal Research* 5(2): 193-237.

Kerlinger, P. 1994. *The Economic Impact of Birding Ecotourism on Communities Surrounding Eight National Wildlife Refuges.* Washington, DC: National Fish and Wildlife Association.

Kerlinger, P. 1999. Birding Tourism and Dauphin Island.

Mathis, M.A. and J.J. Crow, eds. 1983. *The Prehistory of North Carolina: An Archeological Symposium.* Raleigh, North Carolina: North Carolina Division of Archives and History.

Mitsch, W.J. and J.G. Gosselink. 1993. *Wetlands.* Second edition. Van Nostrand Reinhold, New York, New York. 722 pp.

National Audubon Society. 1998. Campaign on HR 3267. National Audubon Society, New York, New York.

New Jersey Department of Environmental Protection. 2000. *Wildlife-associated Recreation on the New Jersey Delaware Bayshore.* New Jersey Division of Fish and Wildlife, Trenton, New Jersey.

North Carolina Employment Security Commission. 1999. Largest Employers by County. www.ncesc.com.

North Carolina Employment Security Commission. 2002. Unemployment Rates by County. www.ncesc.com.

North Carolina Division of Parks and Recreation. 2001. *North Carolina Coastal Plain Paddle Trails Guide.* North Carolina Division of Parks and Recreation, Seven Springs, North Carolina.

Outer Banks Chamber of Commerce. 2003. *History of Dare County.* 5 pp. Outer Banks Chamber of Commerce, Kill Devil Hills, North Carolina.

Perry, M.C., P.C. Osenton, G.A. Gough, J.S. Hatfield and E.J. Lohnes. 1999. *Moist Soil Management of Wetland Impoundments for Plants and Invertebrates.* Washington, DC: U.S. Geological Survey, Biological Research Division.

Pierce, J.W. and D.J. Colquhoun. 1970. Holocene evolution of a portion of the North Carolina coast. *Geological Society of America Bulletin* 81: 3697-3714.

Pilkey, O.H., W.J. Neal, S.R. Riggs, C.A. Webb, D.M. Bush, D.F. Pilkey, J. Bullock and B.A. Cowan. 1998. *The North Carolina Shore and its Barrier Islands: Restless Ribbons of Sand.* Durham, North Carolina: Duke University Press. 318 p.

Reinecke, K.J. and C.K. Baxter. 1996. Waterfowl habitat management in the Mississippi Alluvial Valley. Pages 159–167 in J.T. Ratti, ed., *Seventh International Waterfowl Symposium.* Ducks Unlimited, Memphis, Tennessee.

Riggs, S.R., W.J. Cleary and S.W. Snyder. 1995. Influence of inherited geologic framework on barrier shoreface morphology and dynamics. *Marine Geology* 126: 213-234.

Schafale, M.P. and A.S. Weakely. 1990. *Classification of the Natural Communities of North Carolina: Third Approximation.* North Carolina Natural Heritage Program. Raleigh, North Carolina. 325 pp.

Schmidt, P.R. 1993. Memorandum - Information request regarding impacts of hunting on national wildlife refuges. U.S. Department of the Interior, Fish and Wildlife Service, Office of Migratory Bird Management, Washington, DC. 7 pp.

Sharpe, Bill. 1954. *A New Geography of North Carolina.* Volume 1, 533 pp., illustrated. Raleigh, North Carolina: Sharpe Publishing Company.

Stick, D. 1958. *The Outer Banks of North Carolina: 1584-1958.* Chapel Hill, North Carolina: The University of North Carolina Press. 352 pp.

Thompson, T.A. and W.M. Gardner. 1979. A Cultural Resources and Impact Area Assessment of the Pea Island National Wildlife Refuge, Dare County, North Carolina.

U. S. Department of Agriculture. 1997. *Census of Agriculture, North Carolina, 1997.* Washington, DC: U.S. Department of Agriculture.

U. S. Department of Agriculture, Forest Service. 1991. *Forest Statistics for North Carolina Counties - 1991.* Washington, DC: U.S. Government Printing Office.

U. S. Department of Agriculture, Soil Conservation Service. 1979. *Soil Survey of Dare County, North Carolina.* USDA Soil Conservation Service, Washington, DC.

U. S. Department of Agriculture, Soil Conservation Service. 1992. *Soil Survey of Dare County, North Carolina.* USDA Soil Conservation Service, Washington, DC.

U.S. Department of Agriculture, Soil Conservation Service. 1985. *Hydric Soils of the State of North Carolina, 1985.* U.S. Department of Agriculture, Soil Conservation Service in cooperation with the National Technical Committee for Hydric Soils. Washington, DC. Unpaginated.

U. S. Department of Commerce, Bureau of the Census. 2000a. U.S.A. Counties 2000, General Profile: Dare County, North Carolina. Washington, DC: U.S. Government Printing Office.

U. S. Department of Commerce, Bureau of the Census. 2000b. County Business Patterns, Dare County, North Carolina. Washington, DC: U.S. Government Printing Office.

U. S. Department of Commerce, Bureau of the Census. 2000c. Small Area Income and Poverty Estimates Program. 2000: Model-based Income and Poverty Estimates for Dare County, North Carolina. Washington, DC: U.S. Government Printing Office.

U.S. Department of Interior. 1981. *Report on Fisheries of the South Atlantic States.* U. S. Fish and Wildlife Service, Volume 11, 285 pp.

U.S. Environmental Protection Agency. 1997. Nature-Based Tourism.

U.S. Fish and Wildlife Service. n.d. *Birds of the Outer Banks.* Leaflet published in cooperation with the Eastern National & Coastal Wildlife Refuge Society, Manteo, North Carolina.

U.S. Fish and Wildlife Service. 1981. *Significant Wildlife Resource Areas of North Carolina.* U.S. Fish and Wildlife Service, Asheville Area Office, Asheville, North Carolina. 139 pp.

U.S. Fish and Wildlife Service. 1983. *Distribution of Waterfowl Secies Harvested in States and Counties during 1971–1980 Hunting Seasons.* U.S. Fish and Wildlife Service, Special Scientific Report No. 254, Washington, DC. 114 pp.

U. S. Fish and Wildlife Service. 1996. *National Survey of Fishing, Hunting and Wildlife-associated Recreation.* Washington, DC.

U.S. Fish and Wildlife Service. 2001. *National Survey of Fishing, Hunting, and Wildlife-associated Recreation - North Carolina.* Washington, DC.

Vogelsang, Hans. 2001. *Assessing the Economic Impact of Ecotourism Developments on the Albemarle/Pamlico Region.* Greenville, North Carolina: East Carolina University, Department of Recreation and Leisure Studies.

Appendix III. Relevant Legal Mandates

NATIONAL WILDLIFE REFUGE SYSTEM AUTHORITIES

The mission of the Fish and Wildlife Service is to conserve, protect, and enhance the Nation's fish and wildlife and their habitats for the continuing benefit of the American people. The Service is the primary federal agency responsible for migratory birds, endangered plants and animals, certain marine mammals, and anadromous fish. The Service shares this responsibility to conserve our Nation's fish and wildlife resources with other federal agencies and state and tribal governments.

As part of this responsibility, the Service manages the National Wildlife Refuge System. This system is the only nationwide system of federal land managed and protected for wildlife and their habitats. The mission of the National Wildlife Refuge System is to administer a national network of lands and waters for the conservation, management, and where appropriate, restoration of the fish, wildlife, and plant resources and their habitats within the United States for the benefit of present and future generations of Americans.

The staff manages Pea Island National Wildlife Refuge as part of this system in accordance with the National Wildlife Refuge System Administration Act of 1966, as amended by the National Wildlife Refuge System Improvement Act of 1997, the Refuge Recreation Act of 1962, Executive Order 12996 (Management and General Public Use of the National Wildlife Refuge System), and other relevant legislation, Executive Orders, regulations, and policies.

KEY LEGISLATION AND POLICIES FOR PLAN IMPLEMENTATION

The Pea Island National Wildlife Refuge Comprehensive Conservation Plan describes and illustrates management area projects with standards and guidelines for future decision-making and the Service may adjust it through monitoring and evaluation, as well as amendment and revision. The plan approval establishes conservation and land protection goals, objectives, and specific strategies for the refuge and its expansion. Compatible recreation uses specific to the refuge have been identified and approved by the refuge manager. This plan provides for systematic stepping down from the overall direction as outlined when making project- or activity-level decisions. This level involves site-specific analysis (e.g., Forest Habitat Management Plan) to meet National Environmental Policy Act requirements for decision-making.

Antiquities Act (1906): Authorizes the scientific investigation of antiquities on federal land and provides penalties for unauthorized removal of objects taken or collected without a permit.

Migratory Bird Treaty Act (1918): Designates the protection of migratory birds as a federal responsibility. This Act enables the setting of seasons, and other regulations including the closing of areas, federal or non-federal, to the hunting of migratory birds.

Migratory Bird Conservation Act (1929): Establishes procedures for acquisition by purchase, rental, or gift of areas approved by the Migratory Bird Conservation Commission.

Migratory Bird Hunting and Conservation Stamp Act (1934): Authorized the opening of part of a refuge to waterfowl hunting.

Fish and Wildlife Act (1956): Established a comprehensive national fish and wildlife policy and broadened the authority for acquisition and development of refuges.

Fish and Wildlife Coordination Act (1958): Allows the Fish and Wildlife Service to enter into agreements with private landowners for wildlife management purposes.

Refuge Recreation Act (1962): Allows the use of refuges for recreation when such uses are compatible with the refuge's primary purposes and when sufficient funds are available to manage the uses.

Land and Water Conservation Fund Act (1965): Uses the receipts from the sale of surplus federal land, outer continental shelf oil and gas sales, and other sources for land acquisition under several authorities.

National Wildlife Refuge System Administration Act of 1966 as amended by the National Wildlife Refuge System Improvement Act of 1997, 16 U.S.C. 668dd-668ee. (Refuge Administration Act): Defines the National Wildlife Refuge System and authorizes the Secretary of the Interior to permit any use of a refuge provided such use is compatible with the major purposes for which the Service established the refuge. The Refuge Improvement Act clearly defines a unifying mission for the Refuge System; establishes the legitimacy and appropriateness of the six priority public uses (hunting, fishing, wildlife observation, wildlife photography and environmental education and interpretation); establishes a formal process for determining compatibility; established the responsibilities of the Secretary of the Interior for managing and protecting the System; and requires a Comprehensive Conservation Plan for each refuge by the year 2012. This Act amended portions of the Refuge Recreation Act and National Wildlife Refuge System Administration Act of 1966.

Architectural Barriers Act (1968): Requires federally owned, leased, or funded buildings and facilities to be accessible to persons with disabilities.

National Environmental Policy Act (1969): Requires the disclosure of the environmental impacts of any major federal action significantly affecting the quality of the human environment.

Endangered Species Act (1973): Requires all federal agencies to carry out programs for the conservation of threatened and endangered species.

Rehabilitation Act (1973): Requires that the federal government make any facility funded by the federal government programmatically and physically accessible, ensuring that anyone can participate in any program.

Clean Water Act (1977): Requires consultation with the U.S. Army Corps of Engineers for major wetland modifications.

Executive Order 11988 (1977): Each federal agency shall provide leadership and take action to reduce the risk of flood loss and minimize the impact of floods on human safety, and preserve the natural and beneficial values served by the flood plain.

Emergency Wetlands Resources Act (1986): The purpose of the Act is "To promote the conservation of migratory waterfowl and to offset or prevent the serious loss of wetlands by the acquisition of wetlands and other essential habitat, and for other purposes."

Federal Noxious Weed Act (1990): Requires the use of integrated management systems to control or contain undesirable plant species; and an interdisciplinary approach with the cooperation of other federal and state agencies.

Americans with Disabilities Act (1992): Prohibits discrimination in public accommodations and services.

Executive Order 12996 Management and General Public Use of the National Wildlife Refuge System (1996): Defines the mission, purpose, and priority public uses of the National Wildlife Refuge System. It also presents four principles to guide management of the system.

Executive Order 13007 Indian Sacred Sites (1996): Directs federal land management agencies to accommodate access to and ceremonial use of Indian sacred sites by Indian religious practitioners, avoid adversely affecting the physical integrity of such sacred sites, and where appropriate, maintain the confidentiality of sacred sites.

Emergency Wetland Resources Act of 1986: This Act authorized the purchase of wetlands from Land and Water Conservation Fund moneys, removing a prior prohibition on such acquisitions. The Act also requires the Secretary of the Interior to establish a National Wetlands Priority Conservation Plan, requires the states to include wetlands in their comprehensive outdoor recreation plans, and transfers to the Migratory Bird Conservation Fund an amount equal to import duties on arms and ammunition.

Endangered Species Act of 1973 (16 U.S.C. 1531-1544, 87 Stat. 884), as amended: Public Law 93-205, approved December 28, 1973, repealed the Endangered Species Conservation Act of December 5, 1969 (P.L. 91-135, 83 Stat. 275). The 1969 act amended the Endangered Species Preservation Act of October 15, 1966 (P.L. 89-669, 80 Stat. 926). The 1973 Endangered Species Act provided for the conservation of ecosystems upon which threatened and endangered species of fish, wildlife, and plants depend, both through federal action and by encouraging the establishment of state programs. The Act authorizes the determination and listing of species as threatened and endangered; prohibits unauthorized taking, possession, sale, and transport of endangered species; provides authority to acquire land for the conservation of listed species, using land and water conservation funds; authorizes establishment of cooperative agreements and grants-in-aid to states that establish and maintain active and adequate programs for threatened and endangered wildlife and plants; authorizes the assessment of civil and criminal penalties for violating the Act or regulations; and authorizes the payment of rewards to anyone furnishing information leading to arrest and conviction of anyone violating the Act and any regulation issued thereunder.

Environmental Education Act of 1990(20 USC 5501-5510; 104 Stat. 3325): Public Law 101-619, signed November 16,1990, established the Office of Environmental Education within the Environmental Protection Agency to develop and administer a federal environmental education program. Responsibilities of the Office include developing and supporting programs to improve understanding of the natural and developed environment, and the relationships between humans and their environment; supporting the dissemination of educational materials; developing and supporting training programs and environmental education seminars; managing a federal grant program; and administering an environmental internship and fellowship program. The Act requires the Office to develop and support environmental programs in consultation with other federal natural resource management agencies, including the Fish and Wildlife Service.

Executive Order 11988, Floodplain Management: The purpose of this Executive Order, signed May 24, 1977, is to prevent federal agencies from contributing to the "adverse impacts associated with occupancy and modification of floodplains" and the "direct or indirect support of flood plain development." In the course of fulfilling their respective authorities, federal agencies "shall take action to reduce the risk of flood loss, to minimize the impact of floods on human safety, health and welfare, and to restore and preserve the natural and beneficial values served by flood plains."

Fish and Wildlife Improvement Act of 1978: Congress passed this act to improve the administration of fish and wildlife programs and amend several earlier laws, including the Refuge Recreation Act, the National Wildlife Refuge System Administration Act, and the Fish and Wildlife Act of 1956. It authorizes the Secretary of the Interior to accept gifts and bequests of real and personal property on behalf of the United States. It also authorizes the use of volunteers on Service projects and appropriations to carry out volunteer programs.

Antiquities Act (16 USC 431 - 433)--The Act of June 8, 1906, (34 Stat. 225): This act authorizes the President of the United States to designate as National Monuments objects or areas of historic or scientific interests on lands owned or controlled by the United States. The Act required that applicants obtain a permit for examination of ruins, excavation of archaeological sites and the gathering of objects of antiquity on lands under the jurisdiction of the Secretaries of Interior, Agriculture, and Army, and provided penalties for violations.

Archaeological Resources Protection Act (16 U.S.C. 470aa - 47011)--Public Law 96-95, approved October 31, 1979, (93 Stat. 721): This act largely supplanted the resource protection provisions of the Antiquities Act for archaeological items. It established detailed requirements for issuance of permits for any excavation for or removal of archaeological resources from Federal and Indian lands. It also established civil and criminal penalties for the unauthorized excavation, removal, or damage of any such resources; for any trafficking in such resources removed from Federal and Indian lands in violation of any provision of federal law; and for interstate and foreign commerce in such resources acquired, transported or received in violation of any state or local law.

Public Law 100-588, approved November 3, 1988, (102 Stat. 2983) lowered the threshold value of artifacts triggering the felony provisions of the Act from $5,000 to $500, made attempting to commit an action prohibited by the Act a violation, and required the land managing agencies to establish public awareness programs regarding the value of archaeological resources to the nation.

Archaeological and Historic Preservation Act (16 U.S.C. 469-469c)--Public Law 86-523, approved June 27, 1960, (74 Stat. 220), and amended by Public Law 93-291, approved May 24, 1974, (88 Stat. 174): This act directed federal agencies to notify the Secretary of the Interior whenever a federal, federally assisted, or licensed or permitted project may cause loss or destruction of significant scientific, prehistoric or archaeological data. The Act authorized use of appropriated, donated and/or transferred funds for the recovery, protection and preservation of such data.

Historic Sites, Buildings and Antiquities Act (16 U.S.C. 461-462, 464-467)--The Act of August 21,1935, (49 Stat. 666) popularly known as the Historic Sites Act, as amended by Public Law 89-249, approved October 9,1965, (79 Stat. 971): This act declared it a national policy to preserve historic sites and objects of national significance, including those located on refuges. It provided procedures for designation, acquisition, administration and protection of such sites. Among other things, National Historic and Natural Landmarks are designated under authority of this Act. As of January, 1989, thirty-one national wildlife refuges contained such sites.

National Historic Preservation Act of 1966 (16 U.S.C. 470-470b, 470c-470n)--Public Law 89-665, approved October 15, 1966, (80 Stat. 915) and repeatedly amended: This act provided for preservation of significant historical features (buildings, objects and sites) through a grant-in-aid program to the states. It established a National Register of Historic Places and a program of matching grants under the existing National Trust for Historic Preservation (16 U.S.C. 468-468d).

The Act established an Advisory Council on Historic Preservation, which became a permanent independent agency in Public Law 94-422, approved September 28,1976 (90 Stat. 1319). That Act also created the Historic Preservation Fund. Federal agencies are directed to take into account the effects of their actions on items or sites listed in, or eligible for listing in, the National Register of Historic Places. As of January 1989, 91 such sites on national wildlife refuges are listed in this Register.

Land and Water Conservation Fund Act of 1948: This act provides funding through receipts from the sale of surplus federal land, appropriations from oil and gas receipts from the outer continental shelf, and other sources of land acquisition under several authorities. Agencies may use appropriations from the fund for matching grants to states for outdoor recreation projects and for land acquisition by various federal agencies, including the Fish and Wildlife Service.

Migratory Bird Hunting and Conservation Stamp Act (16 U.S.C. 718-718j, 48 Stat. 452), as amended: The "Duck Stamp Act," of March 16, 1934, requires each waterfowl hunter, 16 years of age or older, to possess a valid federal hunting stamp. Receipts from the sale of the stamp are deposited in a special Treasury account known as the Migratory Bird Conservation Fund and are not subject to appropriations.

National and Community Service Act of 1960 (42 U.S.C. 12401:104 Stat. 3127), Public Law 101-610, signed November 16,1990: This act authorizes several programs to engage citizens of the United States in full- and/or part-time projects designed to combat illiteracy and poverty, provide job skills, enhance educational skills, and fulfill environmental needs. Several provisions are of particular interest to the Fish and Wildlife Service.

American Conservation and Youth Service Corps: A federal grant program established under Subtitle C of the law, the Corps offers an opportunity for young adults between the ages of 16-25, or in the case of summer programs, 15-21, to engage in approved human and natural resources projects which benefit the public or are carried out on Federal or Indian lands. To be eligible for assistance, natural resource programs must focus on improvement of wildlife habitat and recreational areas, fish culture, fishery assistance, erosion, wetlands protection, pollution control and similar projects. Agencies will pay a stipend of not more than 100 percent of the poverty level to participants. A Commission established to administer the Youth Service Corps will make grants to States, the Secretaries of Agriculture and Interior and the Director of ACTION to carry out these responsibilities.

National Environmental Policy Act of 1959 (P.L. 91-190,42 U.S.C. 4321-4347, January 1, 1970, 83 Stat. 852) as amended by Public Law 94-52, July 3, 1975, 89 Stat. 258, and Public Law 94-83, August 9,1975, 89 Stat. 424): Title I of the 1969 National Environmental Policy Act requires that all federal agencies prepare detailed environmental impact statements for "every recommendation or report on proposals for legislation and other major federal actions significantly affecting the quality of the human environment." The 1969 statute stipulated the factors to be considered in environmental impact statements, and required that federal agencies employ an interdisciplinary approach in related decision-making and develop means to ensure that unquantified environmental values are given appropriate consideration, along with economic and technical considerations. Title II of this statute requires annual reports on environmental quality from the President to the Congress, and established a Council on Environmental Quality in the Executive Office of the President with specific duties and functions.

National Wildlife Refuge System Improvement Act of 1997: Public Law 105-57, amended the National Wildlife Refuge System Act of 1966 (16 U.S.C. 668dd-ee), and provided guidance for management and public use of the Refuge System. The Act mandates that the Service consistently direct and manage the Refuge System as a national system of lands and waters devoted to wildlife conservation and management. The Act establishes priorities for recreational uses of the Refuge System. Six wildlife-dependent uses are specifically named in the Act: hunting, fishing, wildlife observation, wildlife photography, and environmental education and interpretation. The Service will promote these activities in the Refuge System, while all nonwildlife-dependent uses are subject to compatibility determinations. A compatible use is one that, in the sound professional judgment of the Refuge Manger, will not materially interfere with, or detract from, fulfillment of the National Wildlife Refuge System mission or refuge purpose(s). As stated in the Act, "The mission of the system is to administer a national network of lands and waters for the conservation, management, and where appropriate, restoration of the fish, wildlife, and plant resources and their habitats within the United States for the benefit of present and future generations of Americans." The Act also requires the development of a comprehensive conservation plan for each refuge and that management be consistent with the plan. When writing a plan for expanded or new refuges, and when making management decisions, the Act requires effective coordination with other federal agencies, state fish and wildlife or conservation agencies, and refuge neighbors. A refuge must also provide opportunities for public involvement when making a compatibility determination.

North American Wetlands Conservation Act (103 Stat. 1968; 16 U.S.C. 4401~4412) Public Law 101-233, enacted December 13, 1989: This act provides funding and administrative direction for implementation of the North American Waterfowl Management Plan and the Tripartite Agreement on Wetlands between Canada, the United States and Mexico. The Act converts the Pittman-Robertson account into a trust fund, with the interest available without appropriation through the year 2006, to carry out the programs authorized by the Act, along with an authorization for annual appropriation of $15 million plus an amount equal to the fines and forfeitures collected under the Migratory Bird Treaty Act. The Service may spend available funds, upon approval of the Migratory Bird Conservation Commission, for payment of not to exceed 50 percent of the United States' share of the cost of wetlands conservation projects in Canada, Mexico, or the United States (or 100 percent of the cost of projects on federal lands). At least 50 percent and no more than 70 percent of the funds received are to go to Canada and Mexico each year.

Refuge Recreation Act of 1952: This Act authorizes the Secretary of the Interior to administer refuges, hatcheries, and other conservation areas for recreational use, when such uses do not interfere with the area's primary purposes. It authorizes construction and maintenance of recreational facilities and the acquisition of land for incidental fish and wildlife oriented recreational development or protection of natural resources. It also authorizes the charging of fees for public uses.

Refuge Revenue Sharing Act (16 U.S.C. 715s): Section 401 of the Act of June 15, 1935, (49 Stat. 383) provided for payments to counties in lieu of taxes, using revenues derived from the sale of products from refuges. Public Law 88-523, approved August 30,1964, (78 Stat. 701) made major revisions by requiring that all revenues received from refuge products, such as animals, timber and minerals, or from leases or other privileges, be deposited in a special Treasury account and net receipts distributed to counties for public schools and roads. Public Law 93-509, approved December 3, 1974, (88 Stat. 1603) required that moneys remaining in the fund after payments be transferred to the Migratory Bird Conservation Fund for land acquisition under provisions of the Migratory Bird Conservation Act. Public Law 95-469, approved October 17, 1978, (92 Stat. 1319) expanded the revenue-sharing system to include national fish hatcheries and Service research stations. It also included in the Refuge Revenue Sharing Fund receipts from the sale of salmonid carcasses. Payments to counties were established as follows: on acquired land, the greatest amount calculated on the basis of 75 cents per acre, three-fourths of one percent of the appraised value, or 25 percent of the net receipts produced from the land; and on land withdrawn from the public domain, 25 percent of net receipts and basic payments under Public Law 94-565 (31 U.S.C. 1601-1607, 90 Stat. 2662). This amendment also authorized appropriations to make up any difference between the amount in the fund and the amount scheduled for payment in any year. Congress removed the stipulation that payments be used for schools and roads, but required counties to pass payments along to other units of local government within the county that suffer losses in revenues due to the establishment of Service areas.

Wilderness Act of 1964: Public Law 88-577, approved September 3,1964, directed the Secretary of the Interior, within 10 years, to review every roadless area of 5,000 or more acres and every roadless island (regardless of size) within the National Wildlife Refuge System and the National Park System for inclusion in the National Wilderness Preservation System.

Coastal Zone Management Act of 1972 (CZMA): The act was enacted on October 27, 1972 to encourage coastal States, Great Lake States, and United States Territories and Commonwealths to develop comprehensive programs for managing and balancing competing uses of coastal resources. Federal Consistency is the CZMA requirement that Federal agency activities with reasonably predictable effects on any land or water use or natural resource of the coastal zone must be consistent with the enforceable policies of a coastal State's federally approved Coastal Management Program (CMP). Federal Consistency reviews are the responsibility of the lead State agency that implements or coordinates the State's federally approved CMP. At the federal level, the National Oceanic and Atmospheric Administration's (NOAA's) National Ocean Service administers the CZMA and oversees application of Federal Consistency; provides management and legal assistance to coastal States, Federal agencies, Tribes and others; and mediates CZMA related disputes.

Coastal Area Management Act of 1974: In 1972, Congress passed the Coastal Zone Management Act, legislation intended to encourage states to keep coastal areas healthy by establishing programs to manage, protect, and promote our country's fragile coastal resources. In 1974, the North Carolina General Assembly passed the Coastal Area Management Act of 1974 (CAMA). CAMA established the Coastal Resources Commission, required local land use planning in 20 coastal counties, and provided for a permitting program to regulate development. The North Carolina Coastal Management Program was federally approved in 1978.

Appendix IV. Public Involvement

Part 1 – Summary of Public Scoping Meeting Comments

At initial planning meetings, the refuge and planning staff discussed strategies for completing the plan, identified their issues and concerns, and compiled a mailing list of likely interested government agencies, non-governmental organizations, businesses, and individual citizens. The Service invited these agencies, organizations, businesses, and citizens to participate in four public scoping meetings on June 26 and 27, 2000, in Rodanthe and Manteo, North Carolina. The staff introduced them to the refuge and its planning process and asked them to identify their issues and concerns. The staff published announcements giving the location, date, and time for the public meeting in the Federal Register and legal notices in local newspapers. The staff also sent the announcements as press releases to local newspapers and as public service announcements to television and radio stations. The planning staff placed fifty posters announcing the meeting in local post offices, local government buildings, and stores.

The Service expanded the planning team's identified issues and concerns to include those generated by the agencies, organizations, businesses, and citizens from the local community. These issues and concerns formed the basis for the development and comparison of the objectives in the different alternatives described in this environmental assessment.

The alternatives were subjects of discussion at a second round of four public meetings on September 25 and 26, 2000, in Rodanthe and Manteo, North Carolina. The planning staff again published announcements giving the location, date, and time for the public meeting as legal notices in local newspapers. They also sent press releases to local newspapers and as public service announcements to television and radio stations. The staff placed seventy-five posters announcing the meeting in local post offices, local government buildings, and stores.

At the second round of public meeting, members of the public expressed concern that the three alternatives being considered did not represent a wide enough range of alternatives. The refuge staff developed Alternatives 4 and 5 in response to those concerns. Alternative 4 assumes that natural forces will dominate the landscape except impoundments north of the Visitor Center. Alternative 5 assumes that natural forces will dominate the landscape except impoundments throughout the refuge.

PEA ISLAND NATIONAL WILDLIFE REFUGE PLANNING SCOPING ISSUES WORKSHEET				
ACTIVITY	**WHAT WOULD YOU LIKE US TO DO?** (% of 12 Responses)			
	Keep the Same	**Eliminate**	**Increase**	**Decrease**
PUBLIC USE ACTIVITIES				
Wildlife Education (School Students)	25	0	67	8
Wildlife Education (School Teachers)	25	0	67	8
Wildlife Interpretation (Formal Programs)	42	0	50	8
Wildlife Interpretation (Printed Material)	67	8	25	0
Wildlife Interpretation (Facilities)	50	0	42	8
Wildlife Photography Opportunities	50	0	42	8
Wildlife Observation Opportunities	50	0	42	8
Fishing	50	25	25	0
Pedestrian Access to Pond Area	67	8	25	0
Pedestrian Access to Beach	68	16	16	0
Vehicle Parking Lots	50	8	42	0
Access to Sound for Boating, Canoeing	68	16	16	0
Planting, Seeding for Facility Aesthetics	84	0	0	16
HABITAT MANAGEMENT ACTIVITIES				
Prescribed Burning	84	0	0	16
Water Management in Ponds	84	0	8	8
Mechanical Vegetation Management	84	0	8	8
Chemical Vegetation Management	67	25	0	8
Dune/Beach Maintenance	49	17	17	17
Planting, Seeding, Clearing for Habitat	76	0	16	8
Candidate Wilderness (Sound-Islands)	51	8	33	8
LAW ENFORCEMENT ACTIVITIES				
Visitor Protection	84	0	8	8
Wildlife Protection	42	0	50	8
OPERATION AND MAINTENANCE ACTIVITIES				
Dike and Trail Maintenance	59	0	33	8
Facilities Maintenance (Signs, Buildings)	59	0	33	8
North Carolina Highway 12	33	8	43	16

PEA ISLAND NATIONAL WILDLIFE REFUGE PLANNING ALTERNATIVES WORKSHEET			
ACTIVITY	**WHAT WOULD YOU LIKE US TO DO?** (% of 8 Responses)		
	Alternative 1	**Alternative 2**	**Alternative 3**
WILDLIFE MANAGEMENT ACTIVITIES			
Waterfowl	17	0	83
Wading Birds	17	0	83
Shorebirds	17	0	83
All Water Birds	17	0	83
Land Birds	17	0	83
Sea Turtles	17	0	83
HABITAT MANAGEMENT ACTIVITIES			
Barrier Dunes	17	0	83
Estuarine Salt Flats and Ponds	17	0	83
Sound Island Shoals	17	0	83
Threatened and Endangered Plants	17	0	83
Impoundments	17	0	83
Salt Marsh	17	0	83
Maritime Scrub/Shrub	17	0	83
Grasslands and Sand Ridges	17	0	83
PUBLIC USE ACTIVITIES			
Environmental Education	17	0	83
Interpretation	17	0	83
Wildlife Observation	17	17	66
Wildlife Photography	17	17	66
RESOURCE PROTECTION ACTIVITIES			
Wilderness Areas	17	17	66
Permits	17	17	66
Law Enforcement	33	17	50
Corridors and Communication Towers	33	0	67
Cultural Resources	33	17	50

Issues raised at the June 2000 public forums

Area of Concern	Issue	Disposition
Wildlife - Shorebirds	Assess the impact of beach use on shorebirds.	Shorebird survey in plan. Assistance with studies to correlate beach use to shorebird use in plan.
Habitat - General	Use public input for management (local oral history of land cover).	Input solicited from agencies, organizations, and individuals as needed.
	Increase staff to survey and manage habitat.	In plan.
Habitat – Dunes	Allow dunes to drift over the highway.	Cooperation with NCDOT on maintenance in plan.
Habitat – Maritime Shrub	Maintain maritime shrubs for songbirds.	In plan.
Habitat – NC Highway 12 Maintenance	Use sand fence to trap sand.	Dunes are too high and steep to build any more.
Habitat – Prescribed Burning	Maintain prescribed burning program.	In plan.
Public Use - General	Increase staff to conduct public use.	In plan.
Public Use - Fishing	Provide access for surf fishing.	Pedestrian access maintained in plan, no vehicular access to beach provided.
	Eliminate commercial fishing.	Refuge only controls fishing on the refuge.
Public Use – Environmental Education	Develop education program on refuge plants.	In plan.
	Educate public on their role in the ecosystem.	In plan.
Public Use – Interpretation	Enlarge Visitor Center.	Not in plan.

Issues raised at the June 2000 public forums

Area of Concern	Issue	Disposition
Public Use – Wildlife Observation	Provide access to impoundments for birders (boardwalks, towers, trails).	Access to North Pond in plan, access to other ponds limited to reduce wildlife disturbance.
	Provide parking lots for better birder access.	Not in plan. No parking lots will be added for any users.
	Provide wider boardwalks, wide railings on observation platforms on which to place books.	Will be considered in step-down plan.
	Add observation platform on north side of New Field Pond.	Completed.
	Add observation platforms on east side of New Field Pond and South Pond.	Not in plan. Biologists want to minimize disturbance in two ponds.
Public Use – Wildlife Photography	Add photo blinds.	One completed.
Public Use – Outreach	Practice outreach on management issues.	In plan.
Public Use - Access	Provide beach access for vehicles.	Not in plan. Vehicular access on NC12 very close to beach.
	Provide beach access at night.	In plan. Night fishing allowed with a permit.
	Provide better beach access (walkovers, paths through dunes).	Not in plan. Walkovers require extensive maintenance. Seventy to eighty paths already exist.
	Maintain NC Highway 12.	Cooperation with NCDOT on maintenance in plan.
	Develop NC Highway 12 emergency contingency plans.	Cooperation with NCDOT on maintenance in plan.
	Move NC Highway 12 into the sound.	NCDOT decision.
	Limit the numbers of visitors.	Not in plan.
Public Use – Commercial Ecotourism	Allow one bidder to run canoe. kayak concession.	Multiple contractors in plan.

Issues raised at the June 2000 public forums

Area of Concern	Issue	Disposition
Public Use – Non Wildlife Dependent Use	Provide access for surfers (parking lot, legal road shoulder parking).	Not in plan. No parking lots will be added for any users. Road shoulder parking unsafe.
Public Use - Signs	Improve refuge entrance signs.	Sign maintenance in plan.
Resource Protection – Interagency Cooperation	Support Oregon Inlet jetties.	Jetties are not in plan. Council for Environmental Quality opposed the jetties.
Resource Protection – Law Enforcement	Post refuge rules.	Proactive law enforcement outreach in plan.
	Enforce refuge rules.	Proactive law enforcement in plan.
	Practice outreach about refuge rules with realtors, tourist bureau, etc.	Proactive law enforcement outreach in plan.
	Increase staff for law enforcement.	In plan.
	Limit the numbers of pedestrian beach access points.	Not practical.
Resource Protection – Pest Animals	Remove cats.	In plan.
Resource Protection – Pest Plants	Control exotic plants.	In plan.
Resource Protection – Water Quality	Monitor water quality and take measures to improve it.	Monitoring and land management to insure water quality are in plan.
	Link water quality data to state monitoring network.	
Administration – General	Increase staff for maintenance.	In plan.
Administration – NC12 Maintenance	Maintain highway.	NCDOT responsible for maintenance.
	Replace highway with movable gravel road.	Cooperation with NCDOT on maintenance in plan.
Administration – Real Property	Provide for utility right-of-way.	Cooperation with utility companies in plan.
	Improve facilities maintenance.	In plan.

Part 2 - Draft Plan Comments and Service Response

Summary of and the Service's response to public comments received on the Draft Comprehensive Conservation Plan and Environmental Assessment (CCP/EA) for Pea Island National Wildlife Refuge.

Introduction

In February 2006, the Draft Comprehensive Conservation Plan and Environmental Assessment (Draft CCP/EA) for Pea Island National Wildlife Refuge was completed. The Draft CCP/EA outlined five alternative scenarios for managing the refuge over the next 15 years. Alternative 2 was identified as the "Service's Proposed Action" in this document. It is the alternative recommended to best achieve the Refuge System mission, and refuge purposes and goals. The Draft CCP/EA was released for 30 days of public review, with the comment period ending on March 6, 2006.

Notice of the comment period and the open houses was sent to the Virginia Pilot, Raleigh News and Observer, Coastland Times, Daily Advance, and the Outer Banks Sentinel. Flyers were also posted in all area post offices and in many tackle shops, grocery stores, and public areas.

All written and oral comments received during the public comment period were evaluated. This section of the document is the Service's response to the substantive comments that were received. Based on the analysis in the Draft CCP/EA, and evaluation of public comments, the proposed action was modified to include the following changes:

1) During the internal review phase of planning, the North Carolina Wildlife Resources Commission requested that the refuge leave the option of hunting for resident game species open for evaluation. The refuge agreed with the idea and incorporated language to that effect in the document. However, not all of the prohibitive language was removed prior to the Draft CCP/EA. It was removed prior to the printing of the final.

2) Language was edited/added to clarify the treatment of the special use permit that allowed construction of the terminal groin.

3) Two additional legal mandates were added (as suggested by the North Carolina Division of Coastal Management).

Summary of Comments Received

A total of 17 individuals, agencies, and organizations provided comments by way of verbal comments at open houses or through submission of written or electronic documents.

Two public open house-type meetings were held to encourage public involvement:
    February 18, 2006, 10:00 am – 2:00 pm at the Pea Island Refuge Headquarters on Hatteras Island
    February 24, 2006, 5:00 – 9:00 pm at the Refuge Administrative Building in Manteo

Four people called, emailed, or wrote letters requesting paper copies of the plan. These copies were mailed within 24 hours of receiving the requests. One email was received from one of these individuals.

Several people at the open houses indicated they planned to send in written comments; however, none were received. Other written comments came in the form of letters and electronic mail.

One written comment came from the North Carolina Department of Administration and advised that the North Carolina State Clearinghouse had received and distributed the document. A second letter was received which consolidated comments from state agencies. Responses to these comments are addressed as a separate group at the end of this section.

In total, three written comments were received from individuals. Two were by email; one was a written letter. Many comments included in these letters were not relevant to the Pea Island Refuge Draft CCP/EA; therefore, those comments are not addressed in this response. Likewise, participants in the open houses discussed many topics with the staff; however, most discussions were not related to the Draft CCP/EA and are not included here.

In the following discussions, issues and comments during the public comment period and the planning team's responses to them are identified.

Administration and Permits

Comment: A refuge patron questioned whether the table on page 108 meant that under Alternatives 1 and 2, the refuge would not enforce the conditions of the permit for the groin.

Response: The entries into the table were confusing. The conditions of the permit will be enforced in all alternatives. Changes were made to the plan.

Comment: One refuge patron questioned the acquisition and disposal of property, as outlined by the plan.

Response: Property is acquired and disposed of following federally approved guidelines and procedures.

Comment: One refuge patrol questioned the need for outreach, cultural resources surveys, waterfowl production surveys, and bi-weekly wildlife monitoring.

Response: These activities are necessary to accomplish the defined goals and objectives of the refuge.

Wildlife

Comment: Two refuge patrons commented that the resource values, especially in relation to shorebirds, were understated in the plan.

Response: Comment was noted; plan was not changed.

Recreation/Public Use

Comment: A refuge patron commented that in one place Alternatives 2 and 3 allowed for hunting of resident game to be considered, but in the back of the plan, the compatibility determination said that hunting was incompatible.

Response: The plan was changed. The compatibility determination was changed to be incompatible only for migratory bird hunting.

Comment: One refuge patron stated that he opposed killing animals on a refuge. He stated that was a contradiction of the word "refuge" and asked that the refuge be closed to all hunting activity.

Response: Hunting is an approved wildlife-dependent recreational activity for national wildlife refuges. Refuges are places that provide for the needs of migratory birds and other wildlife, especially threatened and endangered species, in order to maintain healthy populations. Hunting is only allowed in cases where the populations are healthy and there is a harvestable surplus. Since Pea Island Refuge is closed to the hunting of migratory birds by Presidential Proclamation, only resident game and non-migratory bird hunting would be considered.

Comment: Several participants at the open houses commented that they supported whatever public closures were necessary to protect wildlife, as determined by the managers and biologists of the refuge.

Response: Comments were noted; plan was not changed.

Access

Comment: Several participants at the open houses requested additional information and decisions relating to the type of public access that would be allowed if the Bonner Bridge Replacement Project chose the "Long Bridge Alternative."

Response: The CCP briefly addresses the future North Carolina Department of Transportation Bonner Bridge replacement project in the Section A: Background/Introduction. Once a final decision has been made by the Department of Transportation as to the bridge replacement, the refuge will begin a planning process to include public access. Public input will be sought as a part of this planning process.

Habitat Management

Comment: A refuge patron sent a rather lengthy email questioning the safety of prescribed burning activities due to the release of harmful particulate matter into the air. He noted that it has been proven to cause a number of diseases and illnesses, especially in young children and older adults.

Response: The refuge does prescribed burning to reduce fuel levels to help prevent catastrophic wildfires, which could threaten life and property and to manage habitat for migratory birds and other wildlife. The refuge burns only within a very narrow window of well-defined conditions. These conditions meet federal and state air quality requirements. Prescribed burns are always conducted under conditions when the least amount of particulate matter will be released and with wind directions and speeds that will allow the least number of people impacted.

Comment: The same refuge patron commented that the bibliography used a majority of very old reference sources.

Response: Some wildlife research is timeless and would be applicable. Planners made every effort to find the most recent and applicable information available.

Comment: The same refuge patron stated he opposed all trapping.

Response: Trapping is proposed only as a means to control species that are causing damage to the habitat or species of higher priority.

Comments were received from the North Carolina Division of Coastal Management through the State Clearinghouse.

Comment 1: "The proposed action will be occurring within Dare County; a coastal county within the meaning to the Coastal Zone Management Act of 1972, as amended (CZMA). The CZMA requires that federal agencies proposing activities within a state's coastal zone to provide the state, in this case, the North Carolina Division of Coastal Management, with a consistency determination prior to implementing the activity to document that the proposed activity would comply with the enforceable policies of North Carolina's approved coastal management program and would be conducted consistent with the State's coastal management program. Conformance of the proposed federal activity with the enforceable policies of the state's certified coastal management program was not evaluated in the Draft."

Response: The refuge is aware of the need to comply with the Coastal Management Act of 1972, as amended, and the North Carolina Coastal Area Management Act. Most of the projects that would trigger a need for coordination are currently unfunded and will only be done as resources become available. Management actions covered by the CCP and others that may arise would be coordinated with the North Carolina Division of Coastal Management for a Consistency Determination as they are funded and finalized. Through a separate process, a general Consistency Determination will be requested for the refuge's CCP, recognizing that specific determinations will be required when projects are ready to be implemented.

Comment 2: "Though <u>not</u> a requirement, 15 CFR 930.31 allows a rederal aency to use its NEPA documents a*s a vehicle* for its consistency determination. Inclusion of the consistency analysis into the environmental documents simplifies the environmental review process and focuses the decision-making process by condensing the required analysis into one document. At this point in time, USFWS may either incorporate the consistency analysis into the final environmental document or it may prepare a stand-alone consistency determination."

Response: Comment noted.

Comment 3: "Moreover, DCM recommends that Appendix II (Relevant Legal Mandates), the Land Use Section, and the Regulatory Effects Section be revised to incorporate a review of the proposed action with the Coastal Zone Management Act and North Carolina' s coastal management program.

Response: We have revised Appendix III in the CCP (Relevant Legal Mandates) to include the Coastal Zone Management Act of 1972, as amended and the North Carolina Coastal Area Management Act. We have revised the section entitled "Regulatory Effects Section" to include reference to the Coastal Zone Management Act of 1972. We were unable to locate the "Land Use Section" in our document.

However, the refuge understands and acknowledges the need for coordination under the Coastal Zone Management Act of 1972, as amended and the North Carolina Coastal Area Management Act of 1974.

Comment 4: "DCM also recommends that the USFWS review the applicability of 15 CFR 930.33(a)(4) and 15 CFR 930.36(c). Pursuant to 15 CFR 930.33(a)(4}, the USFWS may request that environmentally beneficial activities conducted in compliance with the Pea Island National Wildlife Refuge's Comprehensive Conservation Plan be excluded from further consistency review."

Response: Comment noted.

Comment 5: "Furthermore, pursuant to 15 CFR 930.36(c), the USFWS may propose a general consistency determination when a federal agency proposes repeated activities other than development projects where the incremental actions do not affect any coastal use or coastal resource when performed separately. Prior to implementing the proposed CCP, the USFWS will need to submit to DCM a consistency determination and obtain the concurrence of DCM."

Response: The response to Comment 1 addresses Comment 5.

Comment 6: "North Carolina's coastal zone management program consists of, but is not limited to, the Coastal Area Management Act, the State's Dredge and Fill Law, and the land use plan of the county and/or local municipality in which the proposed project is located. In preparing the consistency determination, the USFWS will need to review these documents and to evaluate the conformance of the proposed CCP with the state's coastal program. The website for the Division of Coastal Management can be found at: http://dcm2.enr.state.nc.us/index.htm. The State's consistency webpage is located at: http://dcm2.enr.state.nc.us/Permits/consist.htm. Additionally, NOAA's Office of Ocean and Coastal Resources Management (OCRM) has a webpage on the consistency process at: http://coastalmanagement.noaa.gov/czm/federal_consistency.html."

Response: Comment noted.

Comment 7: "Based on our review of the Draft CCP/EA, the broad goals, objectives, and strategies outlined in the Management Direction Section appear to be consistent with the state's coastal program. Additionally, the Draft CCP/EA appears consistent with the Dare County land-use plan. However, it did not provide sufficient detail to determine whether individual projects that could be implemented would be consistent with the state's coastal management program. As noted above, development projects such as those listed in Tables 21-25 (replacement of pump stations, bulkheads, fuel tanks, and parking lots) will require review by DCM before they can be implemented."

Response: The response to Comment 1 addresses Comment 7.

Comment 8: "Additional potential projects that would require review by DCM include proposed work on the Bonner Bridge, NC-12, and dredging activities."

Response: The refuge does not conduct any management or maintenance activities associate with the Bonner Bridge, NC 12, or dredging activities in adjacent waters. However, when a Special Use Permit is issued by the refuge for another state or federal agency to conduct such activities, a condition of each permit requires the permittee to obtain any and all necessary permits and approvals required by other state and federal agencies.

Comment 9: "Furthermore. proposed management actions by the USFWS that would modify public coastal access opportunities would also subject to DCM review."

Response: The refuge does not anticipate any management actions that would modify public coastal access except to the extent necessary to protect certain fish and wildlife species for achieving the mission of the National Wildlife Refuge System and the purpose for which the refuge was established.

Comment 10: "Should the USFWS have any questions on the consistency process relative to the proposed CCP, please give me a call. Thank you for your consideration of the North Carolina Coastal Management Program."

Response: Comment noted.

Comment 11: During a phone conversation with Mr. Stephen Rynas, DCM Federal Consistency Coordinator, on March 16, 2006, an additional comment was made with regards to a desire by the Coastal Reserve Program to be considered as a partner as conservation plans are prepared and projects are implemented.

Response: The Fish and Wildlife Service in general and the Pea Island National Wildlife Refuge staff in particular welcome the opportunity to partner with the North Carolina Coastal Reserve Program. Through such mutual cooperation, a better understanding of each agency's mission and purpose will occur and the most important aspect is that our natural resources will realize greater benefits through a collaborative effort.

Appendix V. Decisions and Approvals

INTRA-SERVICE SECTION 7 BIOLOGICAL EVALUATION

Originating Person: Mike Bryant
Telephone Number: 252-473-1131, extension 222
E-Mail: mike_bryant@fws.gov
Date:

Project Name: Pea Island National Wildlife Refuge Comprehensive Conservation Plan

I.   **Service Program:**
___ Ecological Services
___ Federal Aid
___ Clean Vessel Act
___ Coastal Wetlands
___ Endangered Species Section 6
___ Partners for Fish and Wildlife
___ Sport Fish Restoration
___ Wildlife Restoration
___ Fisheries
_X_ Refuges/Wildlife

II.   **State/Agency:** North Carolina/ U.S. Fish and Wildlife Service

III.   **Station Name:** Pea Island National Wildlife Refuge

IV.   **Description of Proposed Action (attach additional pages as needed):** Implementation of the Comprehensive Conservation Plan for Pea Island National Wildlife Refuge by adopting the preferred alternative that will provide guidance, management direction, and operation plans for the next 15 years.

V.   **Pertinent Species and Habitat:**

     A. Include species/habitat occurrence map:

Bald eagles are occasionally seen during winter months in the area.

Loggerhead sea turtles nest on the refuge beaches.

Piping plovers occasionally nest behind the groin at the north end of the refuge when habitat is suitable.

B. Complete the following table:

SPECIES/CRITICAL HABITAT	STATUS[1]
Bald Eagle	Threatened
Loggerhead Sea Turtle	Threatened
Leatherback Sea Turtle	Endangered
Green Sea Turtle	Threatened
Hawksbill Sea Turtle	Endangered
Kemp's Ridley Sea Turtle	Endangered
American Alligator	Threatened
Piping Plover	Endangered
Roseate Tern	Endangered
Red-cockaded Woodpecker	Endangered
West Indian Manatee	Endangered
Seabeach Amaranth	Threatened

[1]STATUS: E=endangered, T=threatened, PE=proposed endangered, PT=proposed threatened, CH=critical habitat, PCH=proposed critical habitat, C=candidate species

VI.   Location (attach map):

A. **Ecoregion Number and Name**: Roanoke–Tar–Neuse–Cape Fear, Ecosystem No. 34

B. **County and State**: Dare, North Carolina

C. **Section, township, and range (or latitude and longitude)**:

D. **Distance (miles) and direction to nearest town**: Ten miles south of Nags Head, North Carolina; immediately north of Rodanthe, North Carolina

E. **Species/habitat occurrence**:

Bald Eagle - occasionally observed during winter. No active nests.

Loggerhead Sea Turtle – Record of occurrence within 20 years.

Leatherback Sea Turtle – No record of occurrence.

Green Sea Turtle – Record of occurrence within 20 years.

Hawksbill Sea Turtle – Record of occurrence within 20 years.

Kemp's Ridley Sea Turtle – No record of occurrence.

Piping Plover – Record of occurrence within 20 years.

Roseate Tern – Record of occurrence within 20 years.

Red-cockaded Woodpecker – No record of occurrence.

Roseate Tern – Record of occurrence within 20 years.

West Indian Manatee - Incidental record of occurrence outside of its normal range.

Seabeach Amaranth – Record of occurrence within 20 years.

VII. Determination of Effects:
A. Explanation of effects of the action on species and critical habitats in item V. B (attach additional pages as needed).

SPECIES/ CRITICAL HABITAT	IMPACTS TO SPECIES/CRITICAL HABITAT
Bald Eagle	Disturbance by staff and visitors during nesting season.
Loggerhead Sea Turtle	Disturbance by staff and visitors during nesting season.
Leatherback Sea Turtle	Disturbance by staff and visitors during nesting season.
Green Sea Turtle	Disturbance by staff and visitors during nesting season.
Hawksbill Sea Turtle	Disturbance by staff and visitors during nesting season.
Kemp's Ridley Sea Turtle	Disturbance by staff and visitors during nesting season.
Piping Plover	Disturbance by staff and visitors during nesting season.
Roseate Tern	Disturbance by staff and visitors during nesting season.
West Indian Manatee	Disturbance by boaters and anglers. Water quality degradation and lack of submerged aquatic vegetation.
Seabeach Amaranth	Trampling of plants by staff and visitors before seed maturation.

B.   Explanation of actions to be implemented to reduce adverse effects.

SPECIES/ CRITICAL HABITAT	ACTIONS TO MITIGATE/MIMIMIZE IMPACTS
Bald Eagle	Restrict access to nesting area.
Loggerhead Sea Turtle	Restrict access to nesting area. Monitor nesting and emergence of hatchlings with volunteers.
Leatherback Sea Turtle	Restrict access to nesting area. Monitor nesting and emergence of hatchlings with volunteers.
Green Sea Turtle	Restrict access to nesting area. Monitor nesting and emergence of hatchlings with volunteers.
Hawksbill Sea Turtle	Restrict access to nesting area. Monitor nesting and emergence of hatchlings with volunteers.
Kemp's Ridley Sea Turtle	Restrict access to nesting area. Monitor nesting and emergence of hatchlings with volunteers.
Piping Plover	Restrict access to nesting area.
Roseate Tern	Restrict access to nesting area.
West Indian Manatee	Restrict access when manatees are in the area. Cooperate with state agencies to monitor and improve water quality.
Seabeach Amaranth	Restrict access to areas with plants until after seed maturation.

VIII. Effect Determination and Response Requested:

SPECIES/CRITICAL HABITAT	DETERMINATION1			RESPONSE1 REQUESTED
	NE	NA	AA	
Bald Eagle		X		
Loggerhead Sea Turtle		X		
Leatherback Sea Turtle		X		
Green Sea Turtle		X		
Hawksbill Sea Turtle		X		
Kemp's Ridley Sea Turtle		X		
Piping Plover		X		
Roseate Tern		X		
Red-cockaded Woodpecker		X		
West Indian Manatee		X		
Seabeach Amaranth		X		

[1] *DETERMINATION/RESPONSE REQUESTED:*
NE = no effect. This determination is appropriate when the proposed actions will not directly, indirectly, or cumulatively impact, either positively or negatively, any listed, proposed, candidate species or designated/proposed critical habitat. Response Requested is optional but a "Concurrence" is recommended for a complete Administrative Record.

NA = not likely to adversely affect. This determination is appropriate when the proposed action is not likely to adversely impact any listed, proposed, candidate species or designated/proposed critical habitat or there may be beneficial effects to these resources. Response Requested is a "Concurrence".

AA = likely to adversely affect. This determination is appropriate when the proposed action is likely to adversely impact any listed, proposed, candidate species or designated/proposed critical habitat. Response Requested for listed species is "Formal Consultation." Response Requested for proposed or candidate species is "Conference".

_____ Signed _____   4/12/05

Signature (originating station)   **Date**

REFUGE   MANAGER
Title

IX. Reviewing Ecological Services Office Evaluation:

  A. Concurrence ___X___   Nonconcurrence _____

  B. Formal consultation required _____

  C. Conference required _____

  D. Informal conference required _____

  E. Remarks (attach additional pages as needed):

_____ Signed _____   1/11/6

Signature   **Date**

Field Supervisor
Raleigh - ES

Title   **Office**

COMPATIBILITY DETERMINATIONS

Uses: The following uses were considered for compatibility determination reviews: fishing, wildlife observation, photography, environmental education, and interpretation. A description and anticipated biological impacts for each use are addressed separately in this Compatibility Determination.

Refuge Name: Pea Island National Wildlife Refuge.

Date Established: August 8, 1938.

Establishing and Acquisition Authority(ies): 16 U.S.C. Sec. 664 (Migratory Bird Conservation Act of 1929).

Refuge Purpose: The purpose of Pea Island National Wildlife Refuge, as reflected in the refuge's authorizing legislation, is to protect and conserve migratory birds, and other wildlife resources through the protection of wetlands, in accordance with the following laws:

...as a refuge and breeding ground for protection of migratory waterfowl and other wildlife... (Executive Order 7864, August 8, 1938)

...for use as an inviolate sanctuary, or for any other management purpose, for migratory birds... 16 U.S.C. Sec. 664 (Migratory Bird Conservation Act of 1929)

National Wildlife Refuge System Mission:

The mission of the System, as defined by the National Wildlife Refuge System Improvement Act of 1997, is:

... to administer a national network of lands and waters for the conservation, management, and where appropriate, restoration of the fish, wildlife and plant resources and their habitats within the United States for the benefit of present and future generations of Americans.

Other Applicable Laws, Regulations, and Policies:

Antiquities Act of 1906 (34 Stat. 225)
Migratory Bird Treaty Act of 1918 (15 U.S.C. 703-711; 40 Stat. 755)
Migratory Bird Conservation Act of 1929 (16 U.S.C. 715r; 45 Stat. 1222)
Migratory Bird Hunting Stamp Act of 1934 (16 U.S.C. 718-178h; 48 Stat. 451)
Criminal Code Provisions of 1940 (18 U.S.C. 41)
Bald and Golden Eagle Protection Act (16 U.S.C. 668-668d; 54 Stat. 250)
Refuge Trespass Act of June 25, 1948 (18 U.S.C. 41; 62 Stat. 686)
Fish and Wildlife Act of 1956 (16 U.S.C. 742a-742j; 70 Stat.1119)
Refuge Recreation Act of 1962 (16 U.S.C. 460k-460k-4; 76 Stat. 653)
Wilderness Act (16 U.S.C. 1131; 78 Stat. 890)
Land and Water Conservation Fund Act of 1965
National Historic Preservation Act of 1966, as amended (16 U.S.C. 470, et seq.; 80 Stat. 915)
National Wildlife Refuge System Administration Act of 1966 (16 U.S.C. 668dd, 668ee; 80 Stat. 927)
National Environmental Policy Act of 1969, NEPA (42 U.S.C. 4321, et seq; 83 Stat. 852)
Use of Off-Road Vehicles on Public Lands (Executive Order 11644, as amended by Executive Order 10989)
Endangered Species Act of 1973 (16 U.S.C. 1531 et seq; 87 Stat. 884)
Refuge Revenue Sharing Act of 1935, as amended in 1978 (16 U.S.C. 715s; 92 Stat. 1319)

National Wildlife Refuge Regulations for the Most Recent Fiscal Year (50 CFR Subchapter C; 43 CFR 3101.3-3)
Emergency Wetlands Resources Act of 1986 (S.B. 740)
North American Wetlands Conservation Act of 1990
Food Security Act (Farm Bill) of 1990 as amended (HR 2100)
The Property Clause of The U.S. Constitution Article IV 3, Clause 2
The Commerce Clause of The U.S. Constitution Article 1, Section 8
The National Wildlife Refuge System Improvement Act of 1997 (Public Law 105-57, USC668dd)
Executive Order 12996, Management and General Public Use of the National Wildlife Refuge System. March 25, 1996
Title 50, Code of Federal Regulations, Parts 25-33
Archaeological Resources Protection Act of 1979
Native American Graves Protection and Repatriation Act of 1990

Compatibility determinations for each description listed were considered separately. Although for brevity, the preceding sections from "Uses" through "Other Applicable Laws, Regulations and Policies" are only written once within the plan, they are part of each descriptive use and become part of that compatibility determination if considered outside of the comprehensive conservation plan.

Description of Use: *Fishing*

Sport fishing is a common public use on the state waters of the Atlantic Ocean from the beaches located on the Cape Hatteras National Seashore immediately east of the Pea Island National Wildlife Refuge and in the Pamlico Sound west of the refuge. Fish creel limits, boating safety and license requirements are in accordance with State of North Carolina regulations. Access to the beach is only available by foot; no vehicles are allowed on the beach. A public boat ramp is located at New Inlet in the southern part of the refuge. As identified in the comprehensive conservation plan, the staff will conduct additional fishing events, fisheries surveys, and water quality analysis in order to provide a high quality fishing experience.

Availability of Resources: Based on a review of the refuge's budget allocated for this activity, there is adequate funding to ensure compatibility and to administer the use at its current level. There may be some limited disturbance to certain species of wildlife and some trampling of vegetation; however, in most situations this impact should be short-lived and relatively minor and would not negatively impact wildlife resources of the refuge. One exception is potential disturbance that may disrupt beach-nesting shore and colonial waterbirds at the northern end of the refuge. Nesting areas will be posted as closed to public access during critical nesting periods behind the groin on refuge lands and at the stable upper reaches of the mean high tide line. The actual area and timing of closure necessary to eliminate disturbances will be determined based on the best professional judgment of refuge staff.

Anticipated Impacts of the Use: Recreational fishing should not adversely affect the fisheries resource, wildlife resource, endangered species, or any other natural resource of the refuge.

Public use of the Pea Island National Wildlife Refuge will increase with increased visitation to the Outer Banks and better outreach by the staff, but the staff estimates that the level of use would not cause detrimental wildlife disturbance. Law enforcement activities would control problems associated with littering and illegal take of fish. Providing information to refuge visitors about rules and regulations, along with increased law enforcement patrol, would keep these negative impacts to a minimum.

Public Review and Comment: The period of public review and comment began on February 6, 2006, and ended on March 8, 2006. The following methods were used to solicit public review and comment:

> Public notice was posted at refuge headquarters and Refuge Visitor Center
> Public notice was posted on the refuge web pages.
> Public notice was posted in newspapers with wide local distribution (published in Virginia Pilot on February 17, 2006; The Coastland Times on February 5, 2006, and the Outer Banks Sentinel on February 5, 2006)
> Public meetings (Open Houses) were held on February 16 & 22.

No substantive comments were received relating to this use.

This compatibility determination was part of the Draft Comprehensive Conservation Plan and Environmental Assessment for Pea Island National Wildlife Refuge, which was announced in the *Federal Register* and made available for public comment for 30 days.

Determination (check one below):

_____ Use is Not Compatible

__X__ Use is Compatible with Following Stipulations

Stipulations Necessary to Ensure Compatibility: Conflicts between fishermen or other visitors using the refuge for non-consumptive wildlife recreation have not been a problem in the past and are not expected to be a problem in the future. A continued law enforcement presence can minimize associated violations such as taking under size fish, open fires and littering. Following completion of the comprehensive conservation plan, the refuge staff will develop a Fishing Plan. The following stipulations will help ensure the refuge fishing program is compatible with refuge purposes.

> All fishing tackle must be attended at all times.

> Leaving boats on the refuge overnight is prohibited.

> Fishing allowed during daylight hours only except with night fishing permit.

> Public access to areas where shorebirds, colonial nesting birds, and sea turtles are nesting is prohibited.

Justification: Refuge regulations permit fishing of ocean waters from the beach adjacent to the refuge under State regulations and access across refuge property from North Carolina Highway 12. Recreational fishing is providing a quality fishing experience on a sustainable basis. Fishing is a public use activity that, according to the 1997 National Wildlife Refuge System Improvement Act, the Service should provide and expand where possible. The use is among the 6 priority wildlife-dependent public uses authorized by the National Wildlife Refuge Improvement Act of 1997.

Mandatory 10- or 15-year Re-evaluation Date: _____08/02/21_____

Description of Use: *Wildlife Observation and Photography*

Nonconsumptive wildlife observation uses such as birdwatching, hiking, and nature photography are a major attraction of the refuge due to the area's proximity to bird migration routes and large metropolitan areas and the excellent access and facilities. There are estimates that 1.2 million visits/year are for wildlife observation and related activities.

The staff anticipates that an increase in nonconsumptive wildlife-dependent uses will occur over the next few years as The Service provides facilities and programs and especially as the public and conservation groups become more aware of the excellent birding/wildlife viewing opportunities on the refuge

There are no refuge roads maintained for public vehicle travel. The refuge has a trail around North Pond. There are 13 miles of North Carolina Highway 12 to gain visual access to the refuge and parking lots at which visitors can stop and proceed on foot to observe and photograph wildlife.

Availability of Resources: Based on a review of the refuge's budget allocated for this activity, there is adequate funding to ensure compatibility and to administer the use at its current level. The program functions well due to 30,000 annual volunteer hours and diligent training and supervision of the volunteers by staff.

Anticipated Impacts of the Use: Wildlife observation and photography activities might result in some disturbance to wildlife, especially if visitors venture too close to a impoundment or marsh with resting waterbirds, shorebird nesting area, or a rookery. The staff will locate refuge foot trails, boardwalks and wildlife observation platforms opened to pedestrian use by the public to minimize disturbance that could occur in these sensitive areas. If unacceptable levels of disturbance are identified at any time, the Service will close sensitive sites to public entry. Some minimal trampling of vegetation also may occur.

Construction of foot trails, boardwalks, and observation platforms will alter small portions of the natural environment. Proper planning prior to construction, sediment retention and grade stabilization features will reduce negative impacts to wetlands, threatened and endangered species and species of special concern. Impacts such as trampling vegetation and wildlife disturbance by refuge visitors do occur, but is presently not significant. Visitors cause other potential negative impacts, such as littering or illegally taking plants or animals, violating refuge regulations.

Public Review and Comment: The period of public review and comment began on February 6, 2006, and ended on March 8, 2006. The following methods were used to solicit public review and comment:

> Public notice was posted at refuge headquarters and Refuge Visitor Center
> Public notice was posted on the refuge web pages.
> Public notice was posted in newspapers with wide local distribution (published in Virginia Pilot on February 17, 2006; The Coastland Times on February 5, 2006, and the Outer Banks Sentinel on February 5, 2006)
> Public meetings (Open Houses) were held on February 16 & 22.

No substantive comments were received relating to these uses.

This compatibility determination was part of the Draft Comprehensive Conservation Plan and Environmental Assessment for Pea Island National Wildlife Refuge, which was announced in the *Federal Register* and made available for public comment for 30 days.

Determination (check one below):

_____ Use is Not Compatible

__X__ Use is Compatible with Following Stipulations

Stipulations Necessary to Ensure Compatibility: Prior to construction of any additional facilities, the refuge staff would obtain permits from local, state and federal regulatory agencies to reduce the possibility of negatively impacting wetlands, cultural resources or protected species. Law enforcement patrol of public use areas would continue to minimize violations of refuge regulations. The staff will monitor public use for wildlife observation and photography to document any negative impacts. If any negative impacts become noticeable, the Service will take corrective action reduce or eliminate the effects on wildlife.

Justification: Wildlife observation and photography are an important and preferred public uses on Pea Island National Wildlife Refuge and the National Wildlife Refuge System. The 1997 National Wildlife Refuge System Improvement Act identified wildlife observation and photography as priority pubic recreational uses to be facilitated on refuges. It is through permitted, compatible public uses such as this, that the public becomes aware of and provides support for our national wildlife refuges. The uses are among the 6 priority wildlife-dependent public uses authorized by the National Wildlife Refuge Improvement Act of 1997.

Mandatory 10- or 15-year Re-evaluation Date: ____08/02/21____

Description of Use: *Environmental Education and Interpretation*

Environmental education and interpretation are those activities that seek to increase the public's knowledge and understanding of wildlife, national wildlife refuges, ecology and land management, as well as contribute to the conservation of natural resources. If Service enacts the comprehensive conservation plan, the refuge will further develop its interpretation and environmental education programs. Environmental education and interpretation activities have been very popular in recent years. More than one million visitors come to the refuge for interpretation; more than 1,000 take part in a formal education program. The staff plans to develop these programs further and the development will usually be associated with structured activities conducted by refuge staff or trained volunteers. Refuge staff will also develop and provide curriculum and support materials to area teachers for use both on and off the refuge. They will develop additional informational kiosks and interpretive panels at key refuge entrance points, and wildlife observation platforms constructed as part of the environmental education and interpretation programs.

Availability of Resources: Based on a review of the refuge's budget allocated for these activities, funding is adequate to ensure compatibility and to administer these uses at current or proposed levels. The program functions well due to 30,000 annual volunteer hours and diligent training and supervision of the volunteers by staff. The management of a volunteer program is essential to successfully implement the education and visitor use program. Refuge staff will continue to recruit and train volunteers to assist in developing and implementing environmental education and interpretive programs.

Anticipated Impacts of the Use: Construction of facilities such as board walks, kiosks and observation platforms will alter small portions of the natural environment on the refuge. Proper planning and placement of facilities will ensure that wetlands, threatened or endangered species, or species of special concern are not negatively impacted. The refuge staff will obtain proper permits through the county, state and federal regulatory agencies prior to construction to ensure resource protection. The use of on-site, hands-on, action-oriented activities to accomplish environmental education and interpretive tours may impose a low-level impact on the sites used for these activities. These low-level impacts may include trampling of vegetation and temporary disturbance to wildlife species in the immediate area. Educational activities held off-refuge will not create any biological impacts on the resource.

Public Review and Comment: The period of public review and comment began on February 6, 2006, and ended on March 8, 2006. The following methods were used to solicit public review and comment:

> Public notice was posted at refuge headquarters and Refuge Visitor Center
> Public notice was posted on the refuge web pages.
> Public notice was posted in newspapers with wide local distribution (published in Virginia Pilot on February 17, 2006; The Coastland Times on February 5, 2006, and the Outer Banks Sentinel on February 5, 2006)
> Public meetings (Open Houses) were held on February 16 & 22.

No substantative comments were received relating to this use.

This compatibility determination was part of the Draft Comprehensive Conservation Plan and Environmental Assessment for Pea Island National Wildlife Refuge, which was announced in the *Federal Register* and made available for public comment for 30 days.

Determination (check one below):

_____ Use is Not Compatible

__X__ Use is Compatible with Following Stipulations

Stipulations Necessary to Ensure Compatibility: Zoning of visitor activities by time and space, clustering public use facilities, proper monitoring, educating visitors, and enforcement will ensure compatibility with the purposes of the refuge and mission of the National Wildlife Refuge System. Through periodic evaluation of trails and visitor contact points, the visitor services program will assess resource impacts. If future human impacts are determined through evaluation to be detrimental to important natural resources, the refuge will take actions to reduce or eliminate those impacts. The majority portions of the refuge will remain undeveloped, without public interpretive facilities.

Justification: The 1997 National Wildlife Refuge System Improvement Act identifies interpretation and environmental education as activities that the Service should provide and expand on refuges. Educating and informing the public through structured environmental education courses, interpretive materials, and guided tours about migratory birds, endangered species, wildlife management, and ecosystems will lead to improved support of the Service's mission to protect our natural resources. The uses are among the 6 priority wildlife-dependent public uses authorized by the National Wildlife Refuge Improvement Act of 1997.

Mandatory 10- or 15-year Re-evaluation Date: _____08/02/21_____

Approval of Compatibility Determination

The signature of approval is for all compatibility determinations considered within the comprehensive conservation plan. If one of the descriptive uses is considered for compatibility outside of the comprehensive conservation plan, the approval signature becomes part of that determination.

Refuge Manager: _____Signed_____ 6/16/06
(Signature/Date)

Regional Compatibility
Coordinator: _____Signed_____ 7/25/06
(Signature/Date)

Refuge Supervisor: _____Signed_____ 8/1/06
(Signature/Date)

Regional Chief, National
Wildlife Refuge System,
Southeast Region: _____Signed_____ 8/2/06
(Signature/Date)

Appendix VI. Refuge Biota

ANIMALS	
BIRDS	

COMMON NAME	SCIENTIFIC NAME
Avocet, American	*Recurvirostra americana*
Bittern, American	*Botaurus lentiginosus*
Bittern, Least	*Ixobrychus exilis*
Blackbird, Red-winged	*Agelaius phoeniceus*
Blackbird, Rusty	*Euphagus carolinus*
Bluebird, Eastern	*Sialia sialis*
Bobolink	*Dolichonyx oryzivorus*
Bobwhite, Northern	*Colinus virginianus*
Brant, Atlantic	*Brant bernicla*
Bufflehead	*Bucephala albeola*
Bunting, Indigo	*Passerina cyanea*
Bunting, Painted	*Passerina ciris*
Bunting, Snow	*Plectrophenax nivalis*
Canvasback	*Aythya valisineria*
Cardinal, Northern	*Cardinalis cardinalis*
Chat, Yellow-breasted	*Icteria virens*
Chickadee, Carolina	*Parus carolinensis*
Chuck-will's-widow	*Caprimulgus carolinensis*
Coot, American	*Fulica americana*
Cormorant, Double-crested	*Phalacrocorax auritis*
Cormorant, Great	*Phalacrocorax carbo*
Cowbird, Brown-headed	*Molothrus ater*
Creeper, Brown	*Certhia Americana*
Crow, American	*Corvus brachyrhynchos*
Crow, Fish	*Corvus ossifragus*

ANIMALS	
BIRDS	
COMMON NAME	**SCIENTIFIC NAME**
Cuckoo, Yellow-billed	*Coccyzus americanus*
Curlew, Long-billed	*Numenius americanus*
Dickcissel	*Spiza americana*
Dove, Mourning	*Zenaida macroura*
Dove, Rock	*Columba livia*
Dowitcher, Long-billed	*Limnodromus scolopaceous*
Dowitcher, Short-billed	*Limnodromus griseus*
Duck, American Black	*Anas rubripes*
Duck, Ring-necked	*Aythya collaris*
Duck, Ruddy	*Oxyura jamaicensis*
Duck, Wood	*Aix sponsa*
Dunlin	*Calidris alpina*
Eagle, Bald	*Haliaeetus leucocephalus*
Egret, Cattle	*Bubulcus ibis*
Egret, Great	*Casmerodius albus*
Egret, Reddish	*Egretta rufescens*
Egret, Snowy	*Egretta thula*
Falcon, Peregrine	*Falco peregrinus*
Finch, House	*Carpodacus mexicanus*
Finch, Purple	*Carpodacus purpureus*
Flicker, Northern	*Colaptes auratus*
Flycatcher, Acadian	*Empidonax virescens*
Flycatcher, Great-crested	*Myiarchus crinitus*
Flycatcher, Least	*Empidonax minimus*
Flycatcher, Scissor-tailed	*Tyrannus forficatus*
Flycatcher, Willow/alder	*Empidonax traillii*
Flycatcher, Yellow-bellied	*Empidonax flaviventris*

ANIMALS	
BIRDS	
COMMON NAME	**SCIENTIFIC NAME**
Frigatebird, Magnificent	*Fregata magnificens*
Gadwall	*Anas strepera*
Gallinule, Purple	*Porphyrula martinica*
Gannet, Northern	*Morus bassanus*
Gnatcatcher, Blue-gray	*Polioptila caerulea*
Godwit, Hudsonian	*Limosa haemastica*
Godwit, Marbled	*Limosa fedoa*
Goldeneye, Common	*Bucephala clangula*
Goldfinch, American	*Carduelis tristis*
Goose, "Blue"	*Chen caerulescens*
Goose, Canada	*Branta canadensis*
Goose, Greater Snow	*Chen caerulescens*
Goose, Lesser Snow	*Chen caerulescens*
Goose, Ross'	*Chen rossi*
Grackle, Boat-tailed	*Quiscalus major*
Grackle, Common	*Quiscalus quiscula*
Grebe, Eared	*Podiceps nigricollis*
Grebe, Horned	*Podiceps auritus*
Grebe, Pied-billed	*Podilymbus podiceps*
Grebe, Red-necked	*Podiceps grisegena*
Grosbeak, Blue	*Guiraca caerulea*
Grosbeak, Evening	*Coccothraustes vespertinus*
Grosbeak, Rose-breasted	*Pheucticus ludovicianus*
Gull, Black-headed	*Larus ridibundus*
Gull, Bonaparte's	*Larus philadelphia*
Gull, California	*Larus californicus*
Gull, Glaucous	*Larus hyperboreus*

ANIMALS	
BIRDS	
COMMON NAME	**SCIENTIFIC NAME**
Gull, Greater Black-backed	*Larus marinus*
Gull, Herring	*Larus argentatus*
Guli, Iceland	*Larus glaucoides*
Gull, Laughing	*Larus atricilla*
Gull, Lesser Black-backed	*Larus fuscus*
Gull, Little	*Larus minutus*
Gull, Ring-billed	*Larus delawarensis*
Gull, Thayer's	*Larus thayeri*
Harrier, Northern	*Circus cyaneus*
Hawk, Broad-winged	*Buteo platypterus*
Hawk, Cooper's	*Accipiter cooperii*
Hawk, Red-shouldered	*Buteo lineatus*
Hawk, Red-tailed	*Buteo jamaicensis*
Hawk, Rough-legged	*Buteo lagopus*
Hawk, Sharp-shinned	*Accipiter striatus*
Hummingbird, Ruby-throated	*Archilochus colubris*
Ibis, Glossy	*Plegadis falcinellus*
Ibis, White	*Eudocimus albus*
Jaeger, Parasitic	*Stercorarius parasiticus*
Jaeger, Pomarine	*Stercorarius pomarinus*
Jay, Blue	*Cyanocitta cristata*
Junco, Dark-eyed	*Junco hyemalis*
Kestrel, American	*Falco sparverius*
Killdeer	*Charadrius vociferus*
Kingbird, Eastern	*Tyrannus tyrannus*
Kingbird, Gray	*Tyrannus dominicensis*
Kingbird, Western	*Tyrannus verticalis*

ANIMALS	
BIRDS	
COMMON NAME	**SCIENTIFIC NAME**
Kingfisher, Belted	*Ceryle alcyon*
Kinglet, Golden-crowned	*Regulus satrapa*
Kinglet, Ruby-crowned	*Regulus calendula*
Kittiwake, Black-legged	*Rissa tridactyla*
Knot, Red	*Calidris canutus*
Lark, Horned	*Eremophila alpestris*
Longspur, Lapland	*Calcarius lapponicus*
Loon, Common	*Gavia immer*
Loon, Red-throated	*Gavia stellata*
Mallard	*Anas platyrhynchos*
Martin, Purple	*Progne subis*
Meadowlark, Eastern	*Sturnella magna*
Merganser, Common	*Mergus merganser*
Merganser, Hooded	*Lophodytes cucullatus*
Merganser, Red-breasted	*Mergus serrator*
Merlin	*Falco columbarius*
Moorhen, Common	*Gallinula chloropus*
Nighthawk, Common	*Chordeiles minor*
Nuthatch, Brown-headed	*Sitta pusilla*
Nuthatch, Red-breasted	*Sitta Canadensis*
Oriole, Northern (Baltimore)	*Icterus galbula*
Oriole, Orchard	*Icterus spurius*
Osprey	*Pandion haliaetus*
Ovenbird	*Seiurus aurocapillus*
Owl, Barn	*Tyto alba*
Owl, Eastern screech	*Otus asio*
Owl, Great-horned	*Bubo virginianus*

ANIMALS	
BIRDS	
COMMON NAME	**SCIENTIFIC NAME**
Owl, Northern saw-whet	*Aegolius acadicus*
Owl, Short-eared	*Asio flammeus*
Oystercatcher, American	*Haematopus palliatus*
Parula, Northern	*Parula Americana*
Pelican, American White	*Pelecanus erythrorhynchos*
Pelican, Brown	*Pelecanus occidentalis*
Petrel, Leach's Storm	*Oceanodroma leucorhoa*
Petrel, Wilson's Storm	*Oceanites oceanicus*
Pewee, Eastern Wood	*Contopus virens*
Phalarope, Red	*Phalaropus fulicaria*
Phalarope, Red-necked	*Phalaropus lobatus*
Phalarope, Wilson's	*Phalaropus tricolor*
Pheasant, Ring-necked (Exotic)	*Phasianus colchicus*
Phoebe, Eastern	*Sayornis phoebe*
Pintail, Northern	*Anas acuta*
Pipit, American	*Anthus rubescens*
Plover, Black-bellied	*Pluvialis squatarola*
Plover, Lesser Golden	*Pluvialis dominica*
Plover, Piping	*Charadrius melodus*
Plover, Semipalmated	*Charadrius semipalmatus*
Plover, Wilson's	*Charadrius wilsonia*
Rail, Black	*Laterallus jamaicensis*
Rail, Clapper	*Rallus longirostris*
Rail, King	*Rallus elegans*
Rail, Virginia	*Rallus limicola*
Rail, Yellow	*Coturnicops noveboracensis*
Redhead	*Aythya americana*

ANIMALS	
BIRDS	
COMMON NAME	**SCIENTIFIC NAME**
Redstart, American	*Setophaga ruticilla*
Ruff	*Philomachus pugnax*
Sanderling	*Calidris alba*
Sandpiper, Baird's	*Calidris bairdii*
Sandpiper, Buff-breasted	*Tryngites subruficollis*
Sandpiper, Curlew	*Calidris ferruginea*
Sandpiper, Least	*Calidris minutilla*
Sandpiper, Pectoral	*Calidris melanotos*
Sandpiper, Purple	*Calidris maritima*
Sandpiper, Semipalmated	*Calidris pusilla*
Sandpiper, Solitary	*Tringa solitaria*
Sandpiper, Spotted	*Actitis macularia*
Sandpiper, Stilt	*Calidris himantopus*
Sandpiper, Upland	*Bartramia longicauda*
Sandpiper, Western	*Calidris mauri*
Sandpiper, White-rumped	*Calidris fuscicollis*
Sapsucker, Yellow-bellied	*Sphyrapicus rubber*
Scaup, Greater	*Aythya marila*
Scaup, Lesser	*Aythya affinis*
Scoter, Black	*Melanitta nigra*
Scoter, Surf	*Melanitta perspicillata*
Scoter, White-winged	*Melanitta deglandi*
Shearwater, Audubon's	*Puffinus lherminieri*
Shearwater, Cory's	*Calonectris diomedea*
Shearwater, Greater	*Puffinus gravis*
Shearwater, Manx	*Puffinus puffinus*
Shearwater, Sooty	*Puffinus griseus*

ANIMALS	
BIRDS	
COMMON NAME	**SCIENTIFIC NAME**
Shoveler, Northern	*Anas clypeata*
Siskin, Pine	*Carduelis pinus*
Skimmer, Black	*Rynchops niger*
Snipe, Common (Wilson's snipe)	*Gallinago gallinago*
Sora	*Porzana carolina*
Sparrow, Chipping	*Spizella passerina*
Sparrow, Clay-colored	*Spizella pallida*
Sparrow, Field	*Spizella pusilla*
Sparrow, Fox	*Passerella iliaca*
Sparrow, Grasshopper	*Ammodramus savannarum*
Sparrow, House	*Passer domesticus*
Sparrow, "Ipswich"	*Passerculus sandwichensis princeps*
Sparrow, Vesper	*Pooecetes gramineus*
Sparrow, Lark	*Chondestes grammacus*
Sparrow, Lincoln's	*Melospiza lincolnii*
Sparrow, Nelson's sharp-tailed	*Ammodramus caudacutus nelsoni*
Sparrow, Saltmarsh sharp-tailed	*Ammodramus caudacutus caudacutus*
Sparrow, Savannah	*Passerculus sandwichensis*
Sparrow, Seaside	*Ammodramus maritimus*
Sparrow, Song	*Melospiza melodia*
Sparrow, Swamp	*Melospiza georgiana*
Sparrow, White-crowned	*Zonotrichia leucophrys*
Sparrow, White-throated	*Zonotrichia albicollis*
Stilt, Black-necked	*Himantopus mexicanus*
Swallow, Bank	*Riparia riparia*
Swallow, Barn	*Hirundo rustica*
Swallow, Cliff	*Hirundo pyrrhonota*

ANIMALS	
BIRDS	
COMMON NAME	**SCIENTIFIC NAME**
Swallow, Northern rough-winged	*Stelgidopteryx serripennis*
Swallow, Tree	*Tachycineta bicolor*
Swan, Mute	*Cygnus olor*
Swan, Tundra	*Cygnus columbianus*
Swift, Chimney	*Chaetura pelagica*
Tanager, Scarlet	*Piranga olivacea*
Tanager, Summer	*Piranga rubra*
Teal, Blue-winged	*Anas discors*
Teal, Green-winged	*Anas crecca*
Tern, Black	*Chlidonias niger*
Tern, Caspian	*Sterna caspia*
Tern, Common	*Sterna hirundo*
Tern, Forster's	*Sterna forsteri*
Tern, Gull-billed	*Sterna nilotica*
Tern, Least	*Sterna antillarum*
Tern, Roseate	*Sterna dougallii*
Tern, Royal	*Sterna maxima*
Tern, Sandwich	*Sterna sandvicensis*
Tern, Sooty	*Sterna fuscata*
Thrush, Gray-cheeked	*Catharus minimus*
Thrush, Hermit	*Catharus guttatus*
Thrush, Swainson's	*Catharus ustulatus*
Thrush, Wood	*Hylocichla mustelina*
Titmouse, Tufted	*Parus bicolor*
Towhee, Rufus-sided (eastern)	*Pipilo erythrophthalmus*
Turnstone, Ruddy	*Arenaria interpres*
Veery	*Catharus fuscescens*

ANIMALS	
BIRDS	
COMMON NAME	**SCIENTIFIC NAME**
Vireo, Blue-headed (solitary)	*Vireo solitarius*
Vireo, Philadelphia	*Vireo philadelphicus*
Vireo, Red-eyed	*Vireo olivaceus*
Vireo, Warbling	*Vireo gilvus*
Vireo, White-eyed	*Vireo griseus*
Vireo, Yellow-throated	*Vireo flavifrons*
Vulture, Turkey	*Cathartes aura*
Warbler, Bay-breasted	*Dendroica castanea*
Warbler, Blackburnian	*Dendroica fusca*
Warbler, Blackpoll	*Dendroica striata*
Warbler, Black-and-white	*Mniotilta varia*
Warbler, Black-throated Blue	*Dendroica caerulescens*
Warbler, Black-throated Green	*Dendroica virens*
Warbler, Blue-winged	*Vermivora pinus*
Warbler, Canada	*Wilsonia canadensis*
Warbler, Cape May	*Dendroica tigrina*
Warbler, Chestnut-sided	*Dendroica pennsylvanica*
Warbler, Connecticut	*Oporornis agilis*
Warbler, Golden-winged	*Vermivora chrysoptera*
Warbler, Hooded	*Wilsonia citrina*
Warbler, Kentucky	*Oporornis formosus*
Warbler, Magnolia	*Dendroica magnolia*
Warbler, Mourning	*Oporornis philadelphia*
Warbler, Nashville	*Vermivora ruficapilla*
Warbler, Orange-crowned	*Vermivora celata*
Warbler, Palm	*Dendroica palmarum*
Warbler, Pine	*Dendroica pinus*

ANIMALS	
BIRDS	
COMMON NAME	**SCIENTIFIC NAME**
Warbler, Prairie	*Dendroica discolor*
Warbler, Prothonotary	*Protonotaria citrea*
Warbler, Tennessee	*Vermivora peregrina*
Warbler, Yellow	*Dendroica petechia*
Warbler, Wilson's	*Wilsonia pusilla*
Warbler, Worm-eating	*Helmitheros vermivorus*
Warbler, Yellow-rumped	*Dendroica coronata*
Warbler, Yellow-throated	*Dendroica dominica*
Waterthrush, Northern	*Seiurus noveboracensis*
Waxwing, Cedar	*Bombycilla cedrorum*
Yellowthroat, Common	*Geothlypis trichas*

ANIMALS	
MAMMALS	
COMMON NAME	**SCIENTIFIC NAME**
Bat, Eastern Pipistrelle	Pipistrellus subflavus*
Bat, Evening	Nycticeius humeralis*
Bat, Hoary	Lasiurus cinereus*
Bat, Red	Lasiurus borealis*
Bat, Silver-haired	Lasionycteris noctivagans
Deer, White-tailed	Odocoileus virginianus
Fox, Gray	Urocyon cinereoargenteus
Mink	Mustela vison
Mole, Eastern	Scalopus aquaticus*
Mouse, House	Mus musculus
Mouse, Eastern Harvest	Reithrodontomys humilis*
Mouse, White-footed	Peromyscus leucopus*
Muskrat	Ondatra zibethica

ANIMALS

MAMMALS

COMMON NAME	SCIENTIFIC NAME
Nutria (Exotic)	Myocastor coypu
Opossum	Didelphis marsupialis
Otter, River	Lutra canadensis
Rabbit, Eastern Cottontail	Sylvilagus floridanus
Rabbit, Marsh	Sylvilagus palustris
Raccoon	Procyon lotor
Rat, Hispid cotton	Sigmodon hispidus*
Rat, Norway (Exotic)	Rattus norvegicus
Shrew, Least	Cryptotis parva*
Shrrew, Short-tailed	Blarina brevicauda*
Shrew, Southeastern	Sorex longirostris
Vole, Meadow	Microtus pennsylvanicus

ANIMALS

AMPHIBIANS & REPTILES

COMMON NAME	SCIENTIFIC NAME
Frog, Bull	Rana catesbeiana*
Frog, Green Tree	Hyla gratiosa
Frog, Southern Leopard	Rana utricularia
Frog, Squirrel Tree	Hyla squirella
Lizard, Glass	Ophisaures attenuatus
Racerunner, Six-line	Cnemidophorus sexlineatus*
Skink, Ground	Leiolopisma laterale*
Skink, Five-lined	Eumeces fasciatus*
Snake, Green anole (Carolina) anole)	Anolis carolinensis*
Snake, Copperhead	Agkistrodon contortrix*
Snake, Eastern Cottonmouth	Agkistrodon piscivorus*
Snake, Canebrake Rattle	Crotalus horridus atricaudatus*
Snake, Black Racer	Coluber constrictor constrictor

ANIMALS	
AMPHIBIANS & REPTILES	
COMMON NAME	**SCIENTIFIC NAME**
Snake, Black Rat	Elaphe merican merican*
Snake, Corn	Elaphe guttata guttata
Snake, Eastern Garter	Thamnophis sirtalis sirtalis*
Snake, Eastern Hognose	Heterdon platyrhinos
Snake, Eastern King	Lampropeltis getulus getulus*
Snake, Eastern Ribbon	Thamnophis sauritus sauritus*
Snake, Rough Green	Opheodrys aestivus*
Snake, Brown	Storeria dekayi
Snake, Carolina Salt Marsh	Nerodia sipedon williamengelsi
Toad, Fowler's	Bufo woodhousei fowleri
Turtle, Yellow-bellied Slider	Chrysemys scripta
Turtle, Eastern Mud	Kinosternon subrubrum
Turtle, Common Snapping	Chelydra serpentina
Turtle, Diamondback Terrapin	Malaclemys terrapin
Turtle, Loggerhead Sea	Caretta caretta
Turtle, Green Sea	Chelonia mydas
Turtle, Hawksbill Sea	Eretmochelys imbricata
Turtle, Kemp's-ridleys Sea	Lepidochelys kempii
Turtle, Leatherback Sea	Dermochelys coriacea

ANIMALS	
FISH	
COMMON NAME	**SCIENTIFIC NAME**
Alewife	*Alosa pseudoharengus*
Anchovy, Bay	*Anchoa mitchilli*
Bass, Striped	*Morone saxatilis*
Bluefish	*Pomatomus saltatrix*

ANIMALS	
FISH	
COMMON NAME	**SCIENTIFIC NAME**
Croaker, Atlantic	*Micropogonias undulatus*
Drum, Red	*Sciaenops ocellatus*
Eel, American	*Anguilla rostrata*
Flounder, Southern	*Paralichthys lethostigma*
Flounder, Summer	*Paralichthys dentatus*
Gar, Longnose	*Lepisosteus osseus*
Goby, Darter	*Gobionellus boleosoma*
Goby, Naked	*Gobiosoma bosci*
Herring, Blueback	*Alosa aestivalis*
Killifish, Banded	*Fundulus diaphanus*
Killifish, Marsh	*Fundulus confluentus*
Menhaden, Atlantic	*Brevoortia tyrannus*
Mummichog	*Fundulus heteroclitus*
Minnow, Sheepshead	*Cyprinodon variegates*
Mosquitofish	*Gambusia affinis*
Mullet, Striped	*Mugil cephalus*
Mullet, White	*Mugil curema*
Perch, White	*Morone mericana*
Pinfish	*Lagodon rhomboides*
Pipefish, Gulf	*Syngnathus scovelli*
Seatrout, Spotted	*Cynoscion nebulosus*
Seatrout, Gray	*Cynoscion regalis*
Spot	*Leiostomus xanthurus*

ANIMALS	
FISH	
COMMON NAME	**SCIENTIFIC NAME**
Shad, American	*Alosa sapidissima*
Shad, Gizzard	*Dorosoma cepedianum*
Shad, Hickory	*Alosa mediocris*
Silverside, Tidewater	*Menidia peninsulae*
Snapper, Gray	*Lutjanus griseus*
Shark, Sandbar	*Carcharhinus plumbeus*
Shark, Dogfish	*Mustelus canis*

ANIMALS	
OTHER AQUATIC SPECIES	
COMMON NAME	**SCIENTIFIC NAME**
Clam, Coquina	*Donax variabilis*
Clam, Hard-shelled (Quahog)	*Mercenaria mercenaria*
Crab, Blue	*Callinectes sapidus*
Crab, Brackish-Water Fiddler	*Uca minax*
Crab, Ghost	*Ocypode quadrata*
Crab, Mole	*Emerita talpoida*
Crab, Marsh	*Sesarma reticulatum*
Crab, Mud Fiddler	*Uca pugnax*
Crab, Sand Fiddler	*Uca pugilator*
Jellyfish, Cannonball	*Stomolophus meleagris*
Oyster, Common	*Crassostrea virginica*
Periwinkle, Marsh	*Littorina irrorata*
Scallop, Bay	*Aequipecten irradians*

ANIMALS	
OTHER AQUATIC SPECIES	
COMMON NAME	**SCIENTIFIC NAME**
Sea Squirt	*Styela spp.*
Sea Grape	Molgula spp.
Sea Pork	*Amaroucium spp*
Shrimp, Pink	*Penaeus duorarum*
Shrimp, White	*Penaeus setiferus*
Shrimp, Brown	*Penaeus aztecus*
Star, Common Sea	*Asterias forbesi*

* Denotes species that have not been documented on the refuge but are expected to occur.

Appendix VII. Priority Bird Species and their Habitats

Species	Status	Brackish Marsh	Maritime Shrub	Beach, Dune, Grass and Dry Grassland	Managed Wetlands (Moist-soil Units)
Piping Plover	FL			X	
Bald Eagle	FL	X			
Seabeach Amaranth	FL			X	
Saltmarsh Sharp-tailed Sparrow	FSC	X			
Seaside Sparrow	FSC	X			
Black Rail	FSC	X			
Yellow Rail	FSC	X			
King Rail	FSC	X			
Sedge Wren	FSC	X			X
Prairie Warbler	FSC		X		
Yellow-throated Warbler	FSC		X		
Northern Parula	FSC		X		
Red Knot	FSC			X	
Wilson's Plover	FSC			X	
Least Tern	FSC			X	
Black Skimmer	FSC			X	
American Oystercatcher	FSC			X	
Canada Goose	SMC				X
Snow Goose	SMC				X
Tundra Swan	SMC				X
American Black Duck	SMC	X			X
Mallard	SMC				X
American Widgeon	SMC				X
Blue-winged Teal	SMC				X
Green-winged Teal	SMC				X
Ruddy Duck	SMC				X
Ringneck Duck	SMC				X
Northern Pintail	SMC				X
Greater Scaup	SMC				X
Lesser Scaup	SMC				X
Gull-billed Tern	SMC			X	
Common Tern	SMC			X	

(FL=Federally-listed, FSC=Federal Species of Concern,
SMC=Species of Management Concern on Pea Island National Wildlife Refuge)

Appendix VIII. Budget Requests

REFUGE OPERATION NEEDS SYSTEM (RONS) PROJECTS

Pea Island National Wildlife Refuge is managed as a part of the Alligator River National Wildlife Refuge Complex. Many projects, staff positions, etc., listed here are proposed as Alligator River National Wildlife Refuge projects. They are included here because they will affect management of Pea Island National Wildlife Refuge. Projects are ordered by the first two digits of the project number, which stand for the fiscal year the refuge developed the project to facilitate finding the projects listed in the management alternatives.

Projects are listed as Tier 1 projects that support approved critical mission or approved minimum staff or Tier 2 projects that do not.

Project 97001 (Alligator River)
Tier 2 Project
First Year Request $32,500, Recurring Request $25,000
Station Rank (Alligator River) – 28
This project will provide the funding to hire a half-time GS-5 biological technician to perform threatened and endangered species surveys. Two endangered species are found on the refuge: red-cockaded woodpecker and red wolf. One threatened species is found on the refuge: American alligator. Most of the 152,000-acre refuge is comprised of impenetrable, upland forested swamp, which is very difficult to survey by traditional ground surveys. Additional helicopter surveys are needed to properly survey more than 40,000 acres of suitable red-cockaded woodpecker habitat to locate and evaluate new colony sites. Alligator surveys will be reinitiated to monitor an expanding population. Red wolf aerial surveys will be augmented to better document wolf locations, den sites, mortality, and habitat use.

Project 97002 (Alligator River)
Tier 2 Project
First Year Request $32,500, Recurring Request $30,000
Station Rank (Alligator River) - 31
This project will provide the funding to hire a half-time GS-7 biological technician to perform surveys of neotropical migratory songbirds. These songbirds have drastically declined both regionally and nationally over the last 20 years. Since no comprehensive surveys have been conducted on the refuge, very little is known about the use or the importance of refuge habitat by migrating songbirds. The project will determine seasonal land use and habitat use by bird species. Standard neotropical bird surveys will be conducted each month along four established survey routes through all major habitat types on the refuge. These surveys are essential to determine the effects of management activities on migratory birds; thereby improving management decisions.

Project 97003 (Alligator River)
Tier 2 Project
First Year Request $32,500, Recurring Request $35,000
Station Rank (Alligator River) - 21
This project will provide the funding to hire a half-time GS-9 wildlife biologist to perform surveys of wildlife species on the refuge. The refuge contains much of the suitable wildlife habitat on the mainland portion of Dare County. The project is the best way to gauge the effects of the management activities on the refuge's wildlife and plant communities. The project will improve conservation of these resources. Aerial

waterfowl surveys will be conducted biweekly from September through March. Other wildlife and plant surveys (e.g., black bear, white-tailed deer, woodcock, rail, mourning dove, and moist-soil unit production) will be conducted using standard census techniques along established routes. A Wildlife Inventory Plan will also be developed, approved, and implemented.

Project 97004 (Alligator River)
Tier 2 Project
First Year Request $595,000, Recurring Request $551,000
Station Rank (Alligator River) - 4
This project will provide the funding to hire nine full-time permanent employees (three GS-9 resource specialists, two GS-6 clerical employees, and four WG-8 equipment operators) to conduct prescribed burning. Fire in eastern North Carolina has been aggressively suppressed for the past 50 years. As a result, fire-dependent habitats (e.g., pond pine woodlands and cane brake swamps) have deteriorated. Unique wildlife populations (e.g., black bear, red-cockaded woodpeckers, neotropical migrant songbirds, and red wolves) that are associated with these diverse habitat types have been negatively impacted. A minimum of fourteen sites totaling about 20,000 acres will be prescribed burned on an annual basis to create or improve a diversity of habitat types. An active wildfire detection and suppression program will be improved to protect all refuge resources.

Project 97005 (Alligator River)
Tier 2 Project
First Year Request $162,500, Recurring Request $182,000
Station Rank (Alligator River) -18
This project will provide the funding to hire three full-time permanent employees (one GS-9 forester, one GS-7 forestry technician, and one WG-8 equipment operator) to restore Atlantic white cedar stands on the refuge. Past logging and poor post-harvest management has resulted in over 5,000 acres of Atlantic white cedar clear-cuts on the refuge. These clear-cuts should be restored. Inventories have revealed an adequate stocking of "naturally regenerated" cedar in several of the clear-cuts. However, the cedars are being suppressed by an extremely dense growth of hardwood shrubs. The project involves "releasing" the cedars from hardwood competition by aerial application of an environmentally safe and approved herbicide. This will allow the cedar stands to grow free of competition for a few years. Plans also include planting some stands with seedlings.

Project 97006 (Alligator River)
Tier 2 Project
First Year Request $40,000, Recurring Request $49,000
Station Rank (Alligator River) - 7
This project will provide the funding to hire a full-time permanent GS-5 biological technician to monitor water control structures used to restore hydrology on the refuge. The refuge contains 70,000 acres of forested wetland habitat that has been severely impacted from ditching by prior owners. To restore natural habitats, natural hydrology (water flow and levels) in these wetlands, more than 50 water control structures have been installed at various locations. However, these structures must be frequently monitored and adjusted to prevent timber loss and other impacts from prolonged flooding. To ensure proper monitoring, permanent staff gauges will be installed at each water control structure, along with 20 monitoring wells at various locations.

Project 97007 (Alligator River)
Tier 2 Project
First Year Request $60,000, Recurring Request $5,000
Station Rank (Alligator River) - 15
This project will provide the funding to purchase 500,000 acres of recent infrared aerial photography in an electronically digitized format. The Alligator River Refuge (a forested wetland) and Pea Island Refuge (a coastal barrier island) have many unique and varied plant and animal communities. Good planning is needed to properly manage these resources and up-to-date photography is needed for good planning. This imagery will be used on the refuge's geographic information system computer to assist in all phases of refuge management. It will also be used to document land use changes in the red wolf reintroduction area.

Project 97010 (Alligator River)
Tier 2 Project
First Year Request $40,000, Recurring Request $10,000
Station Rank (Alligator River) - 16
This project will provide the funding to install water quality monitoring stations and conduct monitoring. About 70,000 acres of the refuge are comprised of a variety of wetland habitats. A minimum of 12 water quality monitoring stations will be installed, with at least 1 each in all refuge impoundments, lakes, streams, moist-soil units, selected canals, and adjacent sound and river waters. Data collected will include water level, dissolved oxygen, pH, salinity, and temperature. This data is critically needed to document current water quality conditions and to identify problem areas so that possible solutions can be developed and implemented. A water quality enhancement plan will also be developed, approved, and implemented.

Project 97011 (Alligator River)
Tier 2 Project
First Year Request $65,000, Recurring Request $59,000
Station Rank (Alligator River) - 30
This project will provide the funding to hire a permanent full-time biological technician to develop and implement a Marsh and Water Management Plan. Two new pump sites will be installed to more effectively manage water levels in about 3,000 acres of the 5,400-acre moist-soil and farm unit area. The project will provide more efficient management of water levels in the area for waterfowl food production. At critical times during high rainfall events, it will protect roads from flooding and erosion, thereby preventing unnecessary road closures to the public. Pump sites will be installed at the intersections of Milltail and North Perimeter Roads and at Buffalo City and Sawyer Lake Roads.

Project 97018 (Alligator River)
Tier 2 Project
First Year Request $65,000, Recurring Request $49,000
Station Rank (Alligator River) - 30
This project will provide the funding to purchase a large farm tractor and hire a permanent full-ime WG-5 equipment operator. Within the refuge's 4,500-acre farm unit, about 2,000 acres are diked and managed as moist-oil units for the production of waterfowl food plants. To improve the food-producing potential of these units, increased soil manipulation practices (e.g., disking, plowing, and mowing) must be conducted. However, a farm tractor of sufficient size is not currently available to the refuge to do this type of work. The purchase of a new rubber-tired, four-wheel drive farm tractor with more than 100 horsepower will meet this need.

Project 97021 (Alligator River)
Tier 2 Project
First Year Request $100,000, Recurring Request $138,000
Station Rank (Alligator River) - 6
This project will provide the funding to add 20 new water control structures and hire a GS-9 resource specialist and a WG-8 equipment operator to manage them. The refuge has an ongoing project restoring the natural hydrology of 50,000 acres. However, this project needs to be expanded by adding 20 new water control structures and subsequently manipulating water levels. This will result in the restoration of 20,000 additional wetland acres over 5 years. The refuge contains about 70,000 acres of forested wetlands, most of which were ditched and channelized by prior owners. This resulted in an unnatural water flow in the area. It has caused some areas to be "too wet" and other areas to be "too dry" for extended periods of time, thereby resulting in a loss or degradation of wildlife habitat.

Project 97022 (Alligator River)
Tier 2 Project
First Year Request $85,000, Recurring Request $15,000
Station Rank (Alligator River) - 1
This project will provide the funding to control common reed (*Phragmites australis*) on 600 acres of the refuge. The common reed will be treated with an environmentally safe and approved herbicide by a variety of application methods. Failure to aggressively pursue control will result in the replacement of desirable vegetation, thereby reducing the refuge's ability to provide suitable habitat for waterfowl and other wildlife species. Common reed is an invasive wetland plant species that has little wildlife value. Once established, it chokes out more desirable plants and degrades the habitat for a variety of wildlife species.

Project 97023 (Alligator River)
Tier 2 Project
First Year Request $130,000, Recurring Request $99,000
Station Rank (Alligator River) - 20
This project will provide the funding to purchase equipment and hire a permanent half-time GS-9 forester and a permanent full-time WG-8 equipment operator to restore bottomland hardwood habitat on 500 acres over a 5-year period. Most of the refuge's bottomland hardwood sites were harvested and planted with pine by prior owners. This project will restore bottomland hardwood habitat by harvesting the pine stands, conducting site preparation, and planting with suitable bottomland hardwood species (e.g., oaks, black gum, and hickories). Once established, these sites will improve wildlife diversity and quality for black bear, tree squirrels, migratory birds, white-tailed deer, and other resident wildlife species. This project will also benefit the refuge's hydrology restoration project.

Project 97025 (Alligator River)
Tier 2 Project
First Year Request $38,000, Recurring Request $3,200
Station Rank (Alligator River) - 11
This project will provide the funding to purchase and maintain a globally positioning system (GPS) base station. The base station is needed for the collection of a variety of resource and facility data points (e.g., red wolf locations, red-cockaded woodpecker colony sites, rare plant or habitat types, roads, canals, pump sites, and private land holdings). However, the collection of "accurate and precise data" is essential for successful resource and maintenance management. Accurate and precise GPS data depends on access to a community base station so that post-processing of field data can be efficiently done.

Project 97028 (Alligator River)
Tier 2 Project
First Year Request $130,000, Recurring Request $98,000
Station Rank (Alligator River) - 19
This project will provide the funding to hire two permanent full-time WG-5 maintenance workers to operate pump stations and water control structures to prevent flooding and properly manage water. Roads and dikes fragment the refuge's 4,500-acre farm unit into a number of smaller fields and moist-soil units. Due to past land clearing practices, the farm unit's elevation is about 1.5 to 2 feet below the surrounding woodlands. During any major storm event, such as hurricanes, or any other period of prolonged rainfall, the farm unit readily floods. Farming and moist-soil management activities, which are ongoing, require a timely response (operation of two large pump stations) to those events. Often, these events are outside the normal working hours and occur over an extended period of time, requiring overtime pay for refuge staff.

Project 97030 (Alligator River)
Tier 2 Project
First Year Request $32,500, Recurring Request $25,000
Station Rank (Alligator River) - 33
This project will provide the funding to hire a permanent half-time GS-5 biological technician to develop and conduct a 3-year study to document white-tailed deer mortality causes. Deer/red wolf interactions are a major concern of the local public. Many hunters and non-hunters are concerned that red wolves are taking a significant portion of the healthy deer population in the area. The study will involve the placement of satellite transmitters on deer to document deer mortality causes and the operation of deer check stations to determine the overall health and condition of the deer herd. Findings will be used to present objective information in order to gain public acceptance of the red wolf project.

Project 97031 (Alligator River)
Tier 2 Project
First Year Request $32,500, Recurring Request $30,000
Station Rank (Alligator River) - 34
This project will provide the funding to hire a permanent half-time GS-7 biologist to coordinate with other agencies on refuge activities. Improved coordination is needed with the following agencies: (1) North Carolina Forest Service on wildfire suppression activities in eastern north Carolina via a cooperative agreement; (2) U.S. Department of Defense on red wolf management, red-cockaded woodpecker management, hydrology restoration, and fire research on the 46,000-acre Dare County Bombing Range (an inholding within the refuge); and the North Carolina Wildlife Resources Commission on law enforcement activities. All of these activities affect the day-to-day operation of the refuge.

Project 97033 (Alligator River)
Tier 2 Project
First Year Request $65,000, Recurring Request $69,000
Station Rank (Alligator River) - 23
This project will provide the funding to hire a permanent full-time GS-9 park ranger to educate Service personnel and the public on the concept of ecosystem management. The refuge's wildlife interpretive specialist developed an outreach plan for the Roanoke–Tar–Neuse–Cape Fear Ecosystem Team. The interpretative specialist will be heavily involved in the training aspect of the plan.

Project 97039 (Pea Island)
Tier 2 Project
First Year Request $65,000, Recurring Request $69,000
Station Rank (Pea Island) - 6
This project will provide the funding to hire a permanent full-time GS-9 assistant manager for the Pea Island Refuge to coordinate and administer a growing permit issuance system. The barrier island location of the refuge results in requests for a significant number of permits on an annual basis. Most of the requests are received from: (1) North Carolina Department of Transportation on maintenance issues for North Carolina Highway 12, which bisects the refuge for 12 miles; (2) the U.S. Army Corps of Engineers on Oregon Inlet maintenance dredging and material disposal on refuge beaches; (3) U.S. Navy for maintenance of communication towers; (4) Dare County for storm damage disposal and public use facilities; and (5) university research permits. These requests must be processed through proper environmental agencies.

Project 97040 (Pea Island)
Tier 2 Project
First Year Request $56,000, Recurring Request $84,000
Station Rank (Pea Island) - 3
This project will provide the funding to hire a permanent full-time GS-9 resource specialist to improve coordination with other agencies. The refuge needs better coordination with: (1) National Park Service on public use management, maintenance, visitor comfort station, and law enforcement via a memorandum of understanding; (2) U.S. Army Corps of Engineers on beach nourishment, maintenance dredging, and Oregon Inlet Jetty; (3) North Carolina Department of Transportation on North Carolina Highway 12 issues, terminal groin, and Oregon Inlet Bridge; and (4) North Carolina Wildlife Resources Commission on waterfowl management and law enforcement. All of these activities affect the day-to-day operation of the refuge.

Project 97041 (Pea Island)
Tier 2 Project
First Year Request $82,000, Recurring Request $49,000
Station Rank (Pea Island) - 2
This project will provide the funding to hire a permanent full-time GS-5 biological technician to conduct biweekly aerial waterfowl surveys from September through March and add or increase other wildlife surveys. The other surveys (e.g., shorebird, piping plover, raptor, sea turtle, colonial waterbird, and neotropical songbird) will use standard census techniques. The project is the only way to gauge the effects of high public use and other refuge management programs on the refuge's wildlife resources. The project will improve management of these resources. The Wildlife Census Plan will be updated and implemented. Pea Island Refuge is a 5,800-acre refuge located on a coastal barrier island that has high public use (2 million visitors annually).

Project 97043 (Pea Island)
Tier 2 Project
First Year Request $32,500, Recurring Request $44,000
Station Rank (Pea Island) - 4
This project will provide the funding to hire a permanent full-time GS-5 biological technician to conduct basic nesting and production surveys on black ducks and gadwalls. The surveys will be conducted to document the effects of management on the two species. Based on the survey results, appropriate management activities will be initiated to improve habitat conditions. Black duck and gadwalls have traditionally nested in low, grassy habitat provided on Pea Island Refuge. However, these habitats have started to succeed to more woody and brushy plant communities.

Project 97045 (Pea Island)
Tier 2 Project
First Year Request $195,000, Recurring Request $213,000
Station Rank (Pea Island) - 1
This project will provide the funding to buy equipment and hire two permanent full-time GS-7 park rangers and two WG-6 maintenance workers to serve visitors and maintain facilities and grounds at Pea Island Refuge. Two interactive computer stations will be installed at the Visitor Center to help meet visitors' requests for basic information. The stations will display multimedia information on all eastern North Carolina refuges, the National Wildlife Refuge System, wildlife resources, and local destinations. A weather and vandal-proof station will be located on the outside of the Visitor Center in order to serve visitor needs during times when the Visitor Center is closed. Approximately 2 million visitors use the refuge annually. Some are just passing through; however, a large number stop at the Visitor Center for a variety of reasons.

Project 97046 (Alligator River)
Tier 2 Project
First Year Request $130,000, Recurring Request $92,000
Station Rank (Alligator River) - 17
This project will provide the funding to hire a permanent full-time GS-11 forester to develop a comprehensive forest management program and improve forest health on the refuge. At present, most of the refuge's forests are in poor health. Exploitive logging, lack of basic forest management, and altered hydrology have resulted in undesirable stages of development. A forest ecologist is needed to prepare and implement the plan to correct these problems. The ecologist will also develop plans for the surrounding refuges (Pocosin Lakes and Roanoke River) with similar forest health problems and will develop partnerships with other local agencies (Department of Defense, North Carolina Forest Service, and the North Carolina Wildlife Resources Commission).

Project 97047 (Alligator River)
Tier 1 Project
First Year Request $39,000, Recurring Request $10,000
Station Rank (Alligator River) - 5
This project will provide the funding to improve and upgrade the refuge's information resource management (IRM) capabilities by connecting all office computers and related equipment (e.g., printers, plotters, file servers, and copiers) into a modern, high capacity local area network (LAN). The project will upgrade the existing computers, add file servers, and improve cable and router systems. The project will improve staff efficiency, productivity, and decision-making by using the many advantages of modern technology to get the latest biological reports, transmit information, respond to inquiries, and expand relationships with internal (Ecological Services Office, Migratory Bird Field Office) and external partners (National Park Service, local and state agencies). The LAN will also link all refuge computers to the office's geographic information system (GIS) computer, which will give staff immediate access to current GIS layers, and to high-speed Internet access. It will also help eliminate the need for duplicate office equipment (e.g., color printers and modems) at each employee's workstation.

Project 97048 (Alligator River)
Tier 2 Project
First Year Request $210,000, Recurring Request $10,000
Station Rank (combined Alligator River and Pea Island) - 13
This project will provide the funding to buy a truck-tractor and lowboy trailer for use in all aspects of the refuge's management and maintenance programs. An additional hauling unit will allow the refuge to conduct public use, fire management, endangered species management, and biological management activities in a more efficient manner.

Project 98001 (Alligator River)
Tier 2 Project
First Year Request $95,000, Recurring Request $79,000
Station Rank (Alligator River) - 8
This project will provide the funding to hire a permanent full-time GS-9 biologist to guide management of prescribed burning in a 1,000-acre prime red-cockaded woodpecker habitat and thousands of acres of other woodpecker habitat. Over the past 4 years, the refuge has struggled with a southern pine beetle infestation of epidemic proportion. Due primarily to the overstocking of most of the pond pine stands and overall poor health of these stands, much of the infestation occurred in endangered red-cockaded woodpecker habitat. Several hundred acres of forest has been killed while thousands more are in need of active management. Burning will not only promote natural regeneration of pond pine in the dead areas, but will also reduce competition from other species.

Project 98002 (Alligator River)
Tier 2 Project
First Year Request $85,000, Recurring Request $69,000
Station Rank (Alligator River) - 5
This project will provide the funding to hire a permanent full-time GS-9 entomologist to monitor southern pine beetle populations. As a direct result of poor forest health, the refuge has struggled with a southern pine beetle infestation of epidemic proportions for the past 5 years. Many infestations are still spreading at accelerated rates and need control buffers installed to stop the spread and to protect forest resources. The buffers will also spread as firelanes, which are needed to conduct prescribed burns in these areas in order to promote natural regeneration of the pond pine stands.

Project 98004 (Alligator River)
Tier 2 Project
First Year Request $80,000, Recurring Request $80,000
Station Rank (combined Alligator River and Pea Island) - 32
This project will provide the funding to rent 3,000 square feet of new office space as recommended by a recent office review. The General Services Administration is negotiating a 5-year contract to include new office space. The refuge staff has increased to more than 35 full-time employees (both permanent and seasonal) and increase seasonally with summer interns and researchers. Increased office space will enhance safety, staff efficiency, and morale.

Project 98003 (Alligator River)
Tier 1 Project
One Time Request $432,000
Station Rank (Alligator River) - 4
This project will provide the funding to conduct a comprehensive cultural resources survey on both the 152,000-acre Alligator River Refuge and the 5,800-acre Pea Island Refuge to identify significant cultural resources. No comprehensive cultural resource evaluations have been conducted on either refuge. Both refuges are located in an area rich in significant prehistoric, Native American, and early European colonial history. The Outer Banks of North Carolina, where Pea Island is located, is called the "Graveyard of the Atlantic" for all the shipwrecks along the barrier islands starting in the 16th century. Roanoke Island and the adjoining mainland, where Alligator River Refuge is located, are the site of the first English Colony in America and the site of the famous "lost Colony." This project is essential to ensure the identification and protection of any potentially significant cultural resources on these two refuges. The survey will be conducted by either contract archaeologists or through agreements with local universities.

Project 98005 (Pea Island)
Tier 2 Project
First Year Request $85,000, Recurring Request $84,000
Station Rank (Pea Island) - 7
This project will provide the funding to hire a permanent full-time biological technician to monitor the Army Corps of Engineers dredging operations and their effects on beach-dependent wildlife (e.g., shorebirds and sea turtles). Oregon Inlet is located at the north end of the refuge, which is a coastal barrier island. This inlet is the only passage through the barrier islands from the Pamlico Sound to the Atlantic Ocean and is used heavily by recreational and commercial fishing boats. The Corps of Engineers conducts intensive dredging operations to maintain the inlet's opening. This has disrupted natural coastal processes, resulting in beach erosion on the refuge. Changes in dredging operations will be recommended, as needed, to protect wildlife resources.

Project 98006 (Alligator River)
Tier 2 Project
First Year Request $40,000, Recurring Request $5,000
Station Rank (Alligator River) - 12
This project will provide the funding to conduct a comprehensive fisheries survey of refuge lakes, streams, and other water bodies (e.g., canals, ditches, and ponds) to help develop a Fishery Management Plan. The survey will include an evaluation of each aquatic habitat and its ability to support fish populations. Service fisheries biologists will conduct the survey and plan. Very little is known about the freshwater fishery resources on the refuge. The highly acidic waters associated with organic soils, and the periodic inflow of brackish waters from surrounding sounds, make for a unique combination of aquatic conditions.

Project 98007 (Alligator River)
Tier 2 Project
First Year Request $130,000, Recurring Request $127,000
Station Rank (Alligator River) - 3
This project will provide the funding to equip and hire three permanent full-time employees (two GS-5 biological technicians and a WG-8 equipment operator) to properly manage and restore 70,000 acres of forested wetlands, maintain 80 to 90 miles of refuge roads, and manipulate associated canals, sometimes on a daily basis. Engineering equipment, tractors, and other equipment are critically needed to ensure reliable operations of water control structures, pump stations, and other facilities.

Project 98008 (Alligator River)
Tier 2 Project
First Year Request $235,000, Recurring Request $10,000
Station Rank (Alligator River) - None
This project will provide the funding to purchase a long-reach tracked excavator for use in all aspects of the refuge's management and maintenance programs. At present, the refuge does not have an excavator that is capable of cleaning out the large canals associated with 80 to 90 miles of primary refuge roads. The new excavator will allow the refuge to conduct public use, fire management, endangered species management, and biological activities in a more efficient manner. The lack of this essential equipment will continue to hinder refuge operations and accomplishment of station objectives.

Project 98009 (Alligator River)
Tier 2 Project
First Year Request $65,000, Recurring Request $59,000
Station Rank (Alligator River) - 26
This project will provide the funding to buy a motor-grader and hire a permanent full-time WG-8 equipment operator. A large grader is needed to support all aspects of the refuge's management and maintenance programs. The refuge has 150 miles of primary and secondary roads. Some of the roads need to be maintained on a daily basis so that refuge operations and public use activities can continue unimpeded. The refuge has an insufficient number of motor-graders to meet the daily road maintenance needs. An additional motor-grader will allow public use, fire management, endangered species management, and biological program activities to be conducted in a more efficient manner.

Project 98010 (Alligator River)
Tier 2 Project
First Year Request $200,000, Recurring Request $3,000
Station Rank (Alligator River) - None
This project will provide the funding to purchase 6 new vehicles to meet the needs of new staff members. New staff members (both permanent and seasonal) have been added in recent years; however, no additional vehicles have been purchased. At least 6 new vehicles are needed to properly support all aspects of the refuge's management and maintenance programs. These vehicles will allow the refuge's public use, fire management, endangered species management, and biological program activities to be conducted in a more efficient manner.

Project 98011 (Alligator River)
Tier 2 Project
First Year Request $65,000, Recurring Request $69,000
Station Rank (Alligator River) - 10
This project will provide the funding to hire a permanent full-time GS-9 park ranger to manage the refuge volunteer program. The current refuge volunteer program documents more than 25,000 volunteer hours annually in support of the biological, maintenance, management, and administrative programs. Adding a volunteer coordinator will meet both the current need and assist in securing additional volunteer services on the refuge. Volunteers perform tasks such as sea turtle patrol, visitor contact duties, environmental talks at schools, boundary signing, and clerical duties.

Project 99001 (Alligator River)
Tier 2 Project
First Year Request $130,000, Recurring Request $118,000
Station Rank (Alligator River) - 27
This project will provide the funding to hire a permanent full-time GS-9 refuge operations specialist and a GS-5 administrative assistant to meet the administrative needs of increased activities. Expanded refuge operations and activities in program areas, such as endangered species management, fire management, biological, public use, visitor services, etc., along with increased administrative tasks, have caused a decrease in overall efficiency in completing administrative functions in a timely manner. To improve refuge operations, these administrative positions are needed. The increased emphasis on ecosystem management and the associated workload makes it necessary to have a multi-disciplined staff.

Project 99002 (Alligator River)
Tier 1 Project
One Time Request $30,000
Station Rank (Alligator River) - 3
This project will provide the funding to restore a minimum of 250,000 acres (over a 20-year period) in 8 types of forested habitats found on 5 national wildlife refuges in the coastal plain of eastern North Carolina and southeastern Virginia. In this area, forest types, such as pine pocosins, maritime forests, Atlantic white cedar, bottomland hardwoods, and cypress-gum swamps, are greatly reduced and degraded from exploitive timbering, land clearing, drainage of wetlands, and commercial development. Water quality will improve as the forest types are restored. Endangered red wolves and red-cockaded woodpeckers, wood ducks, American woodcock, migratory songbirds, and the largest remaining black bear population on the mid-Atlantic coast will greatly benefit from the restored forests. Local ecotourism and timber product businesses will also benefit. The refuge will partner with the Department of Defense (45,000-acre U.S. Air Force/Navy Bombing Range), U.S. Geological Survey, U.S. Forest Service (Croatan National Forest), and the North Carolina Forest Service to accomplish the restoration of these biologically and economically important forest resources.

Project 99003 (Alligator River)
Tier 2 Project
First Year Request $65,000, Recurring Request $82,000
Station Rank (Alligator River) - 22
This project will provide the funding to hire a permanent full-time GS-11 park ranger to provide additional educational opportunities to visitors. The geographic area surrounding the refuge has the North Carolina Aquarium on Roanoke Island, the sailing ship Queen Elizabeth II State Historic Site, Cape Hatteras National Seashore, Fort Raleigh National Historic Site, Wright Brothers National Memorial, Nags Head Woods Nature Preserve, and many other natural and cultural history sites. Hundreds of school groups from a 2- to 4-state radius travel here for school field trips in the spring and fall. During the summer months, more than 7 million people visit the Outer Banks. Families seek and attend educational programs that will entertain and educate their children. There are many opportunities for the Fish and Wildlife Service to be involved with these activities, and get the Service's message to the public.

Project 00003 (Alligator River)
Tier 1 Project
First Year Request $65,000, Recurring Request $74,000
Station Rank (Alligator River) - 2
This project will provide the funding to hire a permanent full-time GS-11 forester to develop, coordinate, and implement a forest management program on the heavily forested 152,000-acre refuge. A 1999 Forest Management Review recommended a variety of needed forest habitat improvements to include restoration of hardwoods and Atlantic white cedar (a globally imperiled species), control of forest pest species, and effective management of fire-dependent pine stands. A forester is essential for preparing and implementing site-specific forest management plans that will improve habitat for endangered species (e.g., red-cockaded woodpecker), migratory birds (e.g., waterfowl and songbirds), and important resident wildlife (e.g., black bear and white-tailed deer) on the refuge. The forester will also prepare and administer numerous contracts that will be used to accomplish forest habitat improvements, especially in the area of Atlantic white cedar regeneration, southern pine beetle control, and the establishment of permanent fire lanes (needed for prescribed fire and wildfire protection). The forester will work with the Department of Defense resource managers on the 46,000-acre Dare County Bombing Range, which is surrounded by the refuge, to help implement a coordinated forest management program.

Project 00007 (Alligator River)
Tier 1 Project
First Year Request $65,000, Recurring Request $53,000
Station Rank (Alligator River) - 1
This project will provide the funding to hire a permanent full-time Gs-7 biological technician to improve water management, wildlife monitoring, and interagency coordination on both the 152,000-acre Alligator River Refuge and the 5,800-acre Pea Island Refuge. Effective water management is essential to restoring the natural hydrology on the Alligator River Refuge, which is heavily dissected by roads, drainage canals, and ditches. It is also essential to the proper management of wetland vegetation in three artificial impoundments on Pea Island Refuge, which benefit thousands of migratory waterfowl and shorebirds. An improved hydrology regime on Alligator River Refuge will benefit a variety of important wildlife species (e.g., endangered red wolf, black bear, waterfowl, and white-tailed deer) through an overall improvement of habitat quality and diversity. On both refuges, the biological technician will monitor water quality and quantity, water gauges, and pumps. The technician will also survey and monitor endangered red-cockaded woodpecker colonies, conduct fish population surveys, band migratory birds, control invasive plant species, and monitor endangered sea turtle nesting activities and marine mammal strandings. The effects of Army Corps of Engineers dredging and disposal activities on Pea Island Refuge would be monitored to compile biological information needed for management decisions concerning controversial issues associated with beach nourishment and shorebird feeding and nesting habitat.

Project 00010 (Alligator River)
Tier 2 Project
First Year Request $85,000, Recurring Request $830,000
Station Rank (Alligator River) - 9
This project will provide the funding to hire 13 permanent full-time employees (2 GS-9 refuge operations specialists; 1 GS-11 biologist; 4 GS-9 resource specialists; 4 GS-7 park rangers; and 2 GS-7 administrative assistants) to meet the needs of activities identified in the comprehensive conservation plan. The planning process will be completed for 11 refuges on northeastern North Carolina. The completed plans will be implemented and require a cadre of talented staff: ascertainment biologist, realty specialist, personnel specialist, technical writer, engineering technician, and management and various administrative support personnel. The legally mandated plan and staff support will help conserve wildlife and provide wildlife-dependent recreation for the public. Approximately 40,000 acres have been designated as a Wilderness Study Area.

Project 00011 (Pea Island)
Tier 2 Project
First Year Request $65,000, Recurring Request $54,000
Station Rank (Pea Island) - 5
This project will provide the funding to hire two permanent half-time employees (a GS-7 biological technician and a WG-5 maintenance worker) to survey and post the islands in Pamlico Sound adjacent to Pea Island Refuge. Approximately 180 acres of roadless islands are proposed for wilderness designation and need to be adequately surveyed or posted. These islands are fragile components of the barrier island refuge. Major legal issues have never been addressed and with the controversy surrounding the Oregon Inlet, Bonner Bridge, and North Carolina Highway 12, these islands will be even more controversial in the future. These islands are extremely important to a myriad of migratory birds and serve as a nursery area for many aquatic species.

Project 00012 (Alligator River)
Tier 2 Project
First Year Request $15,800, Recurring Request $7,000
Station Rank (Alligator River) - 25
This project will provide the funding to conduct an internal outreach program. This internal outreach program is very successful in the regions within the Service. Staff members are trained in customer service, public relations, and media relations. Public service announcements are produced using various staff members. The announcements portray the positive attributes of staff and refuge programs. The team approach in training produces a quality product.

Project 00092 (Pea Island)
Tier 1 Project
First Year Request $65,000, Recurring Request $54,000
Station Rank (Pea Island) - 1
This project will provide the funding to hire a permanent full-time WG-8 maintenance worker to help operate and maintain 4 refuge pump stations, numerous water control structures, and other facilities on the 5,800-acre Pea Island Refuge and the nearby 152,000-acre Alligator River Refuge. The pumps and water control structures are used to regulate the flooding and draining of 3 artificial impoundments on Pea Island Refuge and extensive farm management and moist-soil units on the Alligator River Refuge. Effective water management is essential to restoring natural hydrology, which has been degraded by an extensive system of roads, drainage canals, and ditches, on the Alligator River Refuge. It is also essential to the proper management of wetland vegetation in the intensively managed artificial impoundments on the Pea Island Refuge, which benefit thousands of migratory waterfowl and shorebirds. This maintenance worker is essential to the proper operation, maintenance, and repair of refuge pumps, water control structures, and other facilities (e.g., buildings, grounds, trails, vehicles, and equipment) associated with water management and other refuge operations (e.g., public use, biological, and prescribed fire). The harsh climatic and environmental conditions (e.g., corrosive salt air, hurricanes) associated with northeastern North Carolina make it necessary to have a quality preventive and cyclic maintenance program. Refuge facilities are in need of constant maintenance to increase the life-span and efficiency of all refuge operations.

Project 00094 (Alligator River)
Tier 1 Project
First Year Request $65,000, Recurring Request $74,000
Station Rank (Alligator River) - 6
This project will provide the funding to hire a permanent full-time GS-11 computer specialist to improve automated data processing and geographic information system operations on two refuges: Alligator River and Pea Island. Refuge operations and maintenance decisions must be based on the most reliable, up-to-date information available. The use of modern automated data processing and geographic information system technology will allow the two refuges' staff (about 30 employees at present) to obtain the latest biological information, analyze data, transmit information, respond to inquiries, and communicate with partners. A computer specialist would administer and maintain the program. As fast as computer technology is advancing, the ability to efficiently gather, analyze, and disseminate information and data increases staff efficiency and fosters professional operations.

Project 00095 (Pea Island)
Tier 1 Project
First Year Request $65,000, Recurring Request $74,000
Station Rank (Pea Island) - 3
This project will provide the funding to hire a permanent full-time GS-11 wildlife biologist to expand and enhance the biological monitoring program on the 5,800-acre Pea Island Refuge and the

152,000-acre Alligator River Refuge. The field biologist will assist the senior refuge biologist and one biological technician in coordinating and conducting all wildlife and habitat surveys on the two refuges. Having a field biologist to oversee biological operations will allow the senior wildlife biologist to develop various wildlife and habitat management plans, which would then be implemented by the field biologist. These plans are essential to the proper management of a diverse number of endangered species (e.g., red wolf, red-cockaded woodpecker, piping plover, and loggerhead sea turtle) and other important wildlife species (e.g., bald eagle, American alligator, waterfowl, shorebirds, wading birds, songbirds, black bear, and white-tailed deer) that use these two refuges. Habitat and fisheries surveys, based on approved plans, would also be conducted or coordinated by the wildlife biologists in consultation with Service fishery biologists, foresters, and fire management specialists.

Project 00096 (Pea Island)
Tier 1 Project
First Year Request $65,000, Recurring Request $60,000
Station Rank (Pea Island) - 4
This project will provide the funding to hire a permanent full-time WG-10 heavy equipment mechanic to maintain and repair bulldozers, road graders, draglines, farm equipment, over-the-road truck tractors, fire equipment, front-end loaders, and fixed pump stations on two refuges: the 5,800-acre Pea Island Refuge and 152,000-acre Alligator River Refuge. Currently, the refuges have no staff person qualified to maintain and repair heavy equipment (mostly with diesel engines). A qualified diesel mechanic would improve the overall refuge maintenance operations by reducing equipment downtime and by reducing transportation costs to commercial repair facilities. Also, the life of heavy equipment would be extended through an effective preventive and cyclic maintenance program conducted by this mechanic. A large assortment of construction type heavy equipment is used to maintain the two refuges' infrastructure such as roads (more than 150 miles), dikes, water control structures, trails, and firebreaks. These refuge facilities are heavily used by the visiting public and are necessary for completing many management activities. Having a heavy equipment mechanic to properly maintain a viable fleet of equipment is necessary to support all areas of refuge management.

Project 00098 (Pea Island)
Tier 1 Project
First Year Request $65,000, Recurring Request $58,000
Station Rank (Pea Island) - 2
This project will provide the funding to hire a permanent full-time GS-7 park ranger (law enforcement) to ensure a proactive law enforcement program on this 5,800-acre refuge. At present, 4 dual purpose officers provide reactive visitor safety and resource protection on this refuge and the nearby 152,000-acre Alligator River Refuge. These two refuges host more than 2 million annual visitors, with most visiting Pea Island Refuge. However, visitation and crime is increasing annually on both refuges. Therefore, a full-time refuge officer is needed to provide information to the visiting public (while striving for voluntary compliance) and to protect the refuge's numerous visitors from a more sophisticated criminal element. The officer is needed to protect the two refuge's significant wildlife resources, such as black bear (the largest concentration of black bears on the mid-Atlantic coast) and the endangered red wolf on Alligator River Refuge, and endangered sea turtles and piping plovers that nest on Pea Island Refuge. The poaching of other important wildlife (e.g., diamond-backed turtle, white-tailed deer, timber rattlesnake, and yellow-spotted turtle), illegal collecting of cultural and historic resources (e.g., Native American artifacts), and vandalizing of refuge facilities, equipment, and signs would be reduced. The refuge officer will work closely with various local, state, and federal law enforcement agencies (Department of Defense) to improve the coordination and efficiency of law enforcement operations in the vicinity of both refuges.

Project 00099 (Pea Island)
Tier 1 Project
First Year Request $65,000, Recurring Request $74,000
Station Rank (combined Alligator River and Pea Island) - 5
This project will provide the funding to hire a permanent full-time GS-11 park ranger (wildlife interpretive specialist) to plan, design, and coordinate wildlife exhibits, trails, and special events. Over 2 million visitors use Pea Island Refuge and the nearby Alligator River Refuge annually, and the number of visitors is increasing every year. A wildlife interpretive specialist is needed to meet the increasing demand for quality environmental education and wildlife interpretation facilities, programs, and events on the two refuges. Day-to-day public use operations and activities need to be directed at a professional level, which this position will accomplish. The wildlife interpretive specialist will also coordinate the operation of the refuge Visitor Center, environmental education and interpretation programs, and large volunteer program (e.g., regular volunteers from the community, college interns, and workampers). This position will provide the proper oversight and coordination of these programs and an active friends group (Coastal Wildlife Refuge Society).

Project 02001 (Alligator River)
Tier 2 Project
First Year Request $65,000, Recurring Request $69,000
Station Rank (Alligator River) - 2
This project will provide the funding to hire a permanent full-time GS-9 refuge operations specialist to serve as a safety/environmental compliance coordinator and asset manager. The position will meet ever-increasing demands for environmental protection and assurance of a safe visitor experience and employee work environment. This position will serve as the station's safety officer and be responsible for conducting periodic safety inspections, identifying safety issues, managing all safety documentation, and conducting safety meetings. Refuge environmental audits and compliance implementation will be coordinated through this position. The individual will be responsible for managing real property inventory and personal property databases and managing the stations' Service Asset and Maintenance Management System (SAMMS) computerized maintenance management software application to track maintenance maintenance expenditures, capture maintenance needs, quantify maintenance activities, and report maintenance accomplishments. The position will serve both the Alligator River and Pea Island Refuges.

Project 03000 (Alligator River)
Tier 1 Project
First Year Request $65,000, Recurring Request $71,000
Station Rank (Alligator River) - None
This project will provide the funding to hire a permanent full-time GS-9 park ranger to serve as a law enforcement officer. With the Department's mandated reduction in dual purpose law enforcement officers, this refuge will have a lack of law enforcement presence. By providing an additional refuge officer to fill the void, the safety of the visiting public will be increased, as well as our ability to provide much needed protection for refuge natural resources and facilities. The addition of a full-time officer will provide a position whose primary responsibility is protecting the resource. Officer presence, surveillance, and visitor contacts are important to visitor safety and are critical to reducing crime on the refuge.

Project 04001 (Alligator River)
Tier 2 Project
First Year Request $330,000, Recurring Request $41,000
Station Rank (Alligator River) - 24
This project will provide the funding to construct new refuge residences, a "duplex" (in one structure) that has two units (sides), each with 1,500-1,600 square feet. The estimated total cost is $250,000. The justification is the lack of affordable housing in the area for permanent full-time entry-level employees. The high cost of housing (e.g., rentals and sales) negatively affects the refuge's ability to attract the "best and brightest" to the Service in this area. The project includes costs for initial construction and long-term maintenance (including a staff position).

			Cost		
			Tier 1 Refuge Operation Needs System (RONS) Projects (Projects that address critical mission criteria) (Both refuges' projects are listed because most projects are shared and benefit both refuges)		
Refuge	**Number**	**Rank**	**First Year, Recurring, Total First Year**	**FTE**	**Description**
PINWR	00092	1	65K,54K,119K	1.0	Restore and manage important wetlands (maintenance worker).
PINWR	00098	2	65K,58K,123K	1.0	Improve resource and visitor protection (park ranger-enforcement).
PINWR	00095	3	65K,74K,139K	1.0	Expand biological monitoring programs (wildlife biologist).
PINWR	00096	4	65K,60K,125K	1.0	Improve equipment maintenance and repair (heavy equipment mechanic).
PINWR	00099	5	65K,74K,139K	1.0	Enhance public education and outreach programs (park ranger-interpretation).
PINWR	00094	6	65K,74K,139K	1.0	Provide improved computer support (computer specialist).
ARNWR	00007	1	65K,53K,118K	1.0	Improve biological data collection and water management (biological technician).
ARNWR	00003	2	65K,74K,139K	1.0	Implement a comprehensive forest management program (forester).
ARNWR	99002	3	30K,0K,30K	0.0	Restore the ecosystem's coastal plain forests.
ARNWR	98003	4	432K,0K,432K	0.0	Identify and protect cultural resources.
ARNWR	97047	5	39K,10K,49K	0.0	Improve information resource management.

PINWR = Pea Island National Wildlife Refuge
ARNWR = Alligator River National Wildlife Refuge
Project numbers have the fiscal year the project was developed as the first two numbers.

Tier 2 Refuge Operation Needs System (RONS) Projects (Projects that address critical mission criteria) (Both refuges' projects are listed because most projects are shared and benefit both refuges)					
Refuge	Number	Rank	Cost First Year, Recurring, Total First Year	FTE	Description
PINWR	97045	1	195K,213K,408K	4.0	Enhance visitor services and education (park rangers, maintenance workers).
PINWR	97041	2	82K,49K,131K	1.0	Expand wildlife monitoring surveys (biological technician).
PINWR	97040	3	56K,84K,140K	1.0	Improve coordination with other resource and public use agencies (resource specialist).
PINWR	97043	4	32.5K,44K,76.5K	1.0	Improve waterfowl nesting and production surveys (biological technician).
PINWR	00011	5	65K,54K,119K	1.0	Roadless proposed wilderness designations (biological technician, maintenance worker).
PINWR	97039	6	65K,69K,134K	1.0	Improve administration and coordination of special uses (refuge operations specialist).
PINWR	98005	7	85K,84K,169K	1.0	Monitor Oregon inlet dredging operations (biological technician).
ARNWR	97022	1	85K,15K,100K	0.0	Reduce or eradicate invasive "Phragmites" pest plant
ARNWR	02001	2	65K,69K,134K	1.0	Improve safety, environmental compliance, and asset management (assistant manager-facilities)
ARNWR	98007	3	130K,127K,257K	3.0	Improve wetland management and restoration capabilities.
ARNWR	97004	4	595K,551K,1146K	9.0	Improve protection and management of refuge resources with fire management
ARNWR	98002	5	85K,69K,154K	1.0	Control southern pine beetle infestations (entomologist).
ARNWR	97021	6	100K,138K,238K	2.0	Restore hydrology on forested wetlands

PINWR = Pea Island National Wildlife Refuge
ARNWR = Alligator River National Wildlife Refuge
Project numbers have the fiscal year the project was developed as the first two numbers.

Refuge	Number	Rank	Cost First Year, Recurring, Total First Year	FTE	Description
Tier 2 Refuge Operation Needs System (RONS) Projects (continued) (Projects that address critical mission criteria) (Both refuges' projects are listed because most projects are shared and benefit both refuges)					
ARNWR	97006	7	40K,49K,89K	1.0	Improve water level management on forested wetlands (biological technician).
ARNWR	98001	8	95K,79K,174K	1.0	Restore red-cockaded woodpecker habitat in pond pine stands (biologist).
ARNWR	00010	9	85K,830K,915K	13.0	Implement comprehensive conservation planning.
ARNWR	98011	10	65K,69K,134K	1.0	Improve volunteer coordination (park ranger).
ARNWR	97025	11	38K,3.2K,43.2K	0.0	Improve resource management data collection
ARNWR	98006	12	40K,5K,45K	0.0	Improve fisheries management capabilities.
ARNWR	97048	13	210K,10K,220K	0.0	Improve resource management and maintenance operations.
ARNWR	99004	14	48K,0K,48K	0.0	Environmental contaminants study – Dare County Landfill
ARNWR	97007	15	60K,5K,65K	0.0	Improve resource management planning
ARNWR	97010	16	40K,10K,50K		Improve water quality monitoring capabilities
ARNWR	97046	17	130,92K,223K	1.0	Improve health of forest resources (forester).
ARNWR	97005	18	162.5K,182K, 344.5K	3.0	Enhance natural regeneration of Atlantic white cedar
ARNWR	97028	19	130K,98K,228K	2.0	Improve water level management during flood events (maintenance workers).
ARNWR	97023	20	130K,99K,229K	1.5	Restore bottomland hardwoods
ARNWR	97003	21	32.5K,35K,67.5K	0.5	Expand wildlife and plant monitoring surveys (wildlife biologist).
ARNWR	99003	22	65K,82K,147K	1.0	Improve public outreach and education activities (park ranger).

PINWR = Pea Island National Wildlife Refuge
ARNWR = Alligator River National Wildlife Refuge
Project numbers have the fiscal year the project was developed as the first two numbers.

Refuge	Number	Rank	Cost First Year, Recurring, Total First Year	FTE	Description
			Tier 2 Refuge Operation Needs System (RONS) Projects (continued) (Projects that address critical mission criteria) (Both refuges' projects are listed because most projects are shared and benefit both refuges)		
ARNWR	97033	23	65K,69K,134K	1.0	Improve public outreach on ecosystem management (park ranger).
ARNWR	04001	24	330K,41K,371K	0.0	Provide entry level employee housing.
ARNWR	00012	25	15.8K,7K,22.8K	0.0	Implement Ambassador Program.
ARNWR	98009	26	65K,59K,124K	1.0	Improve resource management and maintenance operations (motor-grader)(equipment operator).
ARNWR	99001	27	130K,118K,248K	2.0	Improve administrative support (refuge operations specialist), administrative assistant).
ARNWR	97001	28	32.5K,25K,57.5K	0.5	Improve endangered species monitoring program (biological technician).
ARNWR	97011	29	65K,59K,124K	1.0	Improve water level management in moist-soil/farm units (biological technician).
ARNWR	97018	30	65K,49K,114K	1.0	Improve management of moist-soil units (equipment operator).
ARNWR	97002	31	32.5K,30K,62.5K	0.5	Monitor neotropical bird populations (biological technician).
ARNWR	98004	32	80K,80K,160K	0.0	Increase refuge office space.
ARNWR	97030	33	32.5K,25K,57.5K	0.5	Conduct deer mortality study relative to the reintroduction of the red wolf (biological technician).
ARNWR	97031	34	32.5K,30K,62.5K	0.5	Improve coordination with other resource agencies (biological technician).
ARNWR	03000	99	65K,71K,136K	1.0	Provide refuge officer (park ranger).

PINWR = Pea Island National Wildlife Refuge
ARNWR = Alligator River National Wildlife Refuge
Project numbers have the fiscal year the project was developed as the first two numbers.

Tier 2 Refuge Operation Needs System (RONS) Projects (continued) (Projects that address critical mission criteria) (Both refuges' projects are listed because most projects are shared and benefit both refuges)						
			Cost			
Refuge	Number	Rank	First Year, Recurring, Total First Year	FTE	Description	
ARNWR	98008	99	235K,10K,245K	0.0	Improve resource management and maintenance operations (excavator).	
ARNWR	98010	99	200K,3K,203K	0.0	Improve resource management and maintenance operations (vehicle fleet).	
PINWR = Pea Island National Wildlife Refuge ARNWR = Alligator River National Wildlife Refuge Project numbers have the fiscal year the project was developed as the first two numbers.						

MAINTENANCE MANAGEMENT SYSTEM (MMS) PROJECTS

Project Number	Project Name	Year Planned	Cost	Combined Station Rank (Pea Island Rank)	Station Name
Pea Island Projects					
98014	Replace John Deere 4240 Tractor		**$164,000**	8(2)	Pea Island
98021	Replace South Pond Pumping Station	2008	$388,000	39(7)	Pea Island
98057	Replace 1960 Office, Shop, Garage, and Residence	2010	$800,000	20(4)	Pea Island
00007	Replace Storm Damaged Water Control Structure	2009	$301,000		Pea Island
01046	Replace North Pond Pump Station	2008	$474,000		Pea Island
01047	Replace New Field Pump Station	2008	$479,000	53(8)	Pea Island
03001	Transportation Planning for CCPs	2007	$261,000		Pea Island
04001	Replace Damaged Bulkhead That Protects the North Pond Impoundments (West Side)	2009	$61,000	26(5)	Pea Island
04089	Repair/ Rehabilitate New Inlet Parking Area		$39,000		Pea Island
04090	Repair/ Rehabilitate (New Inlet) Kiosk Parking Area		$27,000		Pea Island
04091	Repair/ Rehabilitate Visitor Center – Wildlife Trail Parking Area		$194,000		Pea Island
04092	Repair/ Rehabilitate Pea Island Parking #2		$131,000		Pea Island

Project Number	Project Name	Year Planned	Cost	Combined Station Rank (Pea Island Rank)	Station Name
Pea Island Projects					
04093	Repair/ Rehabilitate Pea Island (Salt Flats) Parking #5		$66,000		Pea Island
04094	Repair/ Rehabilitate Pea Island Parking #6, #5, #4, North Kiosk, and Visitor Center/Wildlife trail Parking Areas		$62,000		Pea Island
04095	Repair/ Rehabilitate North Kiosk Parking		$34,000		Pea Island
04096	Repair/ Rehabilitate Pea Island Parking #8 (Oregon Inlet)		$57,000		Pea Island
97008	Construct Visitor Center and Administrative Office Complex	2011	$3,724,000	9(7)	Alligator River
98007	Replace Worn Shaft Bearings on Laurel Bay Waterfowl Pumps	2008	$50,000	60(52)	Alligator River
98010	Replace Military Truck Tractor		$104,000		Alligator River
98011	Replace Ford 545 Mowing Tractor		$55,000	41(34)	Alligator River
98012	Replace Secondary Refuge Road System	2008	$125,000	34(29)	Alligator River
98013	Replace Timer Equipment Trailer		$53,000	36(30)	Alligator River
98025	Rehabilitate Primary Refuge Road System	2009	$283,000	33(28)	Alligator River
98029	Replace Mowers		$274,000	50(42)	Alligator River
98030	Rehabilitate Primary Canal System	2007	$164,000	30(25)	Alligator River

Project Number	Project Name	Year Planned	Cost	Combined Station Rank (Pea Island Rank)	Station Name
Pea Island Projects					
98032	Replace 1978 D3 crawler Tractor		$136,000	49(41)	Alligator River
98037	Replace Ford 6610 Mowing Tractor		$88,000	43(36)	Alligator River
98039	Replace 15-Ton Crane and 10-Ton Forklift		$120,000	14(11)	Alligator River
98041	Replace Workhorse Equipment Transport Trailer		$71,000	57(49)	Alligator River
98042	Replace John Deere 644G Front-end Loader		$186,000		Alligator River
98044	Replace Catepillar D6H Crawler Tractor		$235,000		Alligator River
98045	Replace Catepillar EL200B Excavator		$238,000	29(24)	Alligator River
98046	Replace John Deere 770B Road Grader		$230,000		Alligator River
98047	Replace Boat, Motor and Trailer		$55,000		Alligator River
98048	Replace Refuge Road Gates	2007	$31,000	37(31)	Alligator River
98065	Replace Worn Shaft Bearings on Creek Waterfowl Impoundment Pumps	2008	$32,000	59(51)	Alligator River
99001	Replace Nodwell Flex Tracked Vehicle		$82,000	44(37)	Alligator River
99002	Replace Refuge Radio System	2002			Alligator River
99005	Replace Allis Chalmers Front End Loader		$164,000	24(20)	Alligator River
99006	Replace ford L9000 Dump Truck		$120,000	47(40)	Alligator River
99007	Repair Parking Area Surface	2008	$43,000	21(40)	Alligator River

Project Number	Project Name	Year Planned	Cost	Combined Station Rank (Pea Island Rank)	Station Name
Pea Island Projects					
99009	Replace Air Boat		$39,000	38(32)	Alligator River
99011	Replace Spryte Thiokol Marsh Buggy		$110,000	45(38)	Alligator River
01001	Remove Military Facility Structures	2008	$32,000	42(35)	Alligator River
01007	Replace 1994 Ford Truck Tractor		$105,000	46(39)	Alligator River
01010	Replace 1996 Ford L9000 Truck Tractor Hauling Unit		$105,000		Alligator River
01024	Replace 1997 Ford F350 Crewcab Pickup (Fire)		$38,000		Alligator River
01028	Replace Worn 1988 IHC Truck Tractor		$105,000	16(13)	Alligator River
01029	Replace 1979 Osh Kosh Truck Tractor and Trailer		$169,000	15(12)	Alligator River
01030	Replace 1997 Ford Explorer		$31,000		Alligator River
01031	Replace Flex Tracked Fire Fighting Tractor (AX4)		$185,000	51(43)	Alligator River
01032	Replace Flex Tracked Fire Fighting Tractor (AX2)		$233,000	32(27)	Alligator River
01032	Replace Flex Tracked Fire Fighting Tractor (AX2)		$233,000	32(27)	Alligator River
01033	Replace Full Tracked Fire Fighting Tractor (AX6)		$233,000	53(45)	Alligator River
01034	Replace Trailer Mounted Pump Unit Engine (Gator 1)		$21,000	10(8)	Alligator River

Project Number	Project Name	Year Planned	Cost	Combined Station Rank (Pea Island Rank)	Station Name
Pea Island Projects					
01035	Replace Trailer Mounted Pump Unit engine (Gator 2)		$21,000	13(10)	Alligator River
01036	Replace Trailer Mounted 16" Water Pump (Pump 1)		$10,000	12(9)	Alligator River
01037	Replace Trailer Mounted 16" Water Pump (Pump 2)		$10,000	17(14)	Alligator River
01038	Replace Heavy Equipment Transport Trailer (Witzco)		$53000	54(46)	Alligator River
01039	Replace Heavy Equipment Transport Trailer (Boaz)		$53,000	55(47)	Alligator River
01040	Replace Ford 8260 Agricultural Tractor		$58,000		Alligator River
01041	Replace Military Excess Bucyrus Erie Dragline		$287,000	19(16)	Alligator River
01042	Replace Worn Ford 6640 Boomaxe Agricultural Tractor		$79,000	58(50)	Alligator River
01043	Replace Fully Tracked Firefighting (Tractor) Equipment (AX5)		$233,000	52(44)	Alligator River
01048	Replace Military Pettibone Forklift		$169,000	31(26)	Alligator River
02001	Replace 1998 Ford Taurus		$27,000		Alligator River
02003	Replace 1999 Ford F-150		$29,000		Alligator River
02004	Replace 1999 Ford F-150		$29,000		Alligator River
02005	Replace 1999 Chevy C-7500 Dump Truck		$42,000		Alligator River
02006	Replace 2001 Dodge 2500		$29,000		Alligator River

Project Number	Project Name	Year Planned	Cost	Combined Station Rank (Pea Island Rank)	Station Name
Pea Island Projects					
02007	Replace 2001 Dodge 2500		$29,000		Alligator River
02008	Replace 2001 Dodge 2500		$29,000		Alligator River
02009	Replace 2000 Chevy Tahoe		$31,000		Alligator River
02013	Replace 2001 Ford F-150		$29,000		Alligator River
02014	Replace 2001 Ford F-150		$29,000		Alligator River
02015	Replace 2002 Ford F-150		$29,000		Alligator River
02016	Replace 2002 Ford F-150		$29,000		Alligator River
02017	Replace 2002 Ford F-150		$29,000		Alligator River
02018	Replace 2002 Ford F-150		$29,000		Alligator River
02019	Replace 2002 Sterling L-9500		$99,000		Alligator River
02020	Replace 2002 LE Dodge LE 1500		$29,000		Alligator River
02021	Replace 2002 Ford Expedition		$31,000		Alligator River
02024	Replace 2002 Ford F-450		$47,000		Alligator River
02025	Replace Allis Chalmers Forklift		$42,000	40(33)	Alligator River
02026	Replace Catepillar D3C LGP		$73,000		Alligator River
02027	Replace Case 4X4 Front End Loader		$167,000		Alligator River
02029	Replace Dresser TD12 LGP Dozer		$188,000		Alligator River
02030	Replace Trail King Dump Trailer		$42,000		Alligator River
02031	Replace Ford 8160 Agricultural Tractor		$84,000		Alligator River
02032	Replace Ford 8830 Agricultural Tractor		$94,000		Alligator River
02034	Replace Fontaine Low Boy Trailer		$63,000		Alligator River

Project Number	Project Name	Year Planned	Cost	Combined Station Rank (Pea Island Rank)	Station Name
Pea Island Projects					
02035	Replace John Deere 4100 Mowing Tractor		$16,000		Alligator River
02036	Replace John Deere 5400 Mowing Tractor		$31,000		Alligator River
02037	Replace Terez D7F Dozer		$261,000		Alligator River
02038	Replace 45' Bridge Trailer		$31,000		Alligator River
02040	Construct Red Wolf Processing Facility		$131,000	2(2)	Alligator River
02043	Construct Two HAZMAT Storage Buildings		$60,000	1(1)	Alligator River
02044	Construct Biological Program Storage Building		$40,000	3(3)	Alligator River
02128	Replace champion 710A Road grader		$136,000	25(21)	Alligator River
03	Replace Worn/ Deteriorated 2002 Ford F-250				Alligator River
03001	Replace Hyster Forklift		$26,000	23(19)	Alligator River
03002	Replace Worn 2002 Ford Explorer		$31,000		Alligator River
03003	Replace Worn 2002 Ford Explorer		$31,000		Alligator River
03005	Replace Worn 2003 F-150		$31,000		Alligator River
03008	Replace 21' Boston Whaler		$63,000		Alligator River
03009	Replace Water Tender Truck (Tanker)		$73,000		Alligator River
03011	Replace 2 Worn Creef Pump Engines		$94,000	27(22)	Alligator River
03012	Replace 2 Worn Laurel Bay Pump Engines		$94,000	28(23)	Alligator River

Project Number	Project Name	Year Planned	Cost	Combined Station Rank (Pea Island Rank)	Station Name
Pea Island Projects					
03013	Replace Stockpile of Aggregate Road Maintenance Material	2006	$84,000	6(6)	Alligator River
03014	Rehabilitate Station heliport		$29,000	56(48)	Alligator River
03015	Replace Laurel Bay pump Vehicular Crossing		$235,000	18(15)	Alligator River
03017	Replace Worn Catepillar 420D Backhoe/Loader		$84,000		Alligator River
04002	Replace 2004 Ford F150		$30,000		Alligator River
04003	Replace 2004 Ford F650 Service Truck		$62,000		Alligator River
04004	Replace 2004 Ford F650 Service Truck (Fire)		$62,000		Alligator River
04005	Replace 2004 Ford F150 Crew Cab		$30,000		Alligator River
04006	Replace 2004 Ford F150 Crew Cab		$30,000		Alligator River
04007	Replace 2004 Ford Expedition (Fire)		$36,000		Alligator River
04008	Replace 2003 Ford F150		$30,000		Alligator River
04009	Replace 2004 Ford Expedition		$36,000		Alligator River
04011	Replace Worn CAT 320 Long Reach Excavator		$180,000		Alligator River
04097	Replace 2004 Ford F150 Pickup		$30,000		Alligator River
04098	Replace 2004 Ford F150 Pickup		$30,000		Alligator River

Appendix IX. Consultation and Coordination

The Service formed a planning core team composed of representatives from various Service divisions to prepare the Draft Comprehensive Conservation Plan and Environmental Assessment. The members of this planning core team are identified in the following table. Initially, the team focused on identifying the issues and concerns pertinent to refuge management. The team met on several occasions from March to June 2000.

In addition, a biological review team met on the refuges in the ecosystem four times between December 1999 and December 2000 to assess the habitats on the refuges and the needs of wildlife species in the ecosystem, and make recommendations on land management and acquisition needs. The second table lists the members of this biological review team.

Throughout the planning process, the core team also sought the contributions of experts from various fields (third table).

Pea Island National Wildlife Refuge Planning Core Team members

Member	Affiliation
Mike Bryant, Project Leader Scott Lanier, Deputy Project Leader Kathy Whaley, Former Deputy Project Leader John Wallace, Former Deputy Project Leader Jim Wigginton, Assistant Manager Dennis Stewart, Wildlife Biologist Thomas Crews, Fire Management Officer Bonnie Strawser, Supervisory Interpretive Specialist Ann Marie Salewski, Wildlife Interpretive Specialist Kim King-Wrenn, Former Wildlife Interpretive Specialist	Pea Island National Wildlife Refuge Fish and Wildlife Service Manteo, North Carolina
Robert Glennon, Natural Resource Planner David Brown, Former Habitat Protection Biologist	Ecosystem Planning Office Fish and Wildlife Service Edenton, North Carolina

Biological Review Team members, Pea Island National Wildlife Refuge

Member	Affiliation
Bob Noffsinger, Former Supervisory Wildlife Management Biologist	Migratory Bird Field Office Fish and Wildlife Service Manteo, North Carolina
Frank Bowers, Former Migratory Bird Coordinator	Southeast Regional Office Fish and Wildlife Service Atlanta, Georgia
Chuck Hunter, Former Nongame Migratory Bird Coordinator	Southeast Regional Office Fish and Wildlife Service Atlanta, Georgia
Ronnie Smith, Fisheries Biologist	Fisheries Assistance Office Fish and Wildlife Service Edenton, North Carolina
John Stanton, Former Wildlife Biologist	Mattamuskeet National Wildlife Refuge Fish and Wildlife Service Swan Quarter, North Carolina
Wendy Stanton, Wildlife Biologist	Pocosin Lakes National Wildlife Refuge Fish and Wildlife Service Columbia, North Carolina
Dennis Stewart, Wildlife Biologist	Alligator River National Wildlife Refuge Fish and Wildlife Service Manteo, North Carolina
Ralph Keel, Former Wildlife Biologist	Great Dismal Swamp National Wildlife Refuge Fish and Wildlife Service Suffolk, Virginia
John Gallegos, Wildlife Biologist	Back Bay National Wildlife Refuge Fish and Wildlife Service Virginia Beach, Virginia
David Allen, Nongame Wildlife Biologist	North Carolina Wildlife Resources Commission New Bern, North Carolina

Expert contributors to the Pea Island National Wildlife Refuge Comprehensive Conservation Plan and their area(s) of expertise

Name	Field of Expertise
Bill Grabill, Former Refuge Supervisor Fish and Wildlife Service, Refuges Southeast Regional Office, Atlanta, Georgia	Refuge Management
Bruce Bell, Former NEPA Specialist Fish and Wildlife Service, Refuges Southeast Regional Office, Atlanta, Georgia	National Environmental Policy Act (NEPA) Requirements
John Ann Shearer, Private Lands Biologist Fish and Wildlife Service, Ecological Services Raleigh, North Carolina	Waterfowl Management, Refuge Management
Richard Kanaski, Regional Archeologist Fish and Wildlife Service Savannah, Georgia	Cultural Resources

Appendix X. Finding of No Significant Impact

Introduction

The U.S. Fish and Wildlife Service proposes to protect and manage certain fish and wildlife resources in Dare and Hyde Counties, North Carolina, within the Pea Island National Wildlife Refuge. An Environmental Assessment has been prepared to inform the public of the possible environmental consequences of implementing the Comprehensive Conservation Plan for Pea Island National Wildlife Refuge. A description of the alternatives, the rationale for selecting the preferred alternative, the environmental effects of the preferred alternative, the potential adverse effects of the action, and a declaration concerning the factors determining the significance of effects, in compliance with the National Environmental Policy Act of 1969, are outlined below. The supporting information can be found in the Environmental Assessment.

Alternatives

In developing the Comprehensive Conservation Plan for Pea Island National Wildlife Refuge, the Fish and Wildlife Service evaluated five alternatives:

The Service adopted Alternative 2, the "Preferred Alternative," as the comprehensive conservation plan for guiding the direction of the refuge for the next 15 years. The overriding concern reflected in this plan is that wildlife conservation assumes first priority in refuge management; wildlife-dependent recreational uses are allowed if they are compatible with wildlife conservation. Wildlife-dependent recreation uses (e.g., hunting, fishing, wildlife observation, wildlife photography, and environmental education and interpretation) will be emphasized and encouraged.

Alternative 1. No Action Alternative

Alternative 1 represents no change from current management of the refuge. Under this alternative, the Service would continue to protect 5,000 acres of refuge lands for resident wildlife, waterfowl, migratory birds, and threatened and endangered species. The staff would direct all refuge management actions towards achieving the refuge's primary purposes (conserving habitat for migratory and breeding shorebirds, colonial nesting birds, marsh birds, other wildlife, and helping to meet the habitat conservation goals of the North American Waterfowl Management Plan), while contributing to other national, regional, and state goals to protect and restore populations of migratory birds, anadromous fish, and other wildlife.

The staff manages impoundments based on its knowledge of migration patterns, the needs of migrating birds, its knowledge of vegetation growth in response to water depth timing of inundation, and vegetation surveys. It manages marshes with prescribed fire with no survey data on the effects of the burning on the habitat or wildlife populations. The staff currently performs intensive monitoring of sea turtles, waterfowl, wading birds, shorebirds and colonial nesting birds, including piping plovers. Staff members assist other agencies and researchers with other surveys, but perform no others on their own. The staff will maintain active habitat management of marshes and impoundments for moist-soil vegetation and mudflats designed to provide a diverse complex that meets the foraging, resting, and breeding requirements for a variety of species.

The refuge would maintain the current level of wildlife-dependent recreation activities (e.g., fishing, wildlife observation, and environmental education and interpretation opportunities). The refuge's two trails associated with the North Pond and a service road that encircles the same pond for visitor access would be maintained and remain open to the public. The staff would maintain the current wildlife observation sites/platforms and interpretive kiosks. The refuge would continue to evaluate wildlife populations and consider hunting opportunities, if the situation warranted a hunt. It would permit fishing (50,000 annual visitors) along the shorelines of the Atlantic Ocean, Oregon Inlet, and Pamlico Sounds and the banks of the ditches. The staff would continue to conduct extensive environmental education (1,500 annual students on refuge and 1,000 annual students off refuge), interpretive (1.1 million annual visitors) and outreach (annual audience of 5 million) programs and would promote them.

Alternative 2.
The preferred alternative, Alternative 2, is considered to be the most effective management action for meeting the purposes of the refuge by representing a modest improvement in programs with an emphasis on biological and public use. Under this alternative, the Service would protect 5,000 acres of refuge lands for resident wildlife, waterfowl, migratory birds, and threatened and endangered species. The staff would direct all refuge management actions towards achieving the refuge's primary purposes (conserving habitat for migratory and breeding shorebirds, colonial nesting birds, marsh birds, other wildlife, and helping to meet the habitat conservation goals of the North American Waterfowl Management Plan), while contributing to other national, regional, and state goals to protect and restore populations of migratory birds, anadromous fish, and other wildlife.

The staff would continue to develop and implement most refuge management based on databases on primary production in impoundments, waterfowl, wading birds, shorebirds, and sea turtles. The staff would manage impoundments based on its knowledge of migration patterns, the needs of migrating birds, its knowledge of vegetation growth in response to water depth timing of inundation, and vegetation surveys. It would manage marshes with prescribed fire with no survey data on the effects of the burning on the habitat or wildlife populations. The staff would continue to perform intensive monitoring of sea turtles, waterfowl, wading birds, shorebirds, and colonial nesting birds, including piping plovers. It would assist other agencies and researchers with other surveys, but would also survey fish and land birds, and document the presence of invertebrates, reptiles and amphibians on their own. The staff would increase the acres of active habitat management through the management of marshes and impoundments for moist-soil vegetation and mudflats designed to provide a diverse complex that meets the foraging, resting, and breeding requirements for a variety of species.

The refuge would increase its capacity to provide wildlife-dependent recreation activities (e.g., fishing, wildlife observation, and environmental education and interpretation opportunities). The refuge would still have two trails associated with North Pond and the service road that encircles the pond for visitor access. The staff would maintain the current wildlife observation sites/platforms, and interpretive kiosks. The refuge would still continue to evaluate wildlife populations and consider hunting opportunities, if the situation warranted a hunt. It would permit fishing (50,000 annual visitors) along the shorelines of the Atlantic Ocean, Oregon Inlet, and Pamlico Sound and the banks of the ditches; and would promote those opportunities more. The staff would conduct more extensive environmental education (3,000 annual students on refuge and 2,000 annual students off refuge), interpretive (1.4 million visitors) and outreach (annual audience of 10 million) programs to serve a larger audience and would promote them more.

Alternative 3.
The primary focus under Alternative 3 would be a substantial improvement in both the biological and public use programs. Under this alternative, the Service would protect 5,000 acres of refuge lands for resident wildlife, waterfowl, migratory birds, and threatened and endangered species. Most refuge management programs would continue to be developed and implemented with substantial baseline biological information. The staff would direct all refuge management actions towards achieving the

refuge's primary purposes (conserving habitat for migratory and breeding shorebirds, colonial nesting birds, marsh birds, other wildlife, and helping to meet the habitat conservation goals of the North American Waterfowl Management Plan), while contributing to other national, regional, and state goals to protect and restore populations of migratory birds, anadromous fish, and other wildlife.

The staff would continue to perform intensive monitoring of sea turtles, waterfowl, wading birds, shorebirds, and colonial nesting birds, including piping plovers. It would assist other agencies and researchers with other surveys, but would also survey fish, invertebrates, land birds, reptiles, and amphibians on their own. The staff manages impoundments based on its knowledge of migration patterns, the needs of migrating birds, its knowledge of vegetation growth in response to water depth timing of inundation, and vegetation surveys. It would manage marshes with prescribed fire and survey data on the effects of the burning on the habitat or wildlife populations. The staff would survey all the habitats on the refuge on a regular basis. The staff would increase the acres of active habitat management through the management of marshes and impoundments for moist-soil vegetation and mudflats designed to provide a diverse complex of habitats that meets the foraging, resting, and breeding requirements for a variety of species.

The refuge would increase its capacity to provide wildlife-dependent recreation activities (e.g., fishing, wildlife observation, and environmental education and interpretation opportunities) even more than in Alternative 2. The refuge would still have two trails associated with North Pond and the service road that encircles the pond for visitor access. The staff would maintain the current wildlife observation sites/platforms, and interpretive kiosks. The refuge would continue to evaluate wildlife populations and consider hunting opportunities, if the situation warranted a hunt. It would permit fishing (50,000 annual visitors) along the shorelines of the Atlantic Ocean, Oregon Inlet, and Pamlico Sound and the banks of the ditches; and would promote those opportunities more. The staff would conduct more extensive environmental education (4,000 annual students on refuge and 3,000 annual students off refuge), interpretive (1.7 million annual visitors), and outreach programs (annual audience of 25 million) to serve a larger audience and would promote them more than in Alternative 2.

Alternative 4
The staff prepared this alternative assuming that it would allow natural processes to dominate the landscape north of the Visitor Center. It represents a substantial improvement in the biological program, but a reduction in the public use program due to limited access. Under this alternative, the Service would protect 5,000 acres of refuge lands for resident wildlife, waterfowl, migratory birds, and threatened and endangered species. The staff would direct all refuge management actions towards achieving the refuge's primary purposes (conserving habitat for migratory and breeding shorebirds, colonial nesting birds, marsh birds, other wildlife, and helping to meet the habitat conservation goals of the North American Waterfowl Management Plan), while contributing to other national, regional, and state goals to protect and restore populations of migratory birds, anadromous fish, and other wildlife.

Most refuge management programs would continue to be developed and implemented with substantial baseline biological information. The staff manages impoundments based on its knowledge of migration patterns, the needs of migrating birds, its knowledge of vegetation growth in response to water depth timing of inundation, and vegetation surveys. It would manage marshes with prescribed fire and survey data on the effects of the burning on the habitat or wildlife populations. The staff would survey all the habitats on the refuge on a regular basis. The staff would continue active habitat management through the management of marshes and impoundments as long as they remain as manageable units for moist-soil vegetation and mudflats as sea level rises.

The staff would continue to perform intensive monitoring of sea turtles, waterfowl, wading birds, shorebirds, and colonial nesting birds, including piping plovers. It would assist other agencies and researchers with other surveys, but would also survey fish, invertebrates, land birds, reptiles and amphibians on its own. However, impoundment, grassland, marsh, and shrub habitat types will give way to ocean overwash fans in some areas. This would result in shifts in monitoring strategies and monitoring for some species. For example, refuge surveys for waterfowl on the refuge would probably be gradually replaced or would certainly decrease as suitable habitat transitions to overwash fan habitat. Surveys for other species using overwash fan habitat may replace impoundment-based surveys.

The refuge would decrease its capacity to provide wildlife-dependent recreation activities (e.g., fishing, wildlife observation, and environmental education and interpretation opportunities). The refuge would still have two trails associated with North Pond and the service road that encircles the pond for visitor access. The staff would maintain the current wildlife observation sites/platforms and interpretive kiosks. The refuge would continue to evaluate wildlife populations and consider hunting opportunities, if the situation warranted a hunt. It would permit fishing (50,000 annual visitors) along the shorelines of the Atlantic Ocean, Oregon Inlet, and Pamlico Sound and the banks of the ditches. The staff would conduct less extensive interpretation on the refuge (50,000 annual visitors) to serve a smaller audience. Environmental education on the refuge (4,000 annual students) off the refuge (3,000 annual students) and outreach (annual audience of 25 million) would remain the same as Alternative 3.

Alternative 5
The staff prepared this alternative assuming that it would allow natural processes to dominate the landscape throughout the refuge. It represents a substantial improvement in the biological program, but a substantial reduction in the public use program due to limited access. Under this alternative, the Service would protect 5,000 acres of refuge lands for resident wildlife, waterfowl, migratory birds, and threatened and endangered species. The staff would direct all refuge management actions towards achieving the refuge's primary purposes (conserving habitat for migratory and breeding shorebirds, colonial nesting birds, marsh birds, other wildlife, and helping to meet the habitat conservation goals of the North American Waterfowl Management Plan), while contributing to other national, regional, and state goals to protect and restore populations of migratory birds, anadromous fish, and other wildlife.

Most refuge management programs would continue to be developed and implemented with substantial baseline biological information. The staff manages impoundments based on its knowledge of migration patterns, the needs of migrating birds, its knowledge of vegetation growth in response to water depth timing of inundation, and vegetation surveys. It would manage marshes with prescribed fire and survey data on the effects of the burning on the habitat or wildlife populations. The staff would survey all the habitats on the refuge on a regular basis. The staff would implement active habitat management through the management of marshes and impoundments as long as they remain as manageable units for moist-soil vegetation and mudflats as sea level rises.

The staff would continue to perform intensive monitoring of sea turtles, waterfowl, wading birds, shorebirds, and colonial nesting birds, including piping plovers. It would assist other agencies and researchers with other surveys, but would also survey fish, invertebrates, land birds, reptiles, and amphibians on its own. However, impoundment, grassland, marsh, and shrub habitat types will give way to ocean overwash fans in some areas. This would result in shifts in monitoring strategies and monitoring for some species. For example, surveys for waterfowl on the refuge would probably be gradually replaced or would certainly decrease as suitable habitat transitions to overwash fan habitat. Surveys for other species using overwash fan habitat may replace impoundment-based surveys.

The refuge would decrease its capacity to provide wildlife-dependent recreation activities (e.g., fishing, wildlife observation, and environmental education and interpretation opportunities). The refuge would still have two trails associated with North Pond and the service road that encircles the pond for visitor access. The staff would maintain the current wildlife observation sites/platforms, and interpretive kiosks. The refuge would continue to evaluate wildlife populations and consider hunting opportunities, if the situation warranted a hunt. It would permit fishing (50,000 annual visitors) along the shorelines of the Atlantic Ocean, Oregon Inlet, and Pamlico Sound and the banks of the ditches. The staff would conduct a less extensive environmental education program (1,500 annual students on the refuge and 3,000 off the refuge) and interpretation (50,000 annual visitors) on the refuge to serve a smaller audience. Environmental education off the refuge (3,000 annual students) and outreach (annual audience of 25 million) would remain the same as Alternative 3.

Selection Rationale

Alternative 2 is selected for implementation because it directs the development of programs to best achieve the refuge purpose and goals; emphasizes better habitat management and increased public use opportunities, while meeting the refuge's primary purpose of protecting habitat for migratory birds and other wildlife. Specific results will include increased waterfowl, shorebird, wading bird, and songbird use and production; enhanced habitat; increased protection for other wildlife; enhanced resident wildlife populations; optimum wetland conditions; greater opportunities for a variety of compatible wildlife-dependent recreational and environmental education activities; collection of habitat and wildlife data; and ensures long-term achievement of refuge and Service objectives. At the same time, these management actions provide balanced levels of compatible public use opportunities consistent with existing laws, Service policies, and sound biological principles. It provides the best mix of program elements to achieve desired long-term conditions.

Under this alternative, all lands under the management and direction of the refuge will be protected, maintained, and enhanced, and those lands within the approved acquisition boundary will be prioritized for acquisition to best achieve national, ecosystem, and refuge-specific goals and objectives. In addition, the action positively addresses significant issues and concerns expressed by the public.

Environmental Effects

Implementation of the Service's management action is expected to result in environmental, social, and economic effects as outlined in the comprehensive conservation plan. Habitat management, population management, land conservation, and visitor service management activities on Pea Island National Wildlife Refuge would result in continuation of the refuge's current management of impoundments and marshes and monitoring of impoundments, waterfowl, shorebirds, and wading birds; and increasing the opportunities in public use programs for fishing, environmental education interpretation, wildlife observation, wildlife photography, and outreach—would not change the impact on the biological and physical environment. It would pose a slightly positive effect on the social and economic environment. These effects are detailed as follows:

- Protect existing habitat important to migratory birds, mammals, reptiles, amphibians, fish, and invertebrates, provide data on wildlife species and habitats, and improve management for shorebirds in impoundments.

- Increased public use may affect the refuge's wildlife populations due to disturbance and habitat trampling. The staff would concentrate the use on the trail around North Pond, on the observation platforms, and in the Visitor Center to minimize the effects on habitats and wildlife. The refuge would continue to post the nesting areas of shorebirds, colonial nesting birds, and sea turtles.

- Increase in fishing, wildlife observation, wildlife photography, and environmental education and interpretation opportunities; increase in volunteer opportunities; and a slightly positive effect on the social environment of refuge visitors.

- Increased visitation to the refuge and greater purchases of local goods and services in the economy of the surrounding communities.

Potential Adverse Effects and Mitigation Measures

Wildlife Disturbance
Disturbance to wildlife at some level is an unavoidable consequence of any public use program, regardless of the activity involved. Obviously, some activities innately have the potential to be more disturbing than others. The management actions to be implemented have been carefully planned to avoid unacceptable levels of impact.

As currently proposed, the known and anticipated levels of disturbance of the management action are considered minimal and well within the tolerance level of known wildlife species and populations present in the area. Implementation of the public use program would take place through carefully controlled time and space zoning, establishment of protection zones around key sites, closures of all-terrain vehicle trails, and routing of roads and trails to avoid direct contact with sensitive areas, such as nesting bird habitat, etc. All hunting activities (e.g., season lengths, bag limits, number of hunters) would be conducted within the constraints of sound biological principles and refuge-specific regulations established to restrict illegal or non-conforming activities. Monitoring activities through wildlife inventories and assessments of public use levels and activities would be utilized, and public use programs would be adjusted as needed to limit disturbance.

User Group Conflicts
As public use levels expand across time, some conflicts between user groups may occur. Programs would be adjusted, as needed, to eliminate or minimize these problems and provide quality wildlife-dependent recreational opportunities. Experience has proven that time and space zonings, such as establishment of separate use areas, use periods, and restricting numbers of users, are effective tools in eliminating conflicts between user groups.

Effects on Adjacent Landowners
Implementation of the management action would not impact adjacent or in-holding landowners. Essential access to private property would be allowed through issuance of special use permits. Future land acquisition would occur on a willing-seller basis only, at fair market values within the approved acquisition boundary. Lands are acquired through a combination of fee title purchases and/or donations and less-than-fee title interests (e.g., conservation easements, cooperative agreements) from willing sellers. Funds for the acquisition of lands within the approved acquisition boundary would likely come from the Land and Water Conservation Fund or the Migratory Bird Conservation Act. The management action contains neither provisions nor proposals to pursue off-refuge stream bank riparian zone protection measures (e.g., fencing) other than on a volunteer/partnership basis.

Land Ownership and Site Development

Proposed acquisition efforts by the Service would result in changes in land and recreational use patterns, since all uses on national wildlife refuges must meet compatibility standards. Land ownership by the Service also precludes any future economic development by the private sector. Potential development of access roads, dikes, control structures, and visitor parking areas could lead to minor short-term negative impacts on plants, soil, and some wildlife species. When site development activities are proposed, each activity will be given the appropriate National Environmental Policy Act consideration during pre-construction planning. At that time, any required mitigation activities will be incorporated into the specific project to reduce the level of impacts to the human environment and to protect fish and wildlife and their habitats.

As indicated earlier, one of the direct effects of site development is increased public use; this increased use may lead to littering, noise, and vehicle traffic. While funding and personnel resources will be allocated to minimize these effects, such allocations make these resources unavailable for other programs.

The management action is not expected to have significant adverse effects on wetlands and floodplains, pursuant to Executive Orders 11990 and 11988.

Coordination

The management action has been thoroughly coordinated with all interested and/or affected parties. Parties contacted include:

All affected landowners
Congressional representatives
Governor of North Carolina
North Carolina Wildlife Resources Commission
North Carolina Division of Coastal Management
North Carolina State Historic Preservation Officer
Local community officials
Interested citizens
Conservation organizations

Findings

It is my determination that the management action does not constitute a major federal action significantly affecting the quality of the human environment under the meaning of Section 102(2)(c) of the National Environmental Policy Act of 1969 (as amended). As such, an environmental impact statement is not required. This determination is based on the following factors (40 C.F.R. 1508.27), as addressed in the Environmental Assessment for the Pea Island National Wildlife Refuge:

1. Both beneficial and adverse effects have been considered and this action will not have a significant effect on the human environment. (Environmental Assessment, pages 141-150).

2. The actions will not have a significant effect on public health and safety. (Environmental Assessment, pages 141-150).

3. The project will not significantly affect any unique characteristics of the geographic area such as proximity to historical or cultural resources, wild and scenic rivers, or ecologically critical areas. (Environmental Assessment, pages 141-150).

4. The effects on the quality of the human environment are not likely to be highly controversial. (Environmental Assessment, pages 141-150).

5. The actions do not involve highly uncertain, unique, or unknown environmental risks to the human environment. (Environmental Assessment, pages 141-150).

6. The actions will not establish a precedent for future actions with significant effects nor do they represent a decision in principle about a future consideration. (Environmental Assessment, pages 141-150).

7. There will be no cumulatively significant impacts on the environment. Cumulative impacts have been analyzed with consideration of other similar activities on adjacent lands, in past action, and in foreseeable future actions. (Environmental Assessment, pages 141-150).

8. The actions will not significantly affect any site listed in, or eligible for listing in, the National Register of Historic Places, nor will they cause loss or destruction of significant scientific, cultural, or historic resources. (Environmental Assessment, pages 141-150).

9. The actions are not likely to adversely affect threatened or endangered species, or their habitats. (Environmental Assessment, pages 141-150).

10. The actions will not lead to a violation of federal, state, or local laws imposed for the protection of the environment. (Environmental Assessment, pages 141-150).

Supporting References

Fish and Wildlife Service. 2006. Draft Comprehensive Conservation Plan and Environmental Assessment for Pea Island National Wildlife Refuge, Dare and Hyde Counties, North Carolina. U.S. Department of the Interior, Fish and Wildlife Service, Southeast Region.

Document Availability

The Environmental Assessment was Section B of the Draft Comprehensive Conservation Plan for Pea Island National Wildlife Refuge and was made available in March 2006. Additional copies are available by writing: Pea Island National Wildlife Refuge, P.O. Box 1969, Manteo, North Carolina 27954.

Signed _____   7/7/06
Sam D. Hamilton   Date
Regional Director

www.ingramcontent.com/pod-product-compliance
Lightning Source LLC
Chambersburg PA
CBHW081207280526
45787CB00006B/2365